BIRDS OF THE
ROCKY
MOUNTAINS

BY
CHRIS C. FISHER

LONE
PINE

First printed in 1997 10 9 8 7 6 5 4 3 2 1

Printed in Canada

The Publisher: Lone Pine Publishing

206, 10426 – 81 Ave.	202A, 1110 Seymour St.	1901 Raymond Ave. SW, Suite C
Edmonton, AB T6E 1X5	Vancouver, BC V6B 3N3	Renton, WA 98055
Canada	Canada	USA

Canadian Cataloguing in Publication Data

Fisher, Chris C. (Christopher Charles), date–
  Birds of the Rocky Mountains

  Includes bibliographical references and index.
  ISBN 1-55105-091-9

  1. Birds—Rocky Mountains—Identification. I. Title.
QL685.5.R63F57 1997   598'.09711   C97-910763-6

Senior Editor: Nancy Foulds

Editorial: Roland Lines, Lee Craig, Edrea Daniel

Technical Review: Wayne Campbell, Jeff Marks, Greg Butcher

Production Manager: David Dodge

Design and Layout: Federico Caceres, Gregory Brown

Cover Design: Jun Lee

Cover Illustration: Gary Ross

Illustrations: Gary Ross, Ted Nordhagen, Ewa Pluciennik, Horst Krause

Maps: Volker Bodegom

Separations and Film: Elite Lithographers Co., Ltd., Edmonton, Alberta

Printing: Select Colour Press, Edmonton, Alberta

The publisher gratefully acknowledges the assistance of the Department of Canadian Heritage
and Alberta Community Development, and the financial support provided by the Alberta
Foundation for the Arts.

CONTENTS

ACKNOWLEDGMENTS

The foundation of this book, and indeed all celebrations of nature in the Rocky Mountains, goes back hundreds, even thousands, of years. In the production of this volume, it was an honor and a pleasure to experience the rich literature on Rocky Mountain bird life. In reading the words of many of the great North American naturalists, I gleaned information and inspiration that mirrors the grandeur of the Rockies themselves.

The artwork is of utmost importance to a bird guide, and I cannot sufficiently thank Gary Ross and Ted Nordhagen; their illustrative talents grant these species dignity and life. My gratitude also goes to Carole Patterson, who provides stability and support and remains a constant loving force in my life. I thank the team at Lone Pine Publishing—Shane Kennedy, Grant Kennedy, Dave Dodge, Greg Brown, Carol Dragich, Wendy Proudfoot and especially the editorial crew of Roland Lines, Lee Craig and Nancy Foulds—for their gentle nature and professionalism. Linda Kershaw wrote a wonderful introduction to the Rocky Mountains for her book on *Plants of the Rocky Mountains* (also published by Lone Pine), and I am grateful for the opportunity to borrow from it for the introduction to this book.

My thanks also extend to my friends and colleagues, who were generous in sharing their thoughts and observations on various birds, including Marke Ambard, Kevin Aanerud, Nancy Baron, Jim Beck, Barb Beck, Gordon Court, Michael den Otter, Alex Drummond, Geoff Holroyd, Andrea Hoover, Pat Marklevitz, Joseph Morlan, Dennis Paulson, Dave Prescott, Isabelle Richardson, Warren Schaffer, Lisa Takats, Terry Thormin and Jody Watson.

This project would not have been possible without John Acorn and Jim Butler. Not only are they two of the continent's great naturalists, but they also share their talents to inspire and promote the love of wild things. Their influence fills these pages.

I am grateful to Jeff Marks and Greg Butcher, without whose assistance and knowledge this project would not have been completed. And, finally, my special thanks must extend to Wayne Campbell, who painstakingly reviewed the text, with unquestionable expertise, while always having a heart for birds and their meaning to people.

Common Loon	Pied-billed Grebe	Horned Grebe	Red-necked Grebe	Eared Grebe
size 32" • p. 30	size 14" • p. 31	size 14" • p. 32	size 20" • p. 33	size 13" • p. 34

Western Grebe	Clark's Grebe	American White Pelican	Double-crested Cormorant	American Bittern
size 22" • p. 35	size 22" • App., p. 314	size 62" • p. 36	size 29" • p. 37	size 25" • p. 38

Least Bittern	Great Blue Heron	Great Egret	Snowy Egret	Cattle Egret
size 13" • App., p. 314	size 52" • p. 39	size 39" • App., p. 314	size 24" • p. 40	size 20" • App., p. 314

Green Heron	Black-crowned	White-faced Ibis	Greater White-fronted Goose • size 30"	Snow Goose
size 19" • App., p. 315	Night-Heron • size 25" • p. 41	size 23" • p. 42	App., p. 315	size 31" • p. 43

Ross's Goose	Canada Goose	Trumpeter Swan	Tundra Swan
size 24" • App., p. 315	size 40" • p. 44	size 66" • p. 45	size 53" • p. 46

Wood Duck	Gadwall	Eurasian Wigeon	American Wigeon
size 18" • p. 47	size 20" • p. 48	size 18" • App., p. 315	size 21" • p. 49

Mallard
size 24" • p. 50

Blue-winged Teal
size 15" • p. 51

Cinnamon Teal
size 16" • p. 52

Northern Shoveler
size 19" • p. 53

Northern Pintail
size 25" • p. 54

Green-winged Teal
size 14" • p. 55

Canvasback
size 21" • p. 56

Redhead
size 20" • p. 57

Ringed-necked Duck
size 16" • p. 58

Greater Scaup
size 18" • App., p. 316

Lesser Scaup
size 17" • p. 59

Harlequin Duck
size 17" • p. 60

Surf Scoter
size 19" • p. 61

White-winged Scoter
size 22" • p. 62

Oldsquaw
size 19" • App., p. 316

Bufflehead
size 14" • p. 63

Common Goldeneye
size 18" • p. 64

Barrow's Goldeneye
size 18" • p. 65

Hooded Merganser
size 18" • p. 66

Red-breasted Merganser
size 23" • p. 67

Common Merganser
size 25" • p. 68

Ruddy Duck
size 16" • p. 69

Turkey Vulture
size 29" • p. 70

Osprey
size 24" • p. 71

Bald Eagle
37" • p. 72

Northern Harrier
size 20" • p. 73

Sharp-shinned Hawk
size 12" • p. 74

Cooper's Hawk
size 17" • p. 75

Northern Goshawk
size 23" • p. 76

Broad-winged Hawk
size 17" • p. 77

Swainson's Hawk
size 21" • p. 78

Red-tailed Hawk
size 22" • p. 79

Ferruginous Hawk
size 25" • p. 80

Rough-legged Hawk
size 22" • p. 81

Golden Eagle
size 35" • p. 82

American Kestrel
size 8" • p. 83

Merlin
size 11" • p. 84

Prairie Falcon
size 16" • p. 85

Peregrine Falcon
size 17" • p. 86

Gyrfalcon
size 23" • p. 87

Gray Partridge
size 13" • p. 88

Chukar
size 13" • p. 89

Ring-necked Pheasant
size 28" • p. 90

Ruffed Grouse
size 17" • p. 91

Sage Grouse
size 26" • p. 92

Spruce Grouse
size 15" • p. 93

Blue Grouse
size 20" • p. 94

Willow Ptarmigan
size 14" • p. 95

White-tailed Ptarmigan
size 13" • p. 96

Sharp-tailed Grouse
size 18" • p. 97

Wild Turkey
size 43" • p. 98

Virginia Rail
size 10" • p. 99

Sora
size 9" • p. 100

American Coot
size 15" • p.101

Sandhill Crane
size 45" • p. 102

Whooping Crane
size 55" • App., p. 316

Black-bellied Plover
size 12" • App., p. 316

American Golden-Plover
size 11" • App., p. 317

Semipalmated Plover
size 7" • p. 103

Killdeer
size 10" • p. 104

Mountain Plover
size 9" • App., p. 317

Black-necked Stilt
size 15" • p. 105

American Avocet
size 18" • p. 106

Greater Yellowlegs
size 14" • p. 107

Lesser Yellowlegs
size 11" • p. 108

Solitary Sandpiper
size 8" • p. 109

Willet
size 15" • p. 110

Spotted Sandpiper
size 8" • p. 111

Upland Sandpiper
size 12" • p. 112

Long-billed Curlew
size 23" • p. 113

Hudsonian Godwit
size 15" • App., p. 317

Marbled Godwit
size 18" • p. 114

Sanderling
size 8" • App., p. 317

Semipalmated Sandpiper
size 6" • p. 115

Western Sandpiper
size 7" • p. 116

Least Sandpiper
size 6" • p. 117

Baird's Sandpiper
size 7" • p. 118

Pectoral Sandpiper
size 9" • p. 119

Dunlin
size 8" • App., p. 318

Stilt Sandpiper
size 8" • App., p. 318

Short-billed Dowitcher
size 12" • App., p. 318

Long-billed Dowitcher
size 12" • p. 120

Common Snipe
size 11" • p. 121

Wilson's Phalarope
size 9" • p. 122

Red-necked Phalarope
size 7" • p. 123

8

Parasitic Jaeger
size 18" • App., p. 318

Franklin's Gull
size 14" • p. 124

Bonaparte's Gull
size 13" • p. 125

Mew Gull
size 16" • App., p. 319

Ringed-billed Gull
size 19" • p. 126

California Gull
size 19" • p. 127

Herring Gull
size 25" • p. 128

Caspian Tern
size 21" • p. 129

Common Tern
size 15" • p. 130

Forster's Tern
size 15" • p. 131

Black Tern
size 10" • p. 132

Rock Dove
size 13" • p. 133

Band-tailed Pigeon
size 14" • p. 134

Mourning Dove
size 12" • p. 135

Black-billed Cuckoo
size 12" • p. 136

Yellow-billed Cuckoo
size 12" • p. 137

Barn Owl
size 15" • App., p. 319

Flammulated Owl
size 7" • p. 138

Eastern Screech-Owl
size 9" • App., p. 319

Western Screech-Owl
size 9" • p. 139

Great Horned Owl
size 22" • p. 140

Snowy Owl
size 24" • p. 141

Northern Hawk Owl
size 16" • p. 142

Northern Pygmy-Owl
size 7" • p. 143

Burrowing Owl
size 9" • p. 144

Barred Owl
size 21" • p. 145

Great Gray Owl
size 29" • p. 146

Long-eared Owl
size 15" • p. 147

Short-eared Owl
size 15" • p. 148

Boreal Owl
size 11" • p. 149

| Northern Saw-whet Owl size 8" • p. 150 | Common Nighthawk size 9" • p. 151 | Common Poorwill size 8" • p. 152 | Black Swift size 7" • p. 153 | Vaux's Swift size 5" • p. 154 |

White-throated Swift size 7" • p. 155 | Black-chinned Hummingbird size 3" • p. 156 | Calliope Hummingbird size 3" • p. 157 | Broad-tailed Hummingbird size 4" • p. 158 | Rufous Hummingbird size 3" • p. 159

Belted Kingfisher size 13" • p. 160 | Lewis's Woodpecker size 11" • p. 161 | Red-headed Woodpecker size 8" • App., p. 319 | Yellow-bellied Sapsucker size 8" • p. 162 | Red-naped Sapsucker size 9" • p. 163

Williamson's Sapsucker size 9" • p. 164 | Downy Woodpecker size 7" • p. 165 | Hairy Woodpecker size 9" • p. 166 | Three-toed Woodpecker size 9" • p. 167 | Black-backed Woodpecker size 10" • p. 168

Northern Flicker size 13" • p. 169 | Pileated Woodpecker size 18" • p. 170 | Olive-sided Flycatcher size 8" • p. 171 | Western Wood-Pewee size 6" • p. 172 | Alder Flycatcher size 6" • App., p. 320

Willow Flycatcher size 6" • p. 173 | Least Flycatcher size 6" • p. 174 | Hammond's Flycatcher size 6" • p. 175 | Dusky Flycatcher size 6" • p. 176 | Gray Flycatcher size 6" • App., p. 320

Cordilleran Flycatcher	Eastern Phoebe	Say's Phoebe	Ash-throated Flycatcher	Cassin's Kingbird
size 6" • p. 177	size 7" • App., p. 320	size 8" • p. 178	size 8" • App., p. 320	size 9" • App., p. 321

Western Kingbird	Eastern Kingbird	Northern Shrike	Loggerhead Shrike	Plumbeous Vireo
size 9" • p. 179	size 9" • p. 180	size 10" • p. 181	size 9" • p. 182	size 6" • p. 183

Warbling Vireo	Philadelphia Vireo	Red-eyed Vireo	Gray Jay	Steller's Jay
size 6" • p. 184	size 5" • p. 185	size 6" • p. 186	size 12" • p. 187	size 12" • p. 188

Blue Jay	Western Scrub-Jay	Pinyon Jay	Clark's Nutcracker	Black-billed Magpie
size 11" • p. 189	size 12" • p. 190	size 10" • p. 191	size 13" • p. 192	size 20" • p. 193

American Crow	Common Raven	Horned Lark	Purple Martin	Tree Swallow
size 19" • p. 194	size 24" • p. 195	size 7" • p. 196	size 8" • p. 197	size 6" • p. 198

Violet-green Swallow	Northern Rough-winged Swallow • size 6" • p. 200	Bank Swallow	Barn Swallow	Cliff Swallow
size 5" • p. 199		size 5" • p. 201	size 7" • p. 202	size 6" • p. 203

Black-capped Chickadee	Mountain Chickadee	Chestnut-backed Chickadee	Boreal Chickadee	Juniper Titmouse
size 6" • p. 204	size 5" • p. 205	size 5" • p. 206	size 5" • p. 207	size 6" • p. 208

Bushtit	Red-breasted Nuthatch	White-breasted Nuthatch	Pygmy Nuthatch	Brown Creeper
size 5" • p. 209	size 5" • p. 210	size 6" • p. 211	size 4" • p. 212	size 5" • p. 213

Rock Wren	Canyon Wren	Bewick's Wren	House Wren	Winter Wren
size 6" • p. 214	size 6" • p. 215	size 5" • p. 216	size 5" • p. 217	size 4" • p. 218

Marsh Wren	American Dipper	Golden-crowned Kinglet	Ruby-crowned Kinglet	Blue-gray Gnatcatcher
size 5" • p. 219	size 8" • p. 220	size 4" • p. 221	size 4" • p. 222	size 5" • p. 223

Western Bluebird	Mountain Bluebird	Townsend's Solitaire	Veery	Gray-cheeked Thrush
size 7" • p. 224	size 7" • p. 225	size 9" • p. 226	size 7" • p. 227	size 7" • App., p. 321

Swainson's Thrush	Hermit Thrush	American Robin	Varied Thrush	European Starling
size 7" • p. 228	size 7" • p. 229	size 10" • p. 230	size 10" • p. 231	size 9" • p. 232

Gray Catbird
size 9" • p. 233

Northern Mockingbird
size 10" • p. 234

Sage Thrasher
size 9" • p. 235

Brown Thrasher
size 12" • p. 236

American Pipit
size 7" • p. 237

Bohemian Waxwing
size 8" • p. 238

Cedar Waxwing
size 7" • p. 239

Tennessee Warbler
size 5" • p. 240

Orange-crowned Warbler
size 5" • p. 241

Nashville Warbler
size 5" • p. 242

Virginia's Warbler
size 5" • p. 243

Yellow Warbler
size 5" • p. 244

Magnolia Warbler
size 5" • p. 245

Yellow-rumped Warbler
size 6" • p. 246

Black-throated Gray
Warbler • size 5" • p. 247

Townsend's Warbler
size 5" • p. 248

Black-throated
Green Warbler
size 5" • App., p. 321

Palm Warbler
size 6" • p. 249

Bay-breasted Warbler
size 6" • p. 250

Blackpoll Warbler
size 6" • p. 251

Black-and-white Warbler
size 5" • p. 252

American Redstart
size 5" • p. 253

Ovenbird
size 6" • p. 254

Northern Waterthrush
size 6" • p. 255

MacGillivray's Warbler
size 5" • p. 256

Common Yellowthroat
size 5" • p. 257

Wilson's Warbler
size 5" • p. 258

Canada Warbler
size 5" • App., p. 321

Yellow-breasted Chat
size 8" • p. 259

Western Tanager
size 7" • p. 260

13

Green-tailed Towhee	Spotted Towhee	American Tree Sparrow	Chipping Sparrow	Clay-colored Sparrow
size 7" • p. 261	size 8" • p. 262	size 6" • p. 263	size 6" • p. 264	size 5" • p. 265

Brewer's Sparrow	Vesper Sparrow	Lark Sparrow	Sage Sparrow	Black-throated Sparrow
size 5" • p. 266	size 6" • p. 267	size 6" • p. 268	size 6" • p. 269	size 5" • App., p. 322

Lark Bunting	Savannah Sparrow	Baird's Sparrow	Grasshopper Sparrow	LeConte's Sparrow
size 7" • p. 270	size 6" • p. 271	size 5" • App., p. 322	size 5" • p. 272	size 5" • p. 273

Nelson's Sharp-tailed Sparrow • size 5" • p. 274	Fox Sparrow	Song Sparrow	Lincoln's Sparrow	Swamp Sparrow
	size 6" • p. 275	size 6" • p. 276	size 6" • p. 277	size 6" • App., p. 322

White-throated Sparrow	Harris's Sparrow	White-crowned Sparrow	Golden-crowned Sparrow	McCown's Longspur
size 7" • p. 278	size 8" • App., p. 322	size 6" • p. 279	size 7" • p. 280	size 6" • App., p. 323

Lapland Longspur	Chestnut-collared Longspur	Dark-eyed Junco	Snow Bunting	Rose-breasted Grosbeak
size 6" • p. 281	size 6" • App., p. 323	size 6" • p. 282	size 7" • p. 284	size 8" • App., p. 323

14

Black-headed Grosbeak	Blue Grosbeak	Lazuli Bunting	Indigo Bunting	Bobolink
size 8" • p. 285	size 7" • p. 286	size 6" • p. 287	size 6" • App., p. 323	size 7" • p. 288

Red-winged Blackbird	Western Meadowlark	Yellow-headed Blackbird	Rusty Blackbird	Brewer's Blackbird
size 9" • p. 289	size 9" • p. 290	size 10" • p. 291	size 9" • p. 292	size 9" • p. 293

Common Grackle	Brown-headed Cowbird	Baltimore Oriole	Bullock's Oriole	Gray-crowned Rosy-Finch
size 12" • p. 294	size 7" • p. 295	size 8" • p. 296	size 8" • p. 297	size 6" • p. 298

Black Rosy-Finch	Brown-capped Rosy-Finch	Pine Grosbeak	Purple Finch	Cassin's Finch
size 6" • p. 299	size 6" • p. 300	size 9" • p. 301	size 6" • p. 302	size 6" • p. 303

House Finch	Red Crossbill	White-winged Crossbill	Common Redpoll	Hoary Redpoll
size 6" • p. 304	size 6" • p. 305	size 6" • p. 306	size 5" • p. 307	size 5" • p. 308

Pine Siskin	Lesser Goldfinch	American Goldfinch	Evening Grosbeak	House Sparrow
size 5" • p. 309	size 4" • p. 310	size 5" • p. 311	size 8" • p. 312	size 6" • p. 313

ABOUT THIS BOOK

*B*irds of the Rocky Mountains presents a brief introduction into the lives of birds, opening the door to the world of wildness. It is designed for anyone who is interested in learning more about the birds that inhabit the forests, meadows, grasslands, alpine slopes and wetlands of the Rockies, whether that person is a resident who wants to know more about his or her natural surroundings, a curious traveler intrigued with wildlife or an experienced birder looking for a convenient reference for his or her pack.

This book is intended to serve as both a bird identification guide and a bird appreciation guide. Getting to know the names of birds is just the first step toward getting to know the birds. Once we've made contact with a species, we can better relate to its character, mannerisms and ecological role through our first-hand experiences. When we open up to the lives of other species, we expand ourselves by understanding the complex world in which we live.

The best way to develop an appreciation of birds is to spend some time outdoors to gain valuable experience with the local bird community, but this book also strives to serve those who cannot walk the trails of the Rockies. Birds are inevitable parts of all our lives, and everyone can gain a better understanding of the natural world even through the species that share our backyards. If we learn more about the familiar world out our backdoors, we are more capable of transferring our experiences to the unfamiliar. Few peo-ple have seen all the species described in this book, and even those who have were not enriched by the numbers of birds they saw but by the simple encounters.

This guide describes and illustrates all the species of birds that regularly occur in the Rockies from northern New Mexico to northern British Columbia. In addition, species that accidentally occur in our area, whether as rarely seen vagrants or as future residents, are included in the appendix near the end of the book.

If you thumb through this book, the illustrations immediately attract your eyes. Visually relating to the birds is important to developing an understanding of them. Unlike many other field guides, which have birds posed in comparable, but lifeless, positions, this guide highlights the beauty of birds. The high quality illustrations complement the text, or they can stand alone for the browser.

The bird species described in this book are arranged in taxonomic order, following a generally accepted evolutionary sequence from the least to the most advanced birds. (How 'advanced' a bird is refers only to how much it has changed from the prehistoric, ancestral birds; it is not a judgment of its relative success as a species.) The common and scientific names used in this book follow the American Ornithologists' Union *Check-list of North American Birds* (6th edition and its supplements through July, 1997). Unfortunately, bird taxonomists often disagree, and occasionally species are renamed. Undoubtedly, more names will change in the future. Do not be overwhelmed by these often confusing changes; in the birding community, such changes are tolerated in a light-hearted manner—the outdated names used by some birdwatchers can testify to the length of their involvement in the pastime.

American Bittern

As well as discussing the identifying features of the birds, each species account also attempts to bring the birds to life by celebrating their various character traits. I often describe a bird's character in human-related terms, because personifying a bird can help us form a connection with it, but these perceived links between human terms and a bird's 'personality' should not be mistaken for actual behaviors: our interpretations do not fully realize the complexities of bird behavior. Rather, I hope that through a playful delivery, the text will inspire the reader without compromising the wildness of the birds. The leading paragraph in the accounts strives to show birds to the reader in the context of his or her own personal experiences; the more structured information that follows provides factual information for a more advanced level of comprehension.

I.D.

It is difficult to describe the features of a bird without being able to visualize it, so this section should be used in combination with the illustrations. Where appropriate, the description is subdivided to highlight the differences between male and female birds, breeding and non-breeding birds and immature and adult birds. The description uses as few technical terms as possible for the parts of a bird (but see the labeled bird illustration on page 325) in favor of easily understood terms. Bird's don't

Belted Kingfisher

really have jaw lines, ear patches or chins, but these and other terms are easily understood by all readers, in spite of their scientific inaccuracy.

SIZE

The size measurement is an average length of the bird's body from bill to tail. It is an approximate measurement of the bird as it is seen in nature. The size is generally given as a range for larger birds, because there is much variation between individuals. In addition, wingspans are given for some of the larger birds that are often seen in flight.

RANGE

The range section in each description indicates roughly where and when the species can be encountered in the Rockies (see the map on page 22). Because the Rockies represent such a varied environment, it is impossible to definitively describe the abundance of a species throughout the whole region. A general comment, such as common, uncommon or rare, is usually sufficient to describe the trend in a general context. Specific situations are bound to contrast somewhat as migratory pulses and centers of activity tend to concentrate or disperse birds in some situations. These natural variances encourage the habit of keeping precise field notes, so you can keep track of the trends you discover.

HABITAT

Understanding the relationship between habitats and bird species often helps you identify which birds are which. Because you won't find a loon up a tree or a grouse on a lake, habitat is an important thing to note when birdwatching.

The quality of habitat is one of the most powerful factors to influence bird distribution. With experience, you might become amazed by the predictability of some birds within a specific habitat type. The habitats I have listed describe where each species can most commonly be found. In most cases, it is a fairly generalized description, but if a bird is primarily restricted to a specific habitat, it is described more precisely. Birds can turn up in just about any type of habitat (because of the freedom flight gives them), but in most encounters, they will occur in perfectly logical environments.

The various habitats in the Rockies occur within the broader context of

Lewis's Woodpecker

elevational zones: lowlands, foothills, montane, subalpine and alpine. There are rarely clear lines dividing these zones.

The foothills in the Canadian Rockies are generally less clearly defined than those in the U.S. Rockies, because in Canada the mountain forests slowly grade to boreal forest in the northeast and to the Columbian forest in the west, both of which have many environmental characteristics and plant species in common with the Rockies. In the U.S. Rockies, the foothills are generally low-elevation scrublands that form the transition between the prairie and the treed (montane) slopes.

The montane zone supports the greatest variety of wildflowers, trees and shrubs. It generally ranges from open stands at low elevations to dense forests as it merges with the subalpine zone. In the U.S. Rockies, the montane zone is generally defined as the 'forested' zone immediately above the scrublands of the foothills. In Canada, the montane zone is less clearly defined, because the foothills are usually forested as well.

The subalpine zone extends from the upper edge of the montane forest to the lower edge of the treeless, alpine zone. Subalpine forests are sometimes called 'snow forests,' because they grow at elevations where moisture (both rain and snow) is high, and their dense trees protect the thick snowpack from melting and evaporating in spring. The subalpine zone is fairly uniform throughout the Rocky Mountains.

The alpine zone extends from treeline to the mountain peaks. It includes areas of mostly low, matted vegetation, exposed, rocky slopes and permanent snowfields. In this cold, windswept environment, some areas may be free of snow early in spring (and even through most of winter); other areas lie blanketed with drifts for most or all of summer.

Broad-tailed Hummingbird

NESTING

The reproductive strategies used by the different bird species can be very interesting, and even migrant species that breed well outside the Rockies are given a full treatment in this account. Nest location and structure, clutch size, incubation period and parental duties are among the reproductive aspects that are discussed.

Please remember that birdwatching ethics discourage the study of active bird nests. If you disturb a nest, you may drive off the parents during a critical period, and once you have discovered a nest it often becomes exposed to natural predation.

FEEDING

Birds are frequently encountered while they are foraging, so a description of their foraging styles and diets can provide valuable identifying characteristics, as well as interesting dietary facts.

VOICE

You will hear many birds, particularly songbirds, long before you find them in your binoculars, so a memorable paraphrase of the species's most distinctive sounds can often aid in your identification. These paraphrases are intended to be fun, and they loosely resemble the rhythm of the call, song or sound produced by the bird. Should one of my paraphases not work for you, make up your own. This rewarding exercise really reinforces the sound in your mind.

Although this heading is called 'voice,' it sometimes describes noises other than vocalizations, such as the vibrations created by air passing through the stiffly erected feathers of displaying birds. It was impossible to describe all the sounds made by a species; only the most common or distinctive are included here.

SIMILAR SPECIES

Easily confused species are discussed in a brief and concise manner in this section. By concentrating on the most relevant field marks, the subtle differences between species can be reduced to easily identifiable traits. You may find it useful to consult these sections when finalizing your identification between a few species; knowing the most relevant field marks will shortcut the identification process.

Harlequin Duck

Pacific Ocean
BRITISH
COLUMBIA
Cassiar Mtns.
Dawson Creek
Prince
George
Rocky
Mountain
Trench
Columbia
Mountains.
BOREAL FOREST
Jasper NP
Edmonton
Banff NP
Vancouver
Calgary
ALBERTA
WASHINGTON
Spokane
Waterton/Glacier NP
Great
Falls
GREAT
PLAINS
OREGON
Columbia
Plateau
IDAHO
Butte
MONTANA
Boise
Billings
Yellowstone NP
Grand Teton NP
Pocatello
WYOMING
Casper
GREAT
BASIN
Wyoming
Basin
Salt Lake
City
Cheyenne
Rocky Mountain NP
Denver
COLORADO
Colorado Springs
UTAH
Colorado
Plateau
Albuquerque
MOUNTAIN RANGES
Canadian Rockies
northern US Rockies
central US Rockies
southern US Rockies
N

THE ROCKY MOUNTAIN REGION

The Rocky Mountains contain some of the most scenic and ecologically diverse regions in North America. With their snow-capped peaks, clear, sparkling lakes and vast expanses of wilderness, the Rockies are one of the most popular tourist destinations in the world. Because of their unique natural features, many parks and reserves have been established in the Rockies, and most of the millions of tourists who visit the Rockies each year arrive in the mountains expecting to experience nature. Seeing wildlife remains one of the most powerful experiences of wild places for people; many of the animals that live in our parks, including the birds, are charismatic and exceptionally bold, providing ample opportunity to view and appreciate them and to fulfill people's wilderness expectations.

The Rocky Mountains encompass a large, diverse region that is rich in biodiversity. The Rockies do not recognize political boundaries: in their broadest sense, they stretch from the Brooks Range in Alaska to the Sangre de Cristo Mountains in northern New Mexico. Many of the birds described in this book occur in the northern reaches of the Rockies, but this guide focuses on the Rockies south of the Liard River in northern British Columbia. This area can be divided into four main regions: the Canadian Rockies, the northern U.S. Rockies, the central U.S. Rockies and the southern U.S. Rockies (see the map on page 22).

Merlin

GEOLOGY AND LANDFORMS

The **Canadian Rockies** extend from the Liard River in northern B.C. to the southern border of Glacier National Park in Montana. They are bounded by the Great Plains on the east and the Rocky Mountain Trench on the west. (The Rockies in northern Montana are included in the 'Canadian' Rockies because, ignoring political boundaries, they are geologically and biologically a part of these mountains.)

The Canadian Rockies are composed mainly of sedimentary rocks, such as limestone and shale, that were thrust upward about 140 to 145 million years ago. These mountains are relatively young, recently sculpted by glaciers into deep, U-shaped valleys, steep slopes and high peaks. Several glaciers, covering about 115 sq. mi. (300 km^2) along the mountain crests, still remain.

Barred Owl

The Canadian Rockies are generally subdivided into four main sections from east to west: the foothills, the front ranges, the main ranges and the western ranges.

In the U.S., the Rockies are geologically very different from the Canadian Rockies. Many of these mountains are volcanic in origin, and those that are not are generally composed of metamorphic and igneous rocks (such as gneiss and granite), the material the makes up the continental plate ('basement' rock) underlying the Canadian Rockies. Although the U.S. Rockies are generally higher than the Canadian Rockies, the local relief is typically less (the mountains are shorter from base to summit) because the valley bottoms are high to begin with. Also, the U.S. Rockies tend to be less obviously affected by glaciation, with fewer deep, U-shaped valleys or freshly cut mountain peaks.

Bank Swallow

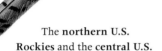
Blue Jay

these dry climates have eroded to the point where they are almost buried by their own debris. Alternating wet periods have produced huge rivers that washed away debris and opened valleys. Continental glaciers have smoothed the plains and some peaks, and alpine glaciers have cut broad U-shaped valleys and dramatic peaks in other areas.

The **northern U.S. Rockies** and the **central U.S. Rockies** are closely related geologically. Volcanic activity has been a major force in their formation, which has generally been associated with the westward movement of the continental plate over a 'hot spot' that is thought to have been initiated about 17 million years ago. Today, the hot spot is located under Yellowstone National Park, as revealed by the many geysers and hot springs in that area.

The northern U.S. Rockies are in western Montana and central Idaho; they are bounded by the Great Plains on the east and by the Columbia Plateau on the south and west. The central U.S. Rockies are in northern and western Wyoming, southeastern Idaho and northeastern Utah; they are bounded by the Great Plains on the east, the Wyoming Basin on the southeast, the Great Basin on the west and the Colorado Plateau on the south.

In some parts of the northern and central U.S. Rockies, spectacular mountains have been produced by massive fault blocks, but over millions of years many mountains in

25

Red-winged Blackbird

The **southern U.S. Rockies**, which extend from southern Wyoming to northern New Mexico, are bounded by the Great Plains on the east, the Wyoming Basin on the northwest and the Colorado Plateau on the southwest. This region contains some of the most extensive alpine areas and the highest mountains in the Rockies, with 54 summits over 14,000 ft. (4250 m).

The southern Rockies can be subdivided into the eastern ranges and the western ranges. Many of the peaks have been sculpted by glaciers, and others show the effects of erosion by wind and water. The result is a variety of mountain types, including glaciated, snow-capped mountains with quartzitic peaks, unglaciated mountains buried in debris, and rounded granite knobs. Many volcanic mountains of lava and ash, with hot springs and geothermal reservoirs, are also found in this region. Ash deposits in these areas have been carved by wind and water to form spectacular canyons and mesas.

CLIMATE

Temperatures are generally cool in the mountains, largely because of the cooling associated with higher elevations: the climate change from a rise in elevation of 1000 ft. (300 m) has been equated to traveling 600 mi. (970 km) north. The local climate varies greatly within the Rockies because this extensive mountain chain covers such a wide range of elevations and latitudes. The annual average temperatures range from about 37° F (3° C) in the Canadian Rockies to about 50° F (10° C) in the southern U.S. Rockies. Above 9000 ft. (2740 m), freezing temperatures can occur on any night of the year.

Differences in temperature have a wide range of

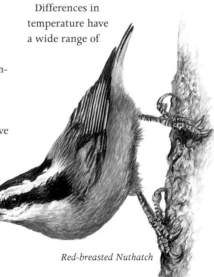

Red-breasted Nuthatch

Dark-eyed Junco

effects on these mountain landscapes. Precipitation is roughly equal from Colorado to Jasper, but southern areas are warmer, and with their higher temperatures they have more evaporation, drier soils, smaller rivers and fewer glaciers. Treeline (the edge of alpine tundra) also increases as you travel south. In Alberta, treeline is generally at 6560–7540 ft. (2000–2300 m), whereas in Colorado it is at 10,820–11,800 ft. (3300–3600 m).

NEIGHBORING REGIONS

Although the Rocky Mountains might appear to stand out on a map, their bird fauna is greatly influenced by the regions that border the Rockies. The northern boreal forest wraps around the northern Canadian Rockies, and as a result it shares much of its bird fauna with that part of the Rockies. Similarly, the distribution of Rocky Mountain birds is influenced by the Columbia

Mountains, the Great Plains, the Great Basin and the arid pinyon-juniper shrublands to the southwest of our area. No sharp boundaries exist between these regions, so their faunas (and floras) mix in transition zones, producing unique combinations of species.

Western Meadowlark

SEASONALITY

The lives of birds are greatly influenced by the seasons. A location that is teeming with activity in late May could appear to be completely devoid of life in February. Throughout our area, spring is a much anticipated event, perhaps first signaled not by the calendar, but by owls and jays that begin their courting in late winter.

The majority of the birds described in this book are migrants that arrive in our area in spring. Many of these birds stay in the Rockies to nest, but many others only stay in our area for a short period of time on their way to more northerly breeding grounds. These migrants pass through the Rockies again in fall, on their way to their winter homes. The flanks of the Rocky Mountains guide several species along their north-south migratory routes. The ridges and the prevailing winds offer lift to many migrants as they skirt along the perimeter of the mountains.

Other bird species nest in the interior of North America and winter to the west of the mountains, and they must cross over the Rockies, usually through low-elevation, east-west passes. These low passes are excellent places to view migratory birds, and they are generally easily accessible (most roadways also lie in low passes).

A few birds migrate into the Rockies during fall and spend winter in our area. Many of these winter residents arrive from the Arctic, while other apparent winter migrants have simply drifted down from higher elevations in the mountains to winter in the milder valleys.

Whether a bird is passing through or stopping to nest, the foraging opportunities that are offered by the Rockies are a necessity. Migrants that are pausing to refuel on mudflats or in treetops use these staging areas and migratory paths as crucial links in their lifecycles. Without these stopovers, trans-Rocky migrants would not be able to complete their migrations and would therefore be unable to reproduce successfully.

Townsend's Warbler

BIRDS OF THE
ROCKY
MOUNTAINS

White-tailed Ptarmigan

COMMON LOON
Gavia immer

A serene symbol of wilderness, Common Loons live in remote, peaceful locales in which humanity's impact on the globe is easily overlooked. ■ Loons are well adapted to their aquatic lifestyle: these natural divers have decreased buoyancy caused by the density of their near solid bones (most birds have hollow bones), and their feet are placed well back on their bodies to propel the birds underwater. ■ Loons require long stretches of open water to take off; occasionally a few are fatally trapped in constricting ice when inland lakes freeze, before migrating to their wintering grounds. ■ Fossils of early loon relatives have been found dating back 65 million years, to the time of the dinosaurs. ■ The word 'loon' may be derived from *lom*, the Scandinavian word for 'clumsy,' referring to this bird's awkwardness on land.

breeding

I.D.: *Sexes similar. Breeding:* green-black head; stout, thick, black bill; white 'necklace'; white breast and underparts; black-and-white 'checkerboard' upperparts; red eyes. *In flight:* long wings beat constantly; hunch-backed appearance; legs trail behind the tail.
Size: L 28–35 in. (71–89 cm).
Range: common breeder in the Canadian Rockies; occasional breeder in Wyoming, Idaho and Montana; spring and fall migrant throughout the Rockies.
Habitat: large wetlands and lakes, often those with islands, that provide undisturbed shorelines for nesting and adequate popula-tions of small fish.
Nesting: on a muskrat lodge, small island or projecting shoreline, always very near water; nest is built of aquatic vegetation; pair shares all

reproductive duties, including nest construction, egg incubation and rearing of the young.
Feeding: pursues small fish underwater to depths of 180 ft. (55 m); occasionally eats large, aquatic invertebrates and larval and adult amphibians.
Voice: alarm call is a 'tremolo,' often called 'loon laughter'; contact call is a long, simple 'wail' note; intimate calls are soft, short 'hoots.' *Male:* territorial call is an undulating, complex 'yodel.'
Similar Species: *Red-throated Loon:* smaller; slender bill; red throat in breeding plumage; white extends from the throat to the chin and ear region in winter plumage.
Pacific Loon: smaller; dusty gray head; a few migrate through low-elevation passes in the Rockies and are most often seen on large lakes in late fall or early spring.

PIED-BILLED GREBE
Podilymbus podiceps

This is the smallest and least colorful of the grebes in our area, and it is heard more frequently than it is seen. Pied-billed Grebes are secretive and inconspicuous, and they can swim and dive without creating a ripple. When frightened by an intruder, these birds might slowly submerge up to their heads, so that only their bill and eyes remain above water. ▪ *Podiceps* is from the Latin *podex*, meaning 'rump,' and *pedis*, meaning 'foot,' in reference to the way the bird's feet are located far back on its body. In flight, the feet extend beyond the tail and help the bird steer.

breeding

I.D.: *Sexes similar. Breeding:* all-brown body; black, vertical band on light-colored bill; bill is flattened on the sides; black throat; very short tail; white undertail coverts; pale belly; white eye ring; black eyes.
Size: *L* 12–15 in. (30–38 cm).
Range: uncommon summer resident and migrant throughout the Rockies.
Habitat: low-elevation wetlands (ponds, marshes, backwaters, etc.) with thick, emergent vegetation.
Nesting: in thick vegetation in lake edges, ponds and marshes; shallow, floating platform nest, made of wet and decaying plants, is anchored to or placed among emergent vegetation; pair incubates 4–5 eggs and raises the striped young.
Feeding: makes shallow dives and gleans the surface for aquatic invertebrates, small fish, adult and larval amphibians and, occasionally, water plants.
Voice: loud, whooping call that begins quickly, then slows down: *kuk-kuk-kuk cow cow cow cowp cowp cowp.*
Similar Species: *Eared Grebe* (p. 34): gold ear tufts; chestnut flanks. *Horned Grebe* (p. 32): gold ear tufts; red neck. *American Coot* (p. 101): all-black body; often seen on land.

HORNED GREBE
Podiceps auritus

Horned Grebes construct floating nests, but the nests ride so low in the water that the eggs often lie in a shallow pool of water. When an incubating parent is frightened off its nest, it will frequently attempt to cover the eggs with wet vegetation before leaving them. ▪ Unlike the fully webbed feet of loons, waterfowl, terns and gulls, grebes' feet are lobed: the three forward-facing toes have individual webbing that is not connected to the other toes. ▪ This bird's common name, and its scientific name *auritus*, meaning 'eared,' refer to the golden 'ears,' or 'horns,' that these grebes acquire in their breeding plumage.

breeding

I.D.: *Sexes similar. Breeding:* rufous neck and flanks; black cheek and forehead; golden ear tufts ('horns'); black back; white underparts; red eyes; flat crown. *In flight:* wings beat constantly; hunchbacked appearance; legs trail behind the tail.

Size: *L* 12–15 in. (30–38 cm).

Range: fairly common spring and fall migrant throughout the Rockies; occasional breeder in the northern U.S. Rockies and in some low-elevation passes.

Habitat: never seen on land. *In migration:* wetlands and larger lakes. *Breeding:* shallow, weedy wetlands.

Nesting: usually nests singly or in groups of 2 or 3 pairs; in thick vegetation in lake edges, ponds, marshes and reservoirs; shallow,

floating platform nest, made of wet and decaying plants, is anchored to or placed among emergent vegetation; pair incubates 4–7 eggs and raises the young together.

Feeding: makes shallow dives and gleans the surface for aquatic insects, crustaceans, mollusks, small fish and adult and larval amphibians.

Voice: loud series of croaks and shrieking notes and a sharp *keark keark* during courtship; usually quiet outside the breeding season.

Similar Species: *Eared Grebe* (p. 34): black neck in breeding plumage. *Pied-billed Grebe* (p. 31): thicker bill; mostly brown body. *Red-necked Grebe* (p. 33): larger; generally louder; white cheek.

RED-NECKED GREBE
Podiceps grisegena

As spring evenings settle upon mountain lakes, the loud, enthusiastic, laughing calls of courting Red-necked Grebes provide an aural backdrop to the wild scene. Although these birds are not as vocally refined and majestic as loons, few birds match the verbal vigor and endurance of a pair of Red-necked Grebes in peak spring passion. ■ All grebes carry their newly hatched young on their backs. The heavily striped young stay aboard even when the parents dive underwater.

■ The scientific name *grisegena* means 'gray cheek,' and it refers to this species's winter plumage. In the Rockies, Red-necked Grebes are only found in their winter plumage briefly during fall migration.

breeding

I.D.: *Sexes similar. Breeding:* red neck; white cheek; black crown; straight, heavy, yellow bill; black upperparts; light underparts; black eyes. *Non-breeding:* grayish-white throat and cheek.
Size: *L* 17–22 in. (43–56 cm).
Range: uncommon breeder and common migrant in the Canadian Rockies; common breeder in western Montana south of Glacier NP; uncommon migrant in the U.S. Rockies.
Habitat: *Breeding:* emergent vegetation in lakes and ponds in the montane and the subalpine. *In migration:* open, deeper lakes.
Nesting: usually nests singly or occasionally in loosely scattered colonies; floating platform nest, made of aquatic vegetation, is anchored to submerged plants; eggs are initially white, but they often become stained by wet vegetation.

Feeding: dives and gleans the surface for small fish, aquatic invertebrates and amphibians.
Voice: often repeated, excited *ah-ooo ah-ooo ah-ooo ah-ah-ah-ah-ah.*
Similar Species: *Horned Grebe* (p. 32): dark cheek. *Eared Grebe* (p. 34): black neck. *Pied-billed Grebe* (p. 31): thicker bill; mostly brown body. *Western Grebe* (p. 35): black upperparts; white underparts. *American Coot* (p. 101): all-black body; often seen on land. *Ducks* (pp. 47–69): all lack the combination of a white cheek and a red neck.

EARED GREBE
Podiceps nigricollis

Like the rest of its clan, the Eared Grebe eats feathers—either old, discarded ones or feathers plucked from its breast. It can eat so many feathers that balls form in its stomach and pack the digestive tract. It is thought that this behavior protects the stomach lining and intestines from sharp fish bones; the feathers might also slow the passage of food through the digestive system, which allows more time for nutrients to be absorbed.

■ These gregarious, colonial birds often replace Horned Grebes in northern areas. ■ The Eared Grebe is a widely distributed species that occurs in western North America, Europe, Asia, Central Africa and South America. ■ The scientific name *nigricollis* means 'black neck,' which is a useful field mark for this species.

breeding

I.D.: *Sexes similar. Breeding:* black neck, cheek, forehead and back; red flanks; gold ear tufts ('horns'); white underparts; thin, straight bill; red eyes; slightly raised crown. *In flight:* wings beat constantly; hunchbacked appearance; legs trail behind the tail.

Size: *L* 12–14 in. (30–36 cm).

Range: fairly common spring and fall migrant throughout the Rockies; locally common breeder in the northern Rockies.

Habitat: never seen on land. *In migration:* wetlands and larger lakes. *Breeding:* shallow, weedy wetlands.

Nesting: usually colonial; in thick vegetation in lake edges, ponds and marshes; shallow, flimsy, floating platform nest, made of wet and decaying plants, is anchored to or placed among emergent vegetation; pair incubates the eggs and raises the young.

Feeding: makes shallow dives and gleans the surface for aquatic insects, crustaceans, mollusks, small fish and larval and adult amphibians.

Voice: usually quiet outside the breeding season; mellow *poo-eee-chk* during courtship.

Similar Species: *Horned Grebe* (p. 32): rufous neck. *Pied-billed Grebe* (p. 31): thicker bill; mostly brown body. *Red-necked Grebe* (p. 33): red neck; white cheek.

WESTERN GREBE
Aechmophorus occidentalis

The courtship display of the Western Grebe is among the most elaborate breeding rituals of North American wildlife. During the 'weed dance,' the male and female both raise their torsos gently out of the water, caressing each other with aquatic vegetation held in their long, rapier-like bills. The pair's bond is fully reinforced by the 'rushing' phase, during which the birds glance at one another before exploding into a sprint across the water's surface. Each grebe stands high, with its wings held back and its cobra-like head and neck rigid, until the race ends with the pair breaking the water's surface in a headfirst dive.

I.D.: *Sexes similar:* long, slender neck; black upperparts, from the base of the bill to the tail; white underparts, from the chin through the belly; long, thin, yellow bill; white cheek; red eyes, surrounded in black.

Size: *L* 20–24 in. (51–61 cm).

Range: common spring and fall migrant throughout the Rockies; locally common summer breeder in the central U.S. Rockies.

Habitat: *Breeding:* large lakes with dense areas of emergent vegetation or thick mats of floating aquatic plants. *In migration:* large, deep lakes.

Nesting: typically on the Great Plains and in the boreal forest; colonial; floating nest, built

of aquatic vegetation, is anchored to submerged plants; pair incubates the eggs for 23 days.

Feeding: gleans the water's surface and dives for small fish and aquatic invertebrates.

Voice: high-pitched *crreeet-crreeet.*

Similar Species: *Double-crested Cormorant* (p. 37): underparts are not clean white. *Common Loon* (p. 30): shorter, stocky neck. *Eared* (p. 34), *Horned* (p. 32) and *Red-necked* (p. 33) grebes: much smaller. *Clark's Grebe* (p. 314): white around the eyes; orange-yellow bill; species ranges overlap in the Great Plains.

AMERICAN WHITE PELICAN
Pelecanus erythrorhynchos

Its wingspan is unsurpassed by any other Rocky Mountain bird, and the purposeful and confident flight of the American White Pelican is an unforgettable experience. These pelicans are often seen skimming low over lakes: their bellies nearly touch the waves as the birds use the subtle air currents rising from the water's surface to help them glide. ■ Watching flocks of white pelicans might let you witness a rare activity among birds: group foraging. Small groups of pelicans typically work together to heard fish into shallow water, where they are easier to catch. ■ The scientific name *erythrorhynchos* is Greek for 'red beak.'

non-breeding

I.D.: *Sexes similar:* very large, stocky, white bird; long, orange bill and throat pouch; black primary and secondary wing feathers; short tail; naked orange skin patch around the eye. *Breeding:* small, keeled plate develops on the upper mandible; pale yellow crest on the back of the head. *Non-breeding* and *Immature:* white plumage is tinged with brown.
Size: *L* 54–70 in. (137–178 cm); *W* 9 ft. (2.8 m).
Range: very uncommon migrant throughout the Rockies; locally common breeder in the greater Yellowstone area.
Habitat: *Breeding:* Yellowstone Lake, Jackson Lake and the Snake River. *In migration:* large, low-elevation lakes.

Nesting: colonial; on bare, low-lying islands; nest scrape is either lined with pebbles and debris or is completely unlined; 2 eggs hatch at different times, after approximately 33 days; young are born naked and helpless.
Feeding: surface dips for small fish and amphibians; small groups of pelicans often feed cooperatively by herding fish into large concentrations.
Voice: generally quiet.
Similar Species: *Snow Goose* (p. 43): smaller; much smaller bill. *Tundra Swan* (p. 46) and *Trumpeter Swan* (p. 45): wing tips are not black; longer, thinner necks.

DOUBLE-CRESTED CORMORANT

Phalacrocorax auritus

This prehistoric-looking bird is the only North American cormorant that is commonly seen in the Rockies.

■ Double-crested Cormorants are often observed with their wings partially spread, drying their flight feathers in the sun and wind. Cormorants lack the ability to waterproof their feathers, which helps them during underwater dives by decreasing their buoyancy. Also aiding the Double-crested Cormorant's aquatic lifestyle are its long, rudder-like tail, its excellent underwater vision and its sealed nostrils. Because these birds cannot breathe through the nose, they can often be identified by their gaping beaks.

■ In South America, cormorants are economically valuable to local people, who mine the birds' guano (excrement) for commercial fertilizer.

breeding

I.D.: *Sexes similar:* large, black water bird; long tail; long neck; thin bill, hooked at the tip; blue eyes. *Breeding:* throat pouch becomes intense orange-yellow; fine, buff plumes trail from the eyebrows. *Immature:* brown upperparts; buff throat and breast; yellowish throat patch. *In flight:* rapid wing beats; kinked neck.

Size: *L* 26–32 in. (66–81 cm); *W* 52 in. (132 cm).

Range: local but common breeder in Idaho and western Montana, in suitable wetland habitat.

Habitat: *Summer:* Yellowstone Lake. *In migration:* large lakes and large, meandering rivers.

Nesting: colonial; on low-lying islands or precariously high in trees; nest platform is made of sticks, aquatic vegetation and guano; often nests on islands with pelicans, terns and gulls.

Feeding: long underwater dives of up to 30 ft. (9 m) after small schooling fish or, rarely, amphibians and invertebrates; young are fed by regurgitation.

Voice: generally quiet; occasional grunts or croaks.

Similar Species: *Common Loon* (p. 30): more colorful; shorter neck. *Canada Goose* (p. 44): white cheek; not completely black. *White-winged Scoter* (p. 62) and *Surf Scoter* (p. 61); shorter necks; shorter tails.

AMERICAN BITTERN
Botaurus lentiginosus

The American Bittern's deep
and mysterious booming call
is as characteristic of the
spring marsh as the sounds of
croaking frogs and nighttime
showers. ▪ When approached
by an intruder, this bird's
first reaction is to freeze: its
bill points skyward and its
brown vertical streaking
blends perfectly with the
surroundings. An American
Bittern will always face an
intruder, and it moves to keep
its streaked breast toward the
danger. Most intruders simply
pass by without noticing the
motionless bird. An American
Bittern will freeze even if it is
encountered in an open area; it is
apparently unaware that a lack of
cover betrays its presence!

I.D.: *Sexes similar:* brown upperparts;
brown streaking from the chin through
the breast; straight, stout bill; yellow legs
and feet; black outer wings; black streaks
from the bill down the neck to the
shoulder; short tail.
Size: *L* 23–27 in. (59–69 cm);
W 42 in. (107 cm).
Range: uncommon breeder in suitable
habitat throughout the Rockies; rare in the
Canadian Rockies, but known to nest in Banff
and Yoho NPs.
Habitat: among tall, dense grasses, bulrushes
and cattails in emergent wetlands, lake edges
and backwaters in the montane.
Nesting: singly; above water-line in dense
vegetation in cattail and bulrush marshes; nest
platform is made of grass, sedges and dead
reeds; nest often has separate entrance and
exit paths.

Feeding: patient stand-and-wait predator;
stabs for small fish, amphibians and aquatic
invertebrates.
Voice: slow, resonant, repetitive *pomp-er-lunk*
or *plum pudding*; most often heard at night.
Similar Species: *Least Bittern* (p. 314):
uncommon; black crown; light, inner wing
linings. *Black-crowned Night-Heron* (p. 41) and
Green Heron (p. 315): immatures lack the
black streak from the bill to the shoulder.

GREAT BLUE HERON
Ardea herodias

The Great Blue Heron is the patient sentry of wetland marshes: it stands motionlessly as it surveys the calm, shallow waters, head-and-shoulders above most other wetland birds. ▪ This heron is often mistaken for a crane because of its similar size, but cranes hold their necks outstretched in flight. Herons and egrets fold their necks back on their shoulders—a specialized vertebra enables herons to contort their necks into an S shape. ▪ Occasionally, people out fishing will catch a large trout that has distinctive triangular scars, which are evidence that the fish survived a heron attack.

breeding

I.D.: *Sexes similar:* large, blue-gray bird; long, curving neck; long, dark legs; blue-gray wing covers and back; straight, yellow bill; chestnut thighs. *Breeding:* colors are more intense; plumes streak from the crown and throat. *In flight:* neck folds back over the shoulders; legs trail behind the body; deep, lazy wing beats.
Size: L 50–54 in. (127–137 cm); W 5 ft. (1.8 m).
Range: most frequently encountered heron through most of the Rockies; common breeder and migrant in the U.S. Rockies; uncommon migrant and summer visitor in the Canadian Rockies.
Habitat: forages along the edges of rivers, lakes and marshes in the montane; also seen in fields and wet meadows.

Nesting: colonial; in a tree; flimsy to elaborate stick and twig platform is added to, often over years, and can be up to 4 ft. (1.2 m) in diameter; pair incubates the eggs for approximately 28 days.
Feeding: patient stand-and-wait predator; stabs for small fish, amphibians, small mammals, aquatic invertebrates and reptiles; occasionally scavenges; occasionally feeds in fields.
Voice: usually quiet; occasionally a deep, harsh *frahnk frahnk frahnk* (usually during take-off).
Similar Species: *Black-crowned Night-Heron* (p. 41): much smaller; shorter legs. *Egrets* (pp. 40 & 314): all are predominantly white. *Sandhill Crane* (p. 102): red cap; flies with its neck outstretched; uncommon in the mountains.

SNOWY EGRET
Egretta thula

While most herons and egrets in the Rockies hunt passively, the Snowy Egret takes a more energetic approach. By waving its yellow feet in shallow wetlands, the Snowy Egret spooks potential prey out of hiding places. When a fish retreats from the bright golden slippers, the bird spots its movement and makes a precise stab with its bill. In an even more devious hunting strategy, Snowies are known to create shade by extending their wings over open water. If a fish is unfortunate enough to be lured into the shaded 'refuge,' it is promptly seized by the waiting egret.

breeding

I.D.: *Sexes similar:* snow white plumage; jet-black bill and legs; bright yellow feet. *Breeding:* elegant plumes on the throat and rump; erect crown; orange-red lore. *Immature:* similar to an adult, but the yellow of the feet extends up the back of the legs. *In flight:* head is folded over the shoulders; legs extend beyond the tail; yellow feet are obvious.
Size: L 22–26 in. (56–66 cm); W 41 in. (104 cm).
Range: uncommon migrant in most of the U.S. Rockies; local breeder in the southern U.S. Rockies; exceptionally rare vagrant in the Canadian Rockies.

Habitat: open edges of rivers, lakes and marshes in the montane.
Nesting: colonial; in trees, bushes and marshes or occasionally on the ground; flimsy nest platform of sticks and twigs is lined with finer plant materials; pair incubates the eggs and raises the young.
Feeding: stirs the substrate with its feet; stands and waits; occasionally hovers and stabs; eats small fish, amphibians and aquatic invertebrates.
Voice: low croaks; bouncy *wulla-wulla-wulla* on breeding grounds.
Similar Species: *Great Egret* (p. 314): larger; yellow bill; black feet. *Cattle Egret* (p. 314): orange-yellow legs and bill.

BLACK-CROWNED NIGHT-HERON

Nycticorax nycticorax

When the setting sun's dim light has driven most of the wetland's waders to their nightly roosts, the Black-crowned Night-Heron arrives to reawaken these feeding areas with its characteristic squawk. A night-heron's eyes are proportionately larger than other herons'—likely an adaptation to foraging in low light. ▪ Most of the night-herons that migrate through low passes in the Rockies have over-wintered in California and are destined to breed on the Great Plains. ▪ This heron's white 'ponytail' is present for most of the year, but it is most noticeable during the breeding season. ▪ *Nycticorax*, meaning 'night raven,' refers to this bird's characteristic nighttime call.

I.D.: *Sexes similar:* black cap and back; white cheek and underparts; gray wings; dull, yellow legs; stout, black bill; large, red eyes. *Breeding:* 2 long, white plumes trail down from the crown. *Immature:* heavily streaked underparts; dull upperparts with light brown spots.
Size: *L* 23–26 in. (58–66 cm); *W* 42 in. (107 cm).
Range: local breeder at Freezeout Lake, Montana; rare to uncommon elsewhere in the Rockies.
Habitat: shallow cattail and bulrush marshes, small lakes and slow rivers.
Nesting: commonly along prairie wetlands;

colonial; in willows and shrubs; loose nest platform of twigs and sticks is lined with finer materials; male gathers the nesting material; female constructs the nest.
Feeding: often at dusk; stands motionless and waits; stabs for small fish, amphibians, aquatic invertebrates, reptiles, young birds and small mammals.
Voice: deep, guttural *quark* or *woc*; often heard as the bird takes flight.
Similar Species: *Great Blue Heron* (p. 39): much larger; longer legs; back is not black. *Green Heron* (p. 315): underparts and flanks are dark.

WHITE-FACED IBIS
Plegadis chihi

In its search for suitable breeding sites in the Great Plains and Great Basin, the White-faced Ibis occasionally finds itself in the Rockies. Its wide-ranging search and nomadic post-breeding dispersal sends it far from its nesting range. ■ The White-faced Ibis is the only North American ibis commonly found in the interior. ■ A trademark of the White-faced Ibis is its heavy, sickle-shaped bill, which it uses so effectively in foraging. *Plegadis* is Greek for 'sickle-shaped.' ■ The White-faced Ibis is superficially very similar to the Glossy Ibis, but the ranges of the two species overlap very little.

breeding

I.D.: *Sexes similar:* dark chestnut plumage; long, downcurved bill; long, dark legs; white feathers bordering a naked facial patch; greenish lower back and wing covers; dark red eyes. *Breeding:* rich red legs and facial patch. *In flight:* outstretched neck; long, downcurved bill is distinctive.
Size: *L* 19–26 in. (48–66 cm); *W* 36 in. (91 cm).
Range: uncommon in the southern U.S. Rockies; rare north of Yellowstone NP.
Habitat: cattail and bulrush marshes, mudflats, brackish wetlands, freshwater marshes.
Nesting: typically on the southern Great Plains and the Great Basin; colonial; in bulrushes or other emergent vegetation; deep cup nest is made of coarse materials and lined with fine plant matter; 3–4 bluish-green eggs.

Feeding: probes mudflats and gleans the ground for aquatic invertebrates, amphibians and other small vertebrates.
Voice: generally quiet; occasionally gives a series of low, duck-like quacks.
Similar Species: *Long-billed Curlew* (p. 113): light brown overall; daintier bill. *Herons and egrets* (pp. 39–41 & 314): all lack the thick, downcurved bill.

SNOW GOOSE
Chen caerulescens

The yearly migrations of Snow Geese are among North America's natural highlights. In spring and fall, great clouds of these white-and-black migrants fill the skies with their calls. Because they are slow to return to their wintering grounds, the fall migration is perhaps the best time to watch for these birds in the mountains. ▪ Snow Geese use low-elevation passes to cross the mountains, and they occasionally stop to feed in low-lying wetlands. ▪ Unlike Canada Geese, which fly in well-formed Vs, migrating Snow Geese usually form unorganized, oscillating, wavy lines. ▪ Tens of thousands of birds gather and cover the fields like snow when they arrive at their wintering grounds in California, New Mexico and Texas.

I.D.: *Sexes similar:* white overall; black wing tips; dark pink feet and bill; dark 'grinning patch' on bill; plumage is occasionally stained rusty by iron in the water. *'Blue Goose':* white head; blue-gray body plumage. *Immature:* gray plumage; dark bill and feet.
Size: *L* 28–33 in. (71–84 cm); *W* 59 in. (150 cm).
Range: common migrant in Idaho and Montana; rare migrant elsewhere in the Rockies.
Habitat: shallow wetlands, lakes and fields in low passes.
Nesting: on the shores of Hudson Bay, the Beaufort Sea and arctic islands; often colonial; on a tussock or other small mound; nest is usually made of mud, grass and moss and lined with down plucked from the female.
Feeding: grazes on waste grain and new sprouts; also eats aquatic vegetation, grass and roots.
Voice: loud, nasal, constant *houk-houk.*
Similar Species: *Ross' Goose* (p. 315): smaller; lacks the black 'grin.' *Tundra Swan* (p. 46) and *Trumpeter Swan* (p. 45): larger; wing tips are not black. *American White Pelican* (p. 36): much larger; larger bill; black in its wings extends much further toward its body.

CANADA GOOSE
Branta canadensis

When most North Americans imagine the sight and sound of a wild goose, it is the Canada Goose that comes immediately to mind, with good reason: this species is the most numerous and the most visible large waterfowl on the continent. The situation is no different in the Rockies. Although Canada Geese are not as abundant here as elsewhere in North America, they are the only geese to nest in the mountains; with persistence, you can find a pair nesting alongside a marsh or even near a golf course. ▪ Although the sight of one of these wetland giants can become quite mundane by the end of summer, the early spring sight of a flock breaking the horizon preludes the excitement of the upcoming season.

I.D.: *Sexes similar:* long, black neck; white cheek; white undertail coverts; light brown underparts; dark brown upperparts; short, black tail.
Size: L 32–48 in. (81–122 cm); W 70 in. (178 cm).
Range: common breeder throughout the Rockies; common winter resident in the U.S. Rockies and southern Canada.
Habitat: lakeshores, riverbanks, ponds and grassy meadows in the montane and the subalpine.
Nesting: on islands and shorelines; usually on the ground, but occasionally on cliffs, Osprey nests or nest platforms; nest is built with grass and other plant materials and lined with down from the female's breast.
Feeding: grazes new sprouts, aquatic vegetation, grass and roots; tips up for roots and tubers.
Voice: loud and familiar *ah-honk*.
Similar Species: *Greater White-fronted Goose* (p. 315): neck is not black; uncommon migrant through the Rockies. *Double-crested Cormorant* (p. 37): cheek and undertail coverts are not white; generally silent in flight.

TRUMPETER SWAN
Cygnus buccinator

The Trumpeter Swan is quickly recovering from being hunted almost to extinction for its feathers and meat early in the 20th century. In fact, biologists are now concerned about the large concentrations of these birds that pack wintering areas throughout western North America. To lessen the threat of disease and the loss of food resources, biologists have been actively transporting swans to less-used sites to ease overcrowding. ■ The best places to see the Trumpeter Swan—the world's largest species of waterfowl—may be in parts of the Rocky Mountains. The Trumpeter Swan is present year-round in the greater Yellowstone area, with hundreds gathering there on open water during winter. ■ Both 'trumpeter' and *buccinator* refer to this species's loud, bugling voice.

I.D.: *Sexes similar:* all-white plumage; large, solid black bill; black feet; no black on wings; no yellow 'teardrop'; neck is held straight, with a kink at the base, while standing or swimming. *Immature:* gray-brown plumage; gray bill.
Size: *L* 59–72 in. (150–183 cm); *W* 8 ft. (2.4 m).
Range: year-round resident in Yellowstone NP, Red Rock Lakes NWR and vicinity; uncommon migrant and breeder in the Canadian Rockies.
Habitat: lakes and large wetlands; locally restricted.

Nesting: builds large mounds of vegetation, often on top of muskrat or beaver lodges, and occasionally on shores; female incubates usually 4–6 eggs.
Feeding: tips up, surface gleans and occasionally grazes for vegetation, primarily sago pondweed, duckweed, tubers and roots.
Voice: loud, resonant and bugle-like *koh-hoh*.
Similar Species: *Tundra Swan* (p. 46): smaller; migrant through the Rockies; yellow 'teardrop' in front of eye; softer, nasal voice. *Snow Goose* (p. 43): smaller; black wing tips; shorter neck.

45

TUNDRA SWAN
Cygnus columbianus

In early spring, Tundra Swans migrate across the mountains through low-elevation passes. The snow and ice that they frequently encounter during their visit in the Rockies will not be the last of their trip; Tundra Swans usually reach their arctic breeding grounds before the spring thaw. ▪ The phrase 'swan song' is derived from this bird's reported habit of cooing a mournful death song after being shot. ▪ Like the Trumpeter Swan, the Tundra Swan's windpipe loops through the bird's sternum, which amplifies its call. ▪ The Lewis and Clark exploration team found this bird near the Columbia River, after which its scientific name was later derived.

I.D.: *Sexes similar:* white plumage; large, black bill; black feet; no black on the wings; yellow 'teardrop' in front of eye; neck is held straight from its base. *Immature:* gray-brown plumage; gray bill.

Size: L 47–58 in. (119–147 cm); W 80 in. (2 m).

Range: common migrant in the lower mountain passes; rare winter resident on open water in the southern U.S. Rockies.

Habitat: *In migration:* shallow areas of montane lakes and wetlands, agricultural fields and flooded pastures.

Nesting: in the Arctic; on a raised mound in a shallow tundra pond or on a shoreline; nest is made of aquatic vegetation and moss; male stands guard while the female incubates the eggs.

Feeding: tips up, dabbles and surface gleans for aquatic vegetation and aquatic invertebrates; grazes for tubers, roots and waste grain.

Voice: high-pitched, quivering *oo-oo-whoo* is constantly repeated by migrating flocks.

Similar Species: *Trumpeter Swan* (p. 45): larger resident; loud bugle-like voice; lacks the yellow 'teardrop' on the bill. *Snow Goose* (p. 43): smaller; black wing tips.

WOOD DUCK
Aix sponsa

The male Wood Duck is one of the most colorful water birds in North America; its image routinely adorns books, magazines, postcards and calendars. To see a male in his breeding finery, perched in a tree, conveys a link between the bird's beauty and its habits. The males molt following breeding, however, and lose much of their extravagant plumage. Most male ducks enter this 'eclipse' plumage stage for a brief period from late summer to fall. They normally molt again into their breeding colors before their fall migration. ▪ Wood Ducks commonly associate with Mallards and American Wigeons in much of the southern Rockies. ▪ The Wood Duck has no close relatives in the Americas. It is in the same genus as the similarly beautiful Mandarin Duck of eastern Asia. ▪ The scientific name *sponsa* is Latin for 'promised bride,' suggesting that the male appears formally dressed for a wedding.

I.D.: *Male:* glossy green head; crest is slicked back from the crown; white chin and throat; chestnut breast is spotted with white; white shoulder slash; golden sides; dark back and hindquarters. *Female:* white, 'teardrop' eye patch; mottled brown breast is streaked with white; brown-gray upperparts; white belly.
Size: *L* 15–21 in. (38–53 cm).
Range: uncommon breeder from Yellowstone NP to the Canadian Rockies; rare migrant in the central and southern U.S. Rockies; rare summer resident in the Canadian Rockies.
Habitat: beaver ponds and backwaters with wooded edges in the foothills and the montane.

Nesting: in a natural hollow or cavity in a tree, often 30 ft. (9.1 m) or more high; also in artificial nest boxes; usually near water; nest is lined with down from the female's breast.
Feeding: surface gleans and tips up for aquatic vegetation, especially duckweed and aquatic sedges and grasses; eats more fruits and nuts than other ducks.
Voice: *Male:* ascending *ter-wee-wee.* *Female:* squeaky *woo-e-e-k.*
Similar Species: *Hooded Merganser* (p. 66): white patch on the crest; slim bill. *Harlequin Duck* (p. 60): no crest; blue-gray overall.

GADWALL
Anas strepera

Although male Gadwalls lack the striking plumage of most other ducks, they nevertheless have a dignified appearance. The intricacies of waterfowl plumage—from the bird's overall color to the structure and shading of individual feathers—is as heightened in Gadwalls as in more showy ducks—it just takes a little more effort to notice. ∎ Although all ducks are capable of diving, those in the genus *Anas* (the dabbling ducks) are more likely to be observed tipping up—except the Gadwall, whose diving habits are more developed than others of this clan. ∎ Gadwalls have recently expanded their range throughout North America.

I.D.: *General:* black-and-white wing patch (often seen in resting birds); white belly. *Male:* mostly gray; black hindquarters; dark bill. *Female:* mottled brown; brown bill with orange sides.
Size: L 18–22 in. (46–56 cm).
Range: uncommon migrant and local breeder in the U.S. Rockies; uncommon migrant and rare visitor to the Canadian Rockies.
Habitat: shallow wetlands, lake borders and beaver ponds in the montane.
Nesting: typically on the Great Plains; in tall vegetation, sometimes far from water; nest is well concealed in a scraped hollow, often with grass arching overhead; nest is made of grass and other dry vegetation and lined with down.

Feeding: dabbles and tips up for leaves, the stems of water plants, tubers and roots; grazes on grass and waste grain during migration; one of the few dabblers to dive routinely for food; also eats aquatic invertebrates, tadpoles and small fish.
Voice: *Male:* simple, singular *quack;* often whistles harshly. *Female:* series of high *kaak kaaak kak-kak-kak,* oscillating in volume.
Similar Species: *American Wigeon* (p. 49): male has a white forehead and a green swipe trailing from each eye; female lacks the black hindquarters and has a green speculum. *Mallard* (p. 50), *Northern Pintail* (p. 54) and *other dabbling ducks* (pp. 49–55): females all generally lack the black hindquarters and the black-and-white wing patch.

AMERICAN WIGEON

Anas americana

The American Wigeon is one of the most common western ducks; the male's characteristic, wheezy laugh is one of the wetland's main voices in the Rocky Mountains. ■ The American Wigeon is generally vegetarian. Although it often dabbles for food, nothing seems to please a wigeon more than wild celery and other pond-bottom plants. Unfortunately for this bird, these plants grow far too deep for a dabbling duck. Instead, pirating wigeons often steal these succulent plants when accomplished divers, such as Canvasbacks, scaups and Redheads, return to the surface with their bottom-dwelling food. When not harassing diving ducks for their lunch, American Wigeons are commonly observed grazing on shore. ■ The American Wigeon's bright white crown and forehead, (in the male) has led some people to call it 'Baldplate.'

I.D.: *General:* large, white wing patch; cinnamon breast and flanks; white belly; gray bill with a black tip; green speculum. *Male:* white forehead; green swipe running back from each eye. *Female:* grayish head; brown underparts.
Size: L 18–23 in. (46–58 cm).
Range: fairly common breeder and resident in the Rockies south of Glacier NP; common migrant and uncommon summer resident in the Canadian Rockies.
Habitat: shallow wetlands, lake edges and ponds in the montane and the lower subalpine.
Nesting: always on dry ground, often far from water; nest is well concealed in tall vegetation and is built with grass, leaves and down; female incubates the white eggs for 23–25 days.
Feeding: dabbles and tips up for aquatic leaves and the stems of pondweeds; also grazes and uproots young shoots in fields; infrequently eats invertebrates.
Voice: *Male:* nasal whistle, *whee WHEE wheew,* frequently repeated. *Female:* soft, seldom heard *quack.*
Similar Species: *Gadwall* (p. 48): lacks the large, white wing patch; male has pure black hindquarters.

MALLARD
Anas platyrhynchos

The Mallard is the most numerous and, with the male's iridescent green head and chestnut breast, the most recognizable duck in the Northern Hemisphere. Its circumpolar distribution makes it a familiar sight through North America, Europe and Asia. Mallards are abundant, year-round residents in the Rockies, tolerating the worst of our weather if water remains open by rivers or hot springs. ▪ Wild Mallards will freely hybridize with domestic ducks. The resulting offspring, frequently seen in city parks, are a confusing blend of both parents. ▪ Most people think of the Mallard's *quack* as the classic duck call. ▪ The scientific name *platyrhynchos* is Greek for 'broad, flat bill.'

I.D.: *General:* dark blue speculum is bordered by white; orange feet. *Male:* glossy green head; yellow bill; chestnut breast; white 'necklace'; gray body plumage; black tail feathers that curl upward. *Female:* mottled brown overall; orange bill is splattered with black.
Size: *L* 20–28 in. (51–71 cm).
Range: abundant year-round resident in the southern Rockies; abundant summer resident, abundant migrant and common winter resident in the northern Rockies.
Habitat: lakes, wetlands, backwaters and springs in the montane and the subalpine.
Nesting: in tall vegetation or under a bush, often near water; nest is made of grass and other plant material and lined with down; female incubates 7–10 light green eggs.
Feeding: tips up and dabbles in shallows for the seeds of sedges, willows and pondweeds; also eats aquatic invertebrates, larval amphibians and fish eggs.
Voice: *Female:* loud quacks; very vocal.
Similar Species: *Northern Shoveler* (p. 53): larger bill; male has a white breast. *American Black Duck:* darker than a female Mallard; purple speculum. *Common Merganser* (p. 68): male lacks the chestnut breast and has snowy white underparts.

BLUE-WINGED TEAL

Anas discors

Of waterfowl migrants, the Blue-winged Teal is one of the champions: individuals that nest in the Rockies frequently winter in the southern U.S. and Mexico. ▪ The white crescent on the male's cheek easily confirms the identity of this small duck. ▪ The Green-winged Teal is not the Blue-winged Teal's closest relative. Blue-wings are more closely related to Cinnamon Teals and Northern Shovelers, as a glance at their broad, flat bills will confirm. These three species also have very similar patterns of wing coloration: a pale-blue forewing and a green speculum. ▪ The scientific name *discors* is Latin for 'without harmony,' possibly in reference to this bird's call as it takes flight.

I.D.: *Male:* blue-gray head; white crescent on the face; breast and sides are spotted with black. *Female:* mottled brown overall. *In flight:* blue forewing patch; green speculum.
Size: L 14–16 in. (36–41 cm).
Range: common migrant and uncommon breeder throughout the Rockies.
Habitat: shallow lake edges and wetlands in the montane; prefers areas of short but dense emergent vegetation.
Nesting: primarily on prairie potholes; in grass along shorelines and in wet meadows, usually very near water; nest is built with grass

and considerable amounts of down; female incubates 8–11 eggs for 24 days.
Feeding: gleans the water surface for sedge and grass seeds, pondweeds, duckweeds and aquatic invertebrates.
Voice: *Male:* soft *keck-keck-keck*. *Female:* soft quacks.
Similar Species: *Harlequin Duck* (p. 60): blue-gray overall; white shoulder slash. *Cinnamon Teal* (p. 52) and *Green-winged Teal* (p. 55): lack the white crescent on the cheek. *Northern Shoveler* (p. 53): male has a green head and lacks the spotting on the body.

CINNAMON TEAL
Anas cyanoptera

When the morning sun strikes a spring wetland, male Cinnamon Teals glow upon the waters like embers. These handsome ducks are frequently seen swimming along the surface of wetlands, their heads partially submerged, skimming aquatic life from the pond's surface. Often, a series of ducks can be seen following a lead foraging individual, taking advantage of the sediments the lead duck stirs up with its paddling feet. ▪ Female Cinnamon Teals have been known to put on a 'broken wing' act to distract predators from their ducklings. The male Cinnamon Teal, unlike most male ducks, often stays with his mate through most of the incubation; sometimes the male has been seen accompanying his mate and her brood. ▪ The scientific name—from *cyano*, 'blue,' and *ptera*, 'wing'—reinforces the similarities of this species to the Blue-winged Teal, with which it has been known to interbreed.

I.D.: *General:* long, broad bill; blue forewing patch; green speculum. *Male:* rich cinnamon-red head, neck and underparts; red eyes. *Female:* mottled brown overall; dark eyes.
Size: L 15–17 in. (38–43 cm).
Range: common summer breeder in the southern and central U.S. Rockies; uncommon migrant in the Canadian Rockies.
Habitat: shallow wetlands with extensive emergent vegetation and sedge beds.
Nesting: in tall vegetation, occasionally far from water; nest is in a concealed hollow and is built with grass and down; female incubates 7–12 eggs for 21–25 days; ducklings fly after 7 weeks.
Feeding: gleans the water surface for grass and sedge seeds, pondweeds, duckweeds and aquatic invertebrates.
Voice: *Male:* whistled *peep. Female:* rough *karr, karr, karr.*
Similar Species: *Ruddy Duck* (p. 69): male has a white cheek and a blue bill. *Green-winged Teal* (p. 55): gray body; white shoulder slash; green streak trailing from each eye.

NORTHERN SHOVELER

Anas clypeata

The Northern Shoveler's spoon-like bill allows this large duck to strain small invertebrates from a pond's mucky bottom. While most ducks' bills have comb-like structures along the mandible edges, the shoveler's straining structures are more developed and allow it to feed more exclusively. Shovelers eat much smaller organisms than do most other waterfowl, and their intestines are elongated to prolong the digestion of these hard-bodied invertebrates. ■ The Northern Shoveler is most commonly seen lounging in shallow wetlands or grazing hazardously along roadsides. ■ The scientific name *clypeata* is Latin for 'furnished with a shield,' in reference to the shoveler's massive bill.

I.D.: *General:* large, spatulate bill; blue fore-wing patch; green speculum. *Male:* green head; white breast; chestnut sides. *Female:* mottled brown overall; orange-tinged bill.
Size: L 18–20 in. (46–51 cm).
Range: locally common in the U.S. Rockies; uncommon migrant throughout the Rockies.
Habitat: shallow marshes, bogs and lakes with muddy bottoms and emergent vege-tation, in open and semi-open areas in the montane.
Nesting: in a shallow hollow on dry ground, usually within 150 ft. (46 m) of water; female builds the nest with dry grass and down and incubates 10–12 eggs for 25 days; ducklings

show the distinctive, spoon-like bill after 2 weeks.
Feeding: dabbles and gleans the water and mud; strains out plant and animal matter, especially aquatic crustaceans, insect larvae and seeds; rarely tips up.
Voice: generally quiet; occasionally a raspy chuckle or quack, most often heard in the spring courtship.
Similar Species: *Mallard* (p. 50): male has a chestnut breast and white flanks; female lacks the pale blue forewing and has a blue speculum. *Blue-winged Teal* (p. 51): female has a much slimmer bill and is smaller.

NORTHERN PINTAIL
Anas acuta

The male's long, tapering tail feathers and the slender finger of white extending up his neck contribute to the sleek and swift appearance of this striking duck. Whether a Northern Pintail is seen flying overhead or resting on a pond or stubble field, its distinctive shape makes identification simple. ▪ Migrating Northern Pintails are often seen in flocks of 20 to 40 birds, but some flocks can contain as many as 200 birds. ▪ The North American population of pintails has yo-yoed up and down over the last century, but from the overall trend, this widespread duck appears to be in decline. ▪ Pintails' nests are often more exposed than those of other ducks. The nests are usually built near water, but they can be up to half a mile. (0.8 km) away. ▪ The scientific name *acuta* is Latin for 'pointed,' an obvious reference to this bird's tail feathers.

I.D.: *General:* long, slender neck; dark glossy bill. *Male:* chocolate brown head; long, tapering tail feathers; white breast; long neck with a white stripe; dusty gray body plumage. *Female:* mottled light brown overall. *In flight:* slender and sleek.
Size: *Male: L* 25–30 in. (64–76 cm). *Female: L* 20–22 in. (51–56 cm).
Range: uncommon year-round resident south of Yellowstone NP; uncommon to common migrant and uncommon breeder in the northern Rockies.
Habitat: shallow wetlands and lake edges in the montane.

Nesting: in a small depression in vegetation; nest is made of grass, leaves and moss and lined with the female's down; female incubates 6–9 eggs for up to 24 days.
Feeding: tips up and dabbles in shallows for the seeds of sedges, willows and pondweeds; also eats aquatic invertebrates and larval amphibians; eats waste grain in agricultural areas during migration.
Voice: *Male:* soft, whistling call. *Female:* rough quack.
Similar Species: *Mallard* (p. 50) and *Gadwall* (p. 48): females are chunkier and lack the tapering tail. *Blue-winged Teal* (p. 51): female is smaller and has a green speculum.

GREEN-WINGED TEAL
Anas crecca

Small, tight-flying flocks of Green-winged Teals are among the most speedy and maneuverable of waterfowl. When intruders cause these small ducks to rocket from wetlands, the ducks circle overhead until the threat departs. ▪ Green-winged Teals can be found farther north through winter than any other teal. ▪ Because feathers gradually wear out and cannot be repaired if they get damaged, all birds molt their old feathers, usually after the breeding season. Many species of ducks are grounded for brief periods during the molting phase, because their set of flight feathers is incomplete. They are generally reclusive and difficult to observe at this time, remaining hidden and quiet in dense vegetation. ▪ The scientific name *crecca* is an imitation of this duck's call.

I.D.: *General:* small bill; green-and-black speculum. *Male:* chestnut head; green swipe running back from the eye; white shoulder slash; creamy breast is spotted with black; pale gray sides. *Female:* mottled brown overall; light belly.
Size: L 12–16 in. (30–41 cm).
Range: fairly common year-round resident in the central U.S. Rockies; rare summer breeder in the southern U.S. Rockies; common migrant and uncommon breeder in the Canadian and northern U.S. Rockies.
Habitat: shallow lakes, wetlands, beaver ponds and meandering rivers in the montane.

Nesting: well-concealed in tall vegetation; nest is built of grass and leaves and lined with down; female incubates 8–9 creamy white eggs.
Feeding: dabbles in shallows for aquatic invertebrates, larval amphibians, sedge seeds and pondweeds.
Voice: *Male:* crisp whistle. *Female:* soft quack.
Similar Species: *American Wigeon* (p. 49): lacks the white shoulder slash and the chestnut head. *Blue-winged Teal* (p. 51): white crescent on the cheek; blue-gray head; light blue speculum.

CANVASBACK
Aythya valisineria

In profile, the Canvasback casts a noble image: its great, sloping bill is an unmistakable field mark, even when viewed from across a pond. Despite its proud proboscis, the 'Can' is named after its clean white back, which appears to be wrapped in a sheet of canvas. ■ This large, fast-flying duck is becoming increasingly difficult to observe in the Rockies, possibly because of habitat destruction on its Great Plains breeding grounds. ■ The scientific name *valisineria* refers to one of the Canvasback's favorite foods—wild celery (*Vallisneria americana*). When the bird was first described by Alexander Wilson, he misspelled *vallisneria* by leaving out an 'l' and adding an 'i.'

I.D.: *General:* head slopes upward from the bill to the forehead. *Male:* canvas-white back; chestnut head; black breast and hindquarters; red eyes. *Female:* brown head, neck and breast; grayish body.
Size: L 19–22 in. (48–56 cm).
Range: uncommon migrant and rare summer resident in the southern Rockies; rare migrant in the northern Rockies.
Habitat: shallow wetlands, lakes and ponds with water plants.
Nesting: typically on the Great Plains; basket nest is well concealed in emergent shoreline vegetation, usually suspended over the water; nest is built with reeds and grass and lined with down; female incubates 7–9 olive green eggs for up to 29 days.
Feeding: dives to depths of up to 30 ft. (9.1 m), but usually 10–12 ft. (3–3.7 m); feeds on roots, tubers, the basal stems of plants (including pondweeds and wild celery) and bulrush seeds; occasionally eats aquatic invertebrates.
Voice: generally quiet. *Male:* occasional *coos* and 'growls' during courtship rituals. *Female:* low, soft, purring *quack* or *kuck*; also 'growls.'
Similar Species: *Redhead* (p. 57): male has a gray back and a bluish bill and lacks the sloped forehead. *Ring-necked Duck* (p. 58): female lacks the straight, sloping bill.

REDHEAD
Aythya americana

Although Redheads are fully equipped with all the features required for diving, they often feed on the surface of wetlands like dabbling ducks. ■ Redheads often build a nest and brood their young as other ducks do, but they occasionally adopt different strategies to reproduce: a female Redhead will occasionally lay some eggs in another hen's nest and incubate only some of her own. ■ Female ducks routinely use up more than 50 percent of their calcium reserves in egg production. ■ Separating Redheads and Canvasbacks is a simple matter of looking at foreheads: Canvasbacks lack a forehead; Redheads look as though they are wearing a ball cap. ■ The genus name *Aythya* has its roots in the Greek word *aithuia*, meaning 'water bird.'

I.D.: *Male:* rounded, red head; black breast and hindquarters; gray back and sides; blue-gray bill is tipped with black. *Female:* dark overall; lighter toward the black-tipped bill.
Size: *L* 18–22 in. (46–56 cm).
Range: uncommon migrant and breeder in the U.S. Rockies; rarely seen in the Canadian Rockies.
Habitat: large wetlands, lakes and rivers, often near emergent vegetation.
Nesting: typically on the Great Plains; deep basket nest is well concealed at the base of emergent vegetation, suspended over water; nest is built with reeds and grass and lined

with fine, white down; female occasionally lays eggs in other ducks' nests.
Feeding: dives to depths of 10 ft. (3 m); primarily eats aquatic vegetation, especially pondweeds and duckweeds, and the leaves and stems of plants; occasionally eats aquatic invertebrates.
Voice: generally quiet. *Male:* courtship call is a cat-like *meow*. *Female:* rolling *kurr-kurr-kurr*, *squak* when alarmed.
Similar Species: *Canvasback* (p. 56): clean white back; bill slopes into the forehead. *Lesser Scaup* (p. 59): female has more white at the base of the bill.

RING-NECKED DUCK
Aythya collaris

For anyone who has seen a Ring-necked Duck, the field mark that immediately strikes the observer is the white ring around the base of the male's bill. For this reason, this stout duck perhaps should have been named the 'Ring-billed Duck'— its neck ring is barely visible. ▪ The Ring-necked Duck normally nests in more northern forests, but in the Rockies it breeds in cool woodland ponds south to Wyoming. ▪ Small flocks of this gregarious bird are often seen in the Rockies. The birds ride high on the surface of wetlands, frequently carrying their tails clear of the water. ▪ The scientific name *collaris* is Latin for 'collar,' a reference to the rarely seen (even by experienced birders), brownish collar around the base of the male's neck.

♂

I.D.: *Male:* dark, angular head with hints of purple; black breast, back and hindquarters; white shoulder slash; gray sides; thin, white ring around the base of the bill; blue-gray bill with black and white banding at the tip. *Female:* dark brown body; light brown head; faint white eye ring.
Size: L 14–18 in. (36–46 cm).
Range: fairly common breeder and migrant in the Canadian and northern U.S. Rockies; common to uncommon migrant in the southern U.S. Rockies.
Habitat: wooded ponds, swamps and marshes and sloughs with emergent vegetation; often associated with yellow waterlilies.

Nesting: frequently over water on a hummock or shoreline; bulky nest is made of grass and moss and lined with down; female incubates 8–10 olive-tan eggs.
Feeding: dives underwater mostly for aquatic vegetation, including seeds, tubers and pondweed leaves; also eats aquatic invertebrates.
Voice: seldom heard. *Male:* low-pitched, hissing whistle. *Female:* growling *churr*.
Similar Species: *Lesser Scaup* (p. 59): lacks the white shoulder slash and the black back; uniform-colored bill, with small black tip. *Redhead* (p. 57): female's head is the same tone as her body.

LESSER SCAUP
Aythya affinis

The Lesser Scaup is the Oreo cookie of the Rocky Mountain duck clan: black at both ends and white in the middle. It is one of the most abundant divers throughout our region, and it can be seen in large rafts during migration. ■ Several female scaups may care for two or more broods of young. Although the ducklings are tended by the females, they feed themselves. ■ Lesser Scaups, also known as Bluebills, leap up neatly before diving underwater, where they propel themselves with powerful strokes of their feet. ■ The scientific name *affinis* is Latin for 'adjacent and allied'—a reference to this scaup's close association to other diving ducks. 'Scaup' may be a reference to this bird's preferred winter food—shellfish bed are called 'scalps' in Scotland—or it may be a phonetic imitation of one of its calls.

I.D.: *Male:* dark head with hints of purple; black breast and hindquarters; yellow eyes; dirty white sides; grayish back; blue-gray bill. *Female:* dark brown; well-defined white patch at the base of the bill.
Size: *L* 15–18 in. (38–46 cm).
Range: locally common breeder and uncommon to common migrant throughout the Rockies.
Habitat: woodland ponds and lake edges with grassy margins.
Nesting: typically on the Great Plains; in tall, concealing vegetation, generally close to water; occasionally on islands; nest hollow is built of grass and lined with down; female incubates 8–10 eggs for about 25 days.
Feeding: dives underwater to depths of about 6 ft. (1.8 m) for aquatic invertebrates, mostly amphipods and insect larvae, and vegetation.
Voice: alarm call is a deep *scaup. Male:* courtship call is a soft *whee-oooh.*
Similar Species: *Ring-necked Duck* (p. 58): male has a white shoulder slash and a black back.

HARLEQUIN DUCK
Histrionicus histrionicus

During late spring and early summer, colorful male Harlequin Ducks can be observed in the roughest mountain waters, either gingerly floating on the surface or standing atop an exposed stream boulder. These scenes are short-lived, however, because in June or early July the males leave the nesting females and travel to the Pacific Coast to molt on marine waters. ▪ A conflict between river rafters and the Harlequin Duck has arisen in some parks. The concern lies with the repeated disturbance to breeding 'Harlies' caused by rafts, which may affect the nesting success of this threatened species. ▪ The Harlequin Duck gets its name from the male's striking plumage—a 'harlequin' is an actor who is colorfully made-up or who wears a mask.

I.D.: *General:* small, rounded duck; round head; short bill; raises and lowers tail while swimming. *Male:* gray-blue body; chestnut sides; white spots and stripes on the head, neck and flanks. *Female:* dusky brown overall; light underparts; 2–3 light patches on the head.
Size: *L* 14–19 in. (36–48 cm).
Range: regular, but local, breeder in the northern Rockies; rare in Colorado and Idaho; more common in Montana, British Columbia and Alberta.
Habitat: shallow, fast-flowing mountain streams from the montane to the lower alpine; prefers undisturbed rivers.
Nesting: under bushes and shrubs or among rocks near streams; shallow nest is lined with grass, plant materials and down; female incubates and rears the young alone.

Feeding: dabbles and dives up to 5 ft. (1.5 m) for aquatic invertebrates, mainly caddisfly and stonefly larvae; searches river bottoms, probing rock crevices for invertebrates and fish eggs.
Voice: generally silent outside the breeding season. *Male:* during courtship, utters squeaky whistles and a descending trill. *Female:* during courtship, utters a harsh *ek ek ek* or a low, croaking call.
Similar Species: *Bufflehead* (p. 63): female is smaller, lacks the white between the eye and the bill and is never found on swift-flowing water. *Surf Scoter* (p. 61) and *White-winged Scoter* (p. 62): females are very similar to a female Harlequin. *Other diving ducks* (pp. 56–59 & 64–69): females have longer necks and their bodies are not as rounded.

SURF SCOTER
Melanitta perspicillata

When spring storms turn mountain lakes into white squalls, migrating Surf Scoters rest comfortably among the crashing waves. Scoters spend their winters just beyond the breaking surf on both the Atlantic and Pacific coasts, and they are well adapted to life on rough water. ■ Scoters use their strong, sturdy bills to wrench shellfish from their winter ocean homes. Their gizzards are exceptionally muscular to help them break the shells. ■ Surf Scoters are often seen in the company of look-alike White-winged Scoters. ■ The Surf Scoter is the most abundant scoter in North America. ■ The genus name *Melanitta* means 'black duck'; *perspicillata* is Latin for 'spectacular,' referring to this bird's colorful bill.

I.D.: *General:* large, stocky, dark duck; large bill; sloping forehead; all-black wings. *Male:* black overall; white on the forehead and the back of the neck; orange bill and legs; black spot, outlined in white, at the base of the bill. *Female:* brown overall; dark gray bill; light patches on the cheek and ear.
Size: *L* 17–21 in. (43–53 cm).
Range: common spring and uncommon fall migrant in the northern Rockies; rare migrant in the southern Rockies; non-breeding birds occasionally summer in the Canadian Rockies.
Habitat: large, deep-water lakes in the montane and the subalpine.

Nesting: typically in northern Canada and Alaska; in a shallow scrape under bushes or branches, usually very near water; female incubates 5–8 buff-colored eggs.
Feeding: dives underwater to depths of 30 ft. (9.1 m); eats the larvae of damselflies, dragonflies, mayflies and caddisflies; occasionally eats aquatic vegetation; primarily eats shellfish when wintering on the coast.
Voice: generally quiet; infrequently utters low, harsh croaks. *Male:* occasionally gives a low, clear whistle. *Female:* guttural *krraak krraak*.
Similar Species: *White-winged Scoter* (p. 62): white wing patches; male lacks the white on the forehead and nape.

WHITE-WINGED SCOTER
Melanitta fusca

As White-winged Scoters race across mountain lakes during migration, their flapping wings reveal their key identifying feature: the white inner-wing patches strike a sharp contrast with the bird's otherwise black plumage. ▪ Scoters are heavy-bodied ducks, and they require long stretches of open water for takeoff. The name 'scoter' is derived from the way these birds scoot across the water's surface, frequently touching cresting waves. Occasionally, scooting is just a way of traveling quickly from one foraging site to another. ▪ White-winged Scoters are the most southerly nesters of the three North American scoters, breeding on occasion in the northwestern U.S. ▪ Black Scoters are the least common of the three scoters in North America. These all-black birds migrate through the Rockies in very small numbers. Large flocks of White-winged Scoters should be thoroughly checked for these rarely seen birds.

I.D.: *General:* largest scoter; stocky, all-dark duck; large, bulbous bill; sloping forehead; base of the bill is fully feathered. *Male:* black overall; white patch below the eye. *Female:* brown overall; gray-brown bill; light patches on the sides of the head. *In flight:* white wing patches.
Size: *L* 19–24 in. (48–61 cm).
Range: common spring and uncommon fall migrant in the northern Rockies; rare migrant in the southern Rockies; non-breeding birds occasionally summer in the Canadian Rockies.
Habitat: large, deep-water lakes and slow-moving streams.
Nesting: typically in Canada and Alaska; among willows or bushes very near shorelines; in a shallow scrape lined with sticks, leaves, grass and down; female incubates 9 eggs for 30 days.
Feeding: deep, underwater dives lasting up to 1 minute; mainly eats crustaceans; frequently takes aquatic insects, such as stonefly and caddisfly larvae, and snails; mainly eats shellfish when wintering on the coast.
Voice: courting pair produces guttural and harsh noises, between a *crook* and a *quack*.
Similar Species: *Surf Scoter* (p. 61): no white wing patches; male has a white forehead and nape.

BUFFLEHEAD
Bucephala albeola

When the morning mist rises from the calm surface of a wetland, a male Buffle-head is often the first duck to be recognized. His simple white-and-dark plumage strikes a vivid contrast to the dark surface of the pond. The white patch on the male's head may serve a role in courtship displays, and it adds to the male's babyface expression. ▪ Buffleheads are among the smallest diving ducks in North America. They seem most comfortable occupying the center of small ponds. ▪ The common name refers to this duck's large head and steep forehead, which are similar in shape to those of a buffalo. The genus name *Bucephala* also refers to the shape of the head: it means 'ox-headed' in Greek. The scientific name *albeola* is from the Latin for 'white,' in reference to the male's plumage.

I.D.: *General:* very small, rounded duck; white speculum in flight; short gray bill; short neck. *Male:* white wedge on the back of the head; head is otherwise dark green; dark back; white body plumage. *Female:* dark brown head; oval, white ear patch; light brown underparts.
Size: L 13–15 in. (33–38 cm).
Range: common migrant and rare breeder in the southern Rockies; common spring migrant and uncommon breeder in the Canadian and northern U.S. Rockies.
Habitat: *In migration:* open water of lakes, ponds and rivers. *Breeding:* small, wooded ponds and small lakes.
Nesting: typically in the boreal forest; often near water; in a tree cavity, usually an abandoned woodpecker nest or a natural cavity; nest chamber may be unlined or filled with a

little down; eggs incubated for 28–33 days; ducklings generally remain in the nest for up to 3 days.
Feeding: dives for aquatic invertebrates, mainly water boatmen and mayfly and damselfly larvae, occasionally snails and crustaceans; sometimes eats small fish and pondweeds.
Voice: *Male:* growling call. *Female:* harsh *quack.*
Similar Species: *Hooded Merganser* (p. 66): white crest is outlined in black. *Harlequin Duck* (p. 60): female has several light spots on the head. *Common Goldeneye* (p. 64) and *Barrow's Goldeneye* (p. 65): males are larger and have a white patch between the eye and the bill. *Other diving ducks* (pp. 56–69): females are much larger.

COMMON GOLDENEYE
Bucephala clangula

The courtship display of the male Common Goldeneye is one of nature's most entertaining slapstick routines. In winter and spring, the male arches his large green head back until his bill points skyward; then he produces a seemingly painful *peent*. Completely unaffected by this chiropractic wonder, he repeatedly performs this ritual, often to rather disinterested females. ▪ Wintering Common Goldeneyes routinely remain in areas of open water across North America. At this time of year they tend to prefer the slow-flowing water of lakes, cooling ponds and reservoirs. ▪ Goldeneyes are frequently called 'whistlers,' because the wind whistles through their wings when they fly.

I.D.: *General:* medium-sized, chunky duck; sloping forehead with a peaked head; black wings with large, white patches; bill is about half as long as the head width; golden eyes. *Male:* dark green head; round, white cheek patch; dark bill; dark back; white sides and belly. *Female:* chocolate brown head; lighter breast and belly; gray-brown body plumage; dark bill, tipped in yellow during summer.
Size: *L* 16–20 in. (41–51 cm).
Range: common winter resident in the southern and central U.S. Rockies; common migrant in the Canadian and northern U.S. Rockies.
Habitat: ponds, lakes and rivers in the montane.

Nesting: typically at low elevations in forested regions of Canada and Alaska; often close to water, but occasionally quite far from it; cavity nest, up to 60 ft. (18 m) high, is lined with wood chips and down; will use nest boxes; female incubates 6–9 eggs for 28–32 days; ducklings leave the nest after 2–3 days.
Feeding: dives underwater for aquatic insect larvae, crustaceans, tubers and sometimes small fish.
Voice: wings whistle in flight. *Male:* courtship calls are a nasal *peent* and a hoarse *kraaagh*. *Female:* harsh croak.
Similar Species: *Barrow's Goldeneye* (p. 65): male has a large, white, crescent-shaped cheek patch and white 'fingerprints' high on the back; female has more orange on the bill.

BARROW'S GOLDENEYE
Bucephala islandica

The Barrow's Goldeneye is one of the most characteristic diving ducks of the Rocky Mountains. It has an amusing foraging style: after making a deep dive for food, the bird pops back up to the surface like a colorful cork. ■ The Barrow's Goldeneye nests primarily west of the Continental Divide, and most of the world's population of this duck breeds in British Columbia, in proximity to wetlands. ■ This species bears the name of Sir John Barrow, secretary to the British Admiralty. Barrow Strait and Barrow, Alaska, are also named after this Englishman, who was committed to finding the Northwest Passage. ■ The scientific name *islandica* is the Latin form of 'Iceland'—Barrow's Goldeneyes also breed in Labrador, Greenland and Iceland.

I.D.: *General:* medium-sized, rounded duck; short bill; steep forehead. *Male:* dark purple head; white crescent on the cheek; white underparts; white 'fingerprints' on the back; dark back and wings. *Female:* chocolate brown head; orange bill is tipped with black during spring/summer; gray-brown body plumage.
Size: *L* 16–20 in. (41–51 cm).
Range: uncommon to common breeder and migrant in the Rockies north of Utah; rare winter resident and migrant in the southern U.S. Rockies.
Habitat: lakes, rivers, ponds and backwaters, usually bordered by deciduous trees; adjacent mixed forests are required for nest sites.

Nesting: in a tree cavity, usually an abandoned woodpecker nest or a natural cavity, up to 50 ft. (15 m) high; down is added to the nest throughout incubation; female incubates 9–10 olive green eggs.
Feeding: dives underwater for aquatic nymphs and larvae, especially damselflies and dragonflies; also eats crustaceans and some aquatic plants.
Voice: generally silent. *Male:* 'mewing' call in spring. *Female:* hoarse 'croaks' in spring.
Similar Species: *Common Goldeneye* (p. 64): male has a small, round, white cheek patch and lacks the white 'fingerprints' on the back; female has a darker bill, which lacks the black tip.

HOODED MERGANSER
Lophodytes cucullatus

The male Hooded Merganser has the most splendid headgear of all birds that breed in the Rocky Mountains. As if that weren't enough, however, he also has a most unusual courtship display: the male routinely performs a complete somersault for a potential mate, taking off and landing perfectly on the water's surface. ■ The male's crest is raised when he is aroused, whether during courtship or out of fear. The raised signal may alert other nearby 'Hoodies' that intruders are present. ■ The Hooded Merganser is the smallest of the mergansers. ■ The genus name of the Hooded Merganser is very appropriate: it means 'crested diver.'

I.D.: *General:* slim duck; crested head; thin, pointed bill. *Male:* black head and back; bold white crest is outlined in black; white breast; 2 white shoulder slashes; rusty sides. *Female:* dusky brown body; shaggy, reddish-brown crest. *In flight:* small, white wing patches.
Size: L 16–19 in. (41–48 cm).
Range: uncommon spring migrant and summer visitor to the Canadian and northern U.S. Rockies; rare migrant and winter resident in the central and southern U.S. Rockies.
Habitat: flooded willows, ponds and occasionally lakes and rivers in the montane and the subalpine.
Nesting: typically in interior B.C. and along the northern Pacific Coast; usually in a tree

cavity 15–20 ft. (4.6–6.1 m) high; rarely on the ground; cavity is lined with leaves, grass and down; female incubates 10–12 white eggs for 29–33 days.
Feeding: very diverse diet; dives for small fish, caddisfly and dragonfly larvae, snails, amphibians and crayfish.
Voice: low grunts and croaks. *Male:* frog-like *crrrrooo* in courtship display. *Female:* generally quiet; occasionally a harsh *gak* or a croaking *croo-croo-crook.*
Similar Species: *Bufflehead* (p. 63): male lacks the black outline to the crest and the white shoulder slashes. *Other small diving ducks* (pp. 58–65 & 69): females lack the crest.

RED-BREASTED MERGANSER
Mergus serrator

The glossy, slicked-back crest and wild, red eyes give the Red-breasted Merganser a crazed, new-age look. ▪ Mergansers are lean, powerful waterfowl designed for the underwater pursuit of fish. All mergansers have specially modified, thin bills with small serrations on the upper and lower mandibles that help them keep a firm grasp on their slippery fish prey. ▪ The scientific name *serrator* is Latin for 'sawyer,' and it refers to this bird's saw-like bill. ▪ Red-breasted Mergansers are infrequently encountered on mountain lakes during their migration between wintering on the coast and breeding in the Arctic.

♂

I.D.: *General:* large, elongated duck; thin, red, serrated bill; shaggy, slicked-back crest. *Male:* green head; light rusty breast is spotted with black; white collar; gray sides; black-and-white wing covers; red eyes. *Female:* gray-brown overall; reddish head. *In flight:* male has 2 white wing patches separated by 2 narrow, black bars; female has 2 white wing patches.
Size: L 19–26 in. (48–66 cm).
Range: locally common east of the Continental Divide in the northern U.S. Rockies during spring migration; rare migrant elsewhere in the Rockies.
Habitat: *In migration:* lakes and large rivers.
Nesting: typically in the boreal forest and taiga; on the ground near a shoreline, under bushes or branches or in dense grass and sedge; well-concealed nest is made with plant material and often lined with down; female builds the nest and incubates the eggs.
Feeding: dives underwater for small fish; also eats aquatic invertebrates, fish eggs and crustaceans.
Voice: generally quiet. *Male:* catlike *yeow* during courtship and feeding. *Female:* harsh *kho-kha*.
Similar Species: *Common Merganser* (p. 68): male lacks the spotted, red breast and the border between the head and breast is more clearly defined; female has a cleanly defined, white throat.

COMMON MERGANSER
Mergus merganser

Looking rather like a large jumbo jet taking off, the Common Merganser runs along the surface of the water, beating its wings until it gains sufficient speed for lift-off. ■ The Common Merganser is the most widespread and the most common merganser in North America. It also occurs in Europe and Asia, where it is called the Goosander—'merganser' is derived from the Latin for 'diving goose.' ■ These ducks are highly social, and they often gather in large assemblies during migration and winter. Whatever the season, Common Mergansers are wary birds that are nervous when they are near humans. ■ When ice forms on northern lakes, Common Mergansers retreat to open water on rivers, cooling ponds and springs.

I.D.: *General:* large, elongated body; long, red bill. *Male:* glossy green head without a crest; brilliant orange bill and feet; white body plumage; black spinal stripe. *Female:* rusty head; clean white neck and throat; gray body. *In flight:* shallow wing beats; body is compressed and arrow-like.
Size: *L* 22–27 in. (56–69 cm).
Range: common migrant and breeder in Yellowstone NP and northward; common winter resident on open water; uncommon migrant and common winter resident in the central and southern U.S. Rockies.
Habitat: large rivers and deep lakes in the montane and the subalpine; on open water during winter.
Nesting: often in a tree cavity 15–20 ft.

(4.6–6.1 m) high; occasionally on the ground, under a bush or log, on a cliff ledge or in a large nest boxes; usually not far from water; female incubates 8–11 eggs for up to 35 days.
Feeding: dives underwater (up to 30 ft. [9.1 m]) for small fish, usually trout, carp, suckers, perch and catfish; young eat aquatic invertebrates.
Voice: *Male:* harsh *uig-a*, like a guitar twang. *Female:* harsh *karr karr*.
Similar Species: *Red-breasted Merganser* (p. 67): shaggy crest; male has a spotted, red breast; female lacks the cleanly defined, white throat. *Mallard* (p. 50): male has a chestnut breast. *Common Goldeneye* (p. 64): male has white cheek patches. *Common Loon* (p. 30): white spotting on the back; bill is not orange.

RUDDY DUCK

Oxyura jamaicensis

Clowns of the wetlands, Ruddy Ducks display energetically on their breeding ponds. With great vigor, the small males pump their bright blue bills, almost touching their breasts. The *plap-plap-plap-plap-plap* of the display increases in speed to its climax: a spasmodic jerk and sputter. ▪ The Ruddy Duck is the only stiff-tailed duck found in the Rockies. It can be seen cocking up its rather long tail as it swims around small ponds. ▪ Female Ruddies commonly lay up to 15 eggs—a remarkable feat, considering that their eggs are bigger than those of a Mallard, even though a Mallard is twice the size of a Ruddy Duck! ▪ Ruddy Ducks often seem reluctant to take flight. When they do, like most diving ducks they must patter across the water for quite a distance before they become air-borne. On land, the Ruddy Duck is almost helpless.

breeding

I.D.: *General:* small duck; large bill and head; short neck; long, stiff tail feathers (often carried cocked upward). *Breeding male:* white cheeks; chestnut-red body; blue bill; black tail and crown. *Female:* brown overall; dark cheek stripe; darker crown and back. *Winter male:* like a female, but with a white cheek.
Size: *L* 15–16 in. (38–41 cm).
Range: common migrant and summer resident in the southern U.S. Rockies; uncommon migrant and summer resident in the central and northern U.S. Rockies and the Canadian Rockies.
Habitat: shallow marshes with dense emergent vegetation (such as cattails or bulrushes) and muddy bottoms.

Nesting: typically on the Great Plains; in cattails, bulrushes or other emergent vegetation; occasionally on a muskrat lodge or a log; basket-like nest is always suspended over water; occasionally uses the abandoned nest of another duck or coot.
Feeding: dives to the bottom of wetlands for the seeds of pondweeds, sedges and bulrushes and for the leafy parts of aquatic plants; also eats a few aquatic invertebrates.
Voice: *Male:* courtship display is *chuck-chuck-chuck-chur-r-r-r. Female:* generally silent.
Similar Species: *Cinnamon Teal* (p. 52): lacks the white cheek and the blue bill. *Diving ducks* (pp. 56–68): females lack the long tail and the dark facial stripe.

TURKEY VULTURE
Cathartes aura

Turkey Vultures are masters of using updrafts and thermals: they are capable of teasing lift from the skies, even when all other soaring birds are grounded. With their wings angled slightly upward, Turkey Vultures rock from side to side, catching rising air as they migrate along the slopes of the Rockies. ▪ The head of a Turkey Vulture is naked, and as a result, the bacteria and parasites they encounter while digging in rotting carcasses can be easily cleaned off. Vultures eat carrion almost exclusively; their bills and feet are not designed to crush or to kill living animals. ▪ Vultures are renowned for their ability to regurgitate their food, which allows parents to transport food to their young and also enables heavy adults to 'lighten up' for a quick take-off. ▪ Recent genetic studies have shown that the American vultures are most closely related to storks, not hawks and falcons.

I.D.: *Sexes similar:* very large, all-black bird. *Adult:* small, featherless, red head. *Immature:* gray head. *In flight:* silver-gray flight feathers; black wing linings; wings are held in a shallow V; head barely visible; tilts when it soars.
Size: L 26–32 in. (66–81 cm); W 68–72 in. (173–183 cm).
Range: common migrant at low elevations in the central and southern U.S. Rockies; uncommon summer resident elsewhere in the U.S. Rockies; rare in the Canadian Rockies.
Habitat: forages over open grasslands, shrublands and agricultural fields.

Nesting: on a cliff ledge, in a cave crevice or among boulders in mountain slopes; no nest material is used; female lays 2 dull-white eggs on bare ground; pair incubates the eggs for up to 41 days.
Feeding: entirely on carrion: ungulates, carnivores, rabbits, fish, domestic animals and rodents; young are fed by regurgitation; vultures are especially abundant when farmers cut crops.
Voice: generally silent; occasionally produces a *hrss* or grunt when threatened.
Similar Species: *Golden Eagle* (p. 82) and *Bald Eagle* (p. 72): wings are held flat in profile; do not rock when soaring; larger heads.

OSPREY

Pandion haliaetus

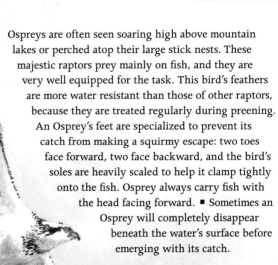

Ospreys are often seen soaring high above mountain lakes or perched atop their large stick nests. These majestic raptors prey mainly on fish, and they are very well equipped for the task. This bird's feathers are more water resistant than those of other raptors, because they are treated regularly during preening. An Osprey's feet are specialized to prevent its catch from making a squirmy escape: two toes face forward, two face backward, and the bird's soles are heavily scaled to help it clamp tightly onto the fish. Osprey always carry fish with the head facing forward. ▪ Sometimes an Osprey will completely disappear beneath the water's surface before emerging with its catch.

I.D.: *General:* large raptor; dark brown upperparts; white underparts; dark eye line; light crown. *Male:* all-white throat. *Female:* fine, dark 'necklace.' *In flight:* long wings are held in a shallow M; dark wrist patches; tail is finely banded with black and white.

Size: *L* 22–25 in. (56–64 cm); *W* 54–72 in. (137–183 cm).

Range: common breeder and migrant northward throughout the Rockies; uncommon in the southern U.S. Rockies.

Habitat: large lakes, slow-flowing rivers and reservoirs.

Nesting: on treetops, usually near lakes, large rivers and reservoirs; also on specially made platforms, utility poles, transmission towers, beacons or pilings, 45–90 ft. (14–27 m) high; large stick nest; male feeds the female while she incubates the eggs.

Feeding: dramatic, feet-first dives into the water; fish, averaging 2 lb. (1 kg), make up 98% of the diet.

Voice: series of melodious ascending notes: *chewk-chewk-chewk*; also an often-heard *kip-kip-kip*.

Similar Species: *Bald Eagle* (p. 72): adult is much larger, has a clean white head and tail, has a dark belly and breast and lacks the wrist patches; subadult is larger, holds its wings flat when soaring and lacks the clean, well-defined dark-and-white patterning.

BALD EAGLE
Haliaeetus leucocephalus

The Rocky Mountains have always been a haven for the Bald Eagle. This easily recognized bird is a source of inspiration and wonder to tourists longing for a wilderness experience. Bald Eagles also cast their spell on native peoples, and this widespread raptor is symbolically represented in their totems. ■ Each fall, large concentrations of Bald Eagles gather to feed on spawning and dying salmon in Glacier National Park. The dying salmon provide a timely bounty for these birds as they enter the lean winter months. ■ The decision to select the Bald Eagle as the United States' national bird was not without controversy. Benjamin Franklin, a respected naturalist, opposed the decision because of this eagle's dishonorable habit of scavenging and stealing fish from Ospreys.

I.D.: *Sexes similar:* very large raptor; unfeathered legs. *Adult:* white head and tail; dark brown body; yellow beak and feet; yellow eyes. *1st-year:* brown overall; dark eyes; dark bill; some white in the underwings. *2nd-year:* wide, white band at the base of the tail; light belly and underwings. *3rd- and 4th-years:* light head; dark eye line; yellow at the base of the bill; variable white body plumage; paler eyes. *In flight:* flaps infrequently; holds wings flat.
Size: L 30–43 in. (76–109 cm); W 5¹/₂–8 ft. (1.7–2.4 m).

Range: locally common migrant and breeder throughout the Rockies; winter resident at open waters throughout the Rockies.
Habitat: *In migration:* large lakes, marshes, rivers and open areas. *Nesting:* forested islands, lakeshores and riverbanks.
Nesting: usually in trees bordering lakes or large rivers; huge stick nest is up to 15 ft. (4.6 m) across—the largest nest of any North American bird.
Feeding: opportunistic; 90% of diet is fish, birds and mammals; fish are caught from swoops at the water's surface, pirated from Ospreys or scavenged from washed up, dead animals on the shore; may also feed on waterfowl; frequently feeds on carrion, especially large mammals in mountain parks.
Voice: thin, weak squeal or gull-like cackle: *kleek-kik-kik-kik* or *kah-kah-kah*.
Similar Species: Adult is distinctive. *Golden Eagle* (p. 82): similar to immature Bald Eagle, but has a golden nape, a smaller bill and heavily feathered feet down to the toes.

NORTHERN HARRIER

Circus cyaneus

The Northern Harrier may be the easiest hawk to identify on the wing, because no other hawk routinely flies so close to the ground. This common hawk cruises low over fields and meadows, seeming to graze the tops of long grass with its belly. Although it relies on excellent vision to detect prey, its owl-like, parabolic facial disc accentuates sounds, allowing the hawk to cue into prey by ear as well. ▪ Sexing a Northern Harrier is nearly as easy as identifying it: males are gray; females are brown. ▪ The genus name *Circus* is a wonderful tribute to this hawk's often erratic flight. ▪ This bird was once known as the Marsh Hawk in North America, and it is called the Hen Harrier in Europe.

I.D.: *General:* medium-sized; long wings and tail; white rump; facial disk. *Male:* gray upperparts; white underparts; black wing tips; indistinct tail bands. *Female:* reddish-brown overall. *Immature:* dark tail bands; heavily streaked breast, sides and flanks.

Size: L 16–24 in. (41–61 cm); W 44–47 in. (112–119 cm).

Range: common migrant in the southern U.S. Rockies; common summer resident in the central U.S. Rockies; uncommon to common breeder and migrant in the Canadian and northern U.S. Rockies.

Habitat: almost any type of open country, including open fields, wet meadows, cattail marshes, agricultural fields, hedgerows and alpine meadows; some migrate at higher elevations in fall.

Nesting: on the ground, often on a raised mound, usually in shrubs, cattails or tall vegetation; flat platform nest is built of grass, sticks and cattails; female incubates 4–6 bluish eggs.

Feeding: hunts by sight and sound in low, coursing flights, often below 30 ft. (9.1 m); eats small mammals, birds, amphibians and reptiles.

Voice: most vocal near nest site and during courtship, but generally quiet; near nest a high-pitch *ke-ke-ke-ke-ke-ke*.

Similar Species: *Red-tailed Hawk* (p. 79): lacks the white rump and the long, narrow tail. *Rough-legged Hawk* (p. 81): broader wings; wrist patches; fan-like tail.

SHARP-SHINNED HAWK

Accipiter striatus

When delivering food to his nestlings, the male Sharp-shinned Hawk is quite cautious around his mate: she is frequently one-third larger than he is. The two sexes prey on different-sized animals, which reduces their competition over food supplies. ▪ 'Accipiters,' named after their genus, are hawks that nest and hunt in woodlands. Their short, rounded wings, long, rudder-like tails and a flap-and-glide flight pattern give these birds the maneuverability to negotiate a maze of tree trunks. ▪ Rural birdfeeders will often attract Sharpies—not for the seeds, but for the finches and sparrows that the seeds attract. ▪ The 'sharp shins' of this hawk serve no purpose in field identification.

I.D.: *Sexes similar. Adult:* small, short, rounded wings; long, straight tail; blue-gray back; red horizontal bars on underparts; red eyes. *Immature:* brown overall; brown eyes; vertical, brown streaking on breast and belly. *In flight:* flap-and-glide flyer; tail is heavily barred and is straight or notched at the end, with a narrow terminal band.

Size: *Male: L* 10–12 in. (25–30 cm); *W* 20–24 in. (51–61 cm). *Female: L* 12–14 in. (30–36 cm); *W* 24–28 in. (61–71 cm).

Range: uncommon year-round resident in the southern U.S. Rockies; common winter resident in the U.S. Rockies; uncommon spring migrant in the Canadian and northern U.S. Rockies.

Habitat: dense to semi-open coniferous or deciduous forests; occasionally along riparian edges. *In migration* (especially in fall): usually seen soaring on thermals in open areas or hunting in alpine areas.

Nesting: new stick or twig nest is usually built each year, normally about 2 ft. (61 cm) across; may remodel an abandoned crow nest; female incubates 4–5 eggs for up to 35 days; male feeds the female during incubation.

Feeding: pursues small birds, such as finches, sparrows, warblers and thrushes, and occasionally woodpeckers and quail, through forests; takes more birds than other accipiters; rarely takes small mammals, amphibians and insects.

Voice: silent, except during the breeding season, when an intense and often repeated *kik-kik-kik-kik* can be heard.

Similar Species: *Cooper's Hawk* (p. 75): usually larger; rounded tail with a broad terminal band. *American Kestrel* (p. 83): long, pointed wings; 2 dark 'sideburns'; often seen in open country. *Merlin* (p. 84): pointed wings; rapid wing beats; lacks the red breast streaks.

74

COOPER'S HAWK

Accipiter cooperii

If a songbird were to dream, the Cooper's Hawk would be the subject of its nightmares. This forest hawk hunts silently, using surprise and speed. Bursting from an overhead perch, a Cooper's Hawk will pursue a songbird, using long legs with sharp talons to grab its quarry in mid-air. ■ Now that the persecution of Cooper's Hawks has been almost eliminated, these forest hawks are recolonizing former habitats. In the northern and western areas of the Rockies, these birds are being observed with increasing frequency. ■ This forest hawk bears the name of William Cooper, one of the many hunters who supplied English and American ornithologists with bird specimens for museum collections during the early 19th century.

I.D.: *Sexes similar. Adult:* medium-sized; short, round wings; long tail; squarish head; blue-gray back; red, horizontal barring on the underparts; red eyes; white, terminal tail band. *Immature:* brown overall; brown eyes; vertical brown streaks on, the breast and belly. *In flight:* flap-and-glide flyer; heavily barred, rounded tail, with a broad, light band at the tip.

Size: *Male: L* 15–17 in. (38–43 cm); *W* 27–32 in. (69–81 cm). *Female: L* 17–19 in. (43–48 cm); *W* 32–37 in. (81–94 cm).

Range: rare to uncommon year-round resident and common migrant throughout the Rockies.

Habitat: mixed coniferous-deciduous woodlands, riparian woodlands and suburban areas. *In migration:* usually seen soaring on thermals in open areas.

Nesting: in the crotch of a coniferous or deciduous tree, often among the outer branches; nest is made of sticks and twigs; may reuse an abandoned crow's nest; female incubates 4–5 bluish eggs for 30–36 days; does not tolerate Sharp-shinned Hawks nesting in the area.

Feeding: pursues prey—mostly thrushes, sparrows, squirrels, woodpeckers, chipmunks and starlings—in flights through forests; often takes prey to a plucking post prior to eating.

Voice: fast, woodpecker-like *cac-cac-cac-cac.*

Similar Species: *Sharp-shinned Hawk* (p. 74): usually smaller; tail is not rounded.

NORTHERN GOSHAWK
Accipiter gentilis

Perhaps the most aggressive and ill-tempered animal in the Rockies, the Northern Goshawk will not hesitate to defend its nest from any perceived threat. It may swoop at intruders, frequently raking their backs or heads with its razor-like talons. The disposition of our largest forest hawk is legendary, and goshawks have been observed preying on any reasonably sized animal. After chasing and catching their prey in a high-speed aerial sprint, these raptors stab repeatedly at the victims, internal organs with their long talons.

- Northern Goshawks require extensive areas of forests in which to hunt and raise their families, and their populations have declined significantly throughout Northern Europe and Asia. They are still found in remote areas of the Rockies.

I.D.: *Sexes similar. Adult:* large forest hawk; rounded wings; dark cap; white eyebrow; blue-gray back; gray, finely barred underparts; long, banded tail; red eyes. *Immature:* brown overall; light underparts; pale eyebrow.

Size: *Male: L* 21–23 in. (53–58 cm); *W* 40–43 in. (102–109 cm).
Female: L 23–25 in. (58–64 cm); *W* 43–47 in. (109–119 cm).

Range: uncommon resident and common fall migrant throughout the Rockies; locally common breeder in the central U.S. Rockies.

Habitat: *Breeding:* mature coniferous, deciduous and mixed woodlands. *Non-breeding:* forest edges, parks, farmlands and alpine areas.

Nesting: in deep woods, in a crotch usually 20–60 ft. (6.1–18 m) up a deciduous tree; bulky nest is built with sticks and twigs, many still green with leaves; nest is often reused; female incubates 3 eggs for 28–32 days.

Feeding: low foraging flights through the forest; feeds primarily on ground-dwelling birds (e.g., grouse and quail), rabbits, ground squirrels and tree squirrels; very opportunistic feeder on anything smaller than a grouse.

Voice: silent, except during the breeding season, when adults utter a loud, shrill and fast *kak-kak-kak-kak* or *gek-gek-gek-gek*.

Similar Species: *Cooper's Hawk* (p. 75) and *Sharp-shinned Hawk* (p. 74): much smaller; adults have red breast bars. *Large hawks* (pp. 77–81): all lack the bold, light eyebrow.

BROAD-WINGED HAWK

Buteo platypterus

In the Rockies, at the fringe of its western range, the small Broad-winged Hawk is an unusual, but not completely unexpected bird in migration. Best known for its flocks of thousands in eastern North America during fall, such spectacular aggregations do not grace Rocky Mountain skies. ▪ The soaring hawks—the genus *Buteo*—have fan-shaped tails and broad wings. They are frequently seen hunting and migrating in open areas, rising and falling on air currents. Even when the exact species of a hawk cannot be determined, it is often possible to know that it is a *Buteo*.

I.D.: *Sexes similar. Light phase adult:* black-and-white tail bands; horizontal russet barring on the breast; brown upperparts. *Dark phase adult:* brown wing linings; dark brown upperparts. *Immature:* brown streaks on a white breast; buffy and dark brown tail bands. *In flight:* broad, short wings; wing linings are slightly darker than the flight feathers; fan-shaped tail.

Size: L 14–19 in. (36–48 cm); W 32–39 in. (81–99 cm).

Range: very rare spring and fall migrant throughout the Rockies east of the Continental Divide.

Habitat: *In migration:* mountain ridges; also in riparian and deciduous forests.

Nesting: typically in eastern North America; usually in a deciduous tree, often near water; occasionally in a coniferous tree; small, bulky stick nest is built in a crotch 15–50 ft. (4.6–15 m) high; usually builds a new nest each year; occasionally reuses hawk, crow or squirrel nests.

Feeding: swoops from a perch for small animals, especially small mammals, amphibians, insects and young birds.

Voice: high-pitched whistle: *peeeo-wee-ee;* generally silent during migration.

Similar Species: *Sharp-shinned Hawk* (p. 74), *Cooper's Hawk* (p. 75) and *Northern Goshawk* (p. 76): long, narrow tails; adults have a blue-gray back. *Red-tailed Hawk* (p. 79) and *Swainson's Hawk* (p. 78): lack the banding on the tail in both the light and dark phases.

SWAINSON'S HAWK
Buteo swainsoni

light phase

This dainty, soaring hawk is the most common
summer raptor in open areas east of the Rockies.
Occasionally, individuals drift into low-elevation
fields and meadows in the mountains to hunt for
small rodents. ▪ The Swainson's Hawk migrates
the farthest of the raptors found in the Rockies:
these narrow-winged hawks winter as far south as
the southern tip of South America.
Unfortunately, the heavy use of insecticides in
Latin America recently caused a massive die-
off of this species. ▪ This hawk bears the
name of Englishman William Swainson,
an early 19th-century illustrator of
natural history.

dark phase

I.D.: *Sexes similar. General:* long, narrow wings;
fan-shaped tail. *Light phase:* dark bib; white
wing linings; dark flight feathers; white belly;
finely barred tail. *Dark phase:* dark wing linings
blend with brown flight feathers; brown overall. *In flight:* conspicuous wing linings and bib;
wings are held in a shallow V.
Size: *Male: L* 19–20 in. (48–51 cm);
W 52 in. (132 cm). *Female: L* 20–22 in.
(51–56 cm); *W* 52 in. (132 cm).
Range: locally common to uncommon
throughout the Rockies east of the
Continental Divide.
Habitat: open fields, grasslands, sagebrush
shelter belts and riparian and agricultural
areas.

Nesting: often in solitary trees in open fields;
builds a large stick nest; often uses the abandoned nests of other raptors, crows, ravens
or magpies; uses the same nest repeatedly;
female incubates 2–3 eggs for about 28–35
days.
Feeding: dives for voles, mice and occasionally ground squirrels; also eats snakes, small
birds and large insects, such as grasshoppers
and crickets.
Voice: high, weak *keeeaar.*
Similar Species: *Red-tailed Hawk* (p. 79):
wings are held flat when soaring; bulkier
overall; lacks the light wing linings and the
dark flight feathers. *Falcons* (pp. 83–87):
pointed wings; long, narrow tail.

RED-TAILED HAWK
Buteo jamaicensis

The Red-tailed Hawk is the most widespread and commonly observed western hawk. It is common throughout the Rocky Mountains and is frequently seen perched in trees, overlooking open fields. ■ The 'Harlan's Hawk' is a dark form of this species that breeds in Alaska and Canada and winters in the central and southern U.S. Rockies. ■ The Red tail's distinctive call is most often heard in spring during courtship, but it can also be heard throughout the remainder of the year. The distinctive scream is commonly used in the background of TV shows and movies to create the sense of wilderness. ■ This hawk occurs from Alaska to Panama and the West Indies. The scientific name *jamaicensis* refers to Jamaica, the source of the first scientifically described specimen of this species.

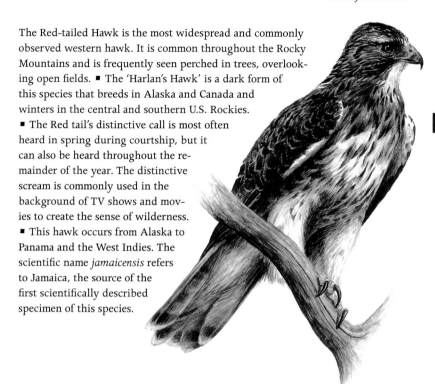

I.D.: *Sexes similar. General adult:* red tail; dark upperparts; light underparts; brown 'belt'; light breast. *Immature:* extremely variable; lacks the red tail; generally darker. *In flight:* fan-shaped tail; dark leading edge on the underwing; light wing linings; dark belt. *'Harlan's Hawk':* very dark; white mottling on back, breast and underwings; gray tail with dark streaks; variable.
Size: *Male: L* 18–23 in. (46–58 cm); *W* 46–58 in. (117–147 cm.). *Female: L* 20–25 in. (51–64 cm.); *W* 46–58 in. (117–147 cm.).
Range: common resident at low elevations from Colorado in southern Montana; common summer breeder and rare winter resident in the Canadian Rockies.
Habitat: open country, utility rights-of-way, roadsides, fields, mixed woodlands; rarely in the high alpine.
Nesting: usually in woodlands adjacent to open fields or shrublands; in a crotch in the crown of a deciduous tree, or occasionally a coniferous tree; rarely on cliffs; bulky stick nest is usually added to each year; both parents incubate the eggs; female alone raises the young, which fly at 6½ weeks.
Feeding: sit-and-wait hunting strategy from a perch on a fencepost, utility pole or tree; swoops down on prey; often dives after prey while soaring; occasionally forages by stalking on the ground; eats voles, mice, rabbits, chipmunks, small to medium-sized birds, amphibians and reptiles.
Voice: down-slurred scream: *keee-rrrr.*
Similar Species: *Swainson's Hawk* (p. 78): present only in summer; dark bib; light leading edge on the underwings. *Ferruginous Hawk* (p. 80): very large; dark legs; light underparts. *Rough-legged Hawk* (p. 81): present only in winter; very dark; white tail base; elbow patches on the underwings.

FERRUGINOUS HAWK
Buteo regalis

Cruising low over the contours of rolling, bare hills, Ferruginous Hawks approach ground squirrel or prairie dog communities. These large, graceful, open-country hawks strike unexpectedly, dropping from the air upon unknowing rodents. Ferruginous Hawks were once shot and poisoned because they were thought to be pests. Because of its largely rabbit and rodent diet, however, the Ferruginous Hawk is actually very beneficial to agriculture. ▪ These threatened hawks breed primarily on the Great Plains and overwinter south and west of the southern Rockies. Artificial nesting platforms have proven to be successful in encouraging nesting hawks. ▪ A very large, noble bird, it is well deserving of the scientific name *regalis*.

I.D.: *Sexes similar. Light phase adult:* rusty red upperparts; very light underparts; dark leggings; light head; light tail is tipped with rust. *Dark phase adult:* dark underparts; white tail; dark wing linings; light flight feathers. *Immature:* may lack the spotting on the legs. *In flight:* dark reddish-brown legs stand out against the white belly; mostly white underparts.
Size: L 22–27 in. (56–69 cm);
W 56 in. (142 cm).
Range: uncommon breeder in the southern and central U.S. Rockies; local breeder in Yellowstone NP; vagrant in the Canadian and northern U.S. Rockies.
Habitat: open grasslands, rangelands and agricultural fields.

Nesting: typically on the Great Plains; usually in a solitary tree, on a cliff or on the ground; large, compact nest is well made of sticks, weeds and cow dung and lined with finer materials; female incubates 2–4 eggs for 32–33 days; male provides food.
Feeding: swoops from high soaring flight; primarily eats ground squirrels, prairie dogs, rabbits and hares; also takes snakes and small birds.
Voice: alarm call is a loud, squealing *kreeah*, usually dropping at the end.
Similar Species: *Red-tailed Hawk* (p. 79): smaller; underparts are generally darker; red tail. *Swainson's Hawk* (p. 78): much smaller; dark flight feathers; light wing linings. *Rough-legged Hawk* (p. 81): present only in winter; dark 'elbow' patches.

ROUGH-LEGGED HAWK

Buteo lagopus

This Arctic-nesting hawk follows fall frosts south to overwinter in parts of southern Canada and the northern states. It is well adapted to cold climates, having feet that are fully feathered right down to the toes. ▪ Foraging Rough-legged Hawks can easily be identified at great distances— they are one of the few large hawks to routinely hover over prey. ▪ Populations of these hawks cycle with the populations of northern lemmings. When the number of small mammals is high, Rough-legs can produce up to seven young; in years of low mammal numbers, a pair may be fortunate to produce a single chick. ▪ The name *lagopus*, meaning 'hare's (or rabbit's) foot,' refers to this bird's distinctive feathered feet.

I.D.: *Sexes similar:* feet are feathered to the toes. *Light phase adult:* light, black-tipped tail; wide, dark 'belt'; streaked breast; dark upperparts; light head. *Dark phase adult:* dark wing linings, body and underparts; light flight feathers and undertail; very dark tail. *Immature:* unstreaked breast; unmarked undertail. *In flight:* light underwings with dark 'elbow' patches; long wings; frequently hovers.

Size: L 19–24 in. (48–61 cm); W 48–56 in. (122–142 cm).

Range: irregularly common winter resident and migrant in the central and southern U.S. Rockies; uncommon migrant and rare winter visitor in the Canadian and northern U.S. Rockies.

Habitat: *Winter:* open grasslands, agricultural fields, meadows and sagebrush flats with few trees.

Nesting: in the Arctic; on steep cliff ledges; occasionally in tall conifers; nest is built with grass and sticks; male or female incubates 2–7 eggs for up to 31 days; brood size depends on food availability.

Feeding: flies to a potential hunting area, then hangs and hovers, searching for prey; primarily eats small rodents; occasionally eats birds, amphibians, reptiles and large insects.

Voice: alarm call is a cat-like *kee-eer*, usually dropping at the end.

Similar Species: *Red-tailed* (p. 79), *Swainson's* (p. 78) and *Ferruginous* (p. 80) hawks: rarely hover; adults lack the dark 'elbow' patches and the dark, banded tail. *Northern Harrier* (p. 73): slimmer; long tail; facial disc.

GOLDEN EAGLE
Aquila chrysaetos

If the Rockies could be represented by just one bird, it would surely be the Golden Eagle. From its alpine, 'Rocky Mountain high' soaring to its low flights over the front ranges, the noble eagle embodies the wonder and wildness of the landscape. ■ The northern Rockies host one of the world's greatest raptor migrations: the spring and fall passing of Golden Eagles. Thousands of Golden Eagles ride the thermals of the Rockies to their breeding and wintering grounds each year. ■ Sometimes called the 'king of birds,' the Golden Eagle has been highly regarded by some cultures and persecuted by others. The tail and flight feathers of these eagles were used in the headdresses of many native groups living on the Great Plains.

I.D.: *Sexes similar. Adult:* large, brown raptor; golden tint to the neck and head; legs are fully feathered; brown eyes; brown tail is slightly banded with white; yellow feet; dark bill. *Immature:* white tail base; white patches in the wings. *In flight:* smallish head; long tail; occasional light patches.
Size: L 30–40 in. (76–102 cm); W 6¹/₂–7¹/₂ ft. (2–2.3 m).
Range: common winter resident in the Colorado and Wyoming Rockies; common spring migrant and uncommon breeder north of Colorado and throughout the Canadian Rockies.
Habitat: *Summer:* open and semi-open mountainous areas in the subalpine and alpine. *Winter:* lower elevations; occasionally seen at landfills.

Nesting: usually on a cliff overlooking an open area with a good population of small mammals; infrequently in a tree; nest is built of sticks, branches and roots and measures up to 10 ft. (3 m) across; site is often reused, and it may become stained white from droppings.
Feeding: swoops on prey from a soaring flight; very opportunistic feeder on ground squirrels, marmots and grouse; often eats carrion; can kill the young of goats, sheep or deer.
Voice: generally quiet; rarely a short bark.
Similar Species: *Bald Eagle* (p. 72): immature lacks the feathers down the legs, shows more white in the wings and has a larger head and heavier bill. *'Harlan's' Red-tailed Hawk* (p. 79): much smaller; hints of red in the tail.

AMERICAN KESTREL

Falco sparverius

The American Kestrel is the smallest and most common falcon in the Rockies, and it is frequently seen hovering, beating its wing into a blur, while looking for prey. A kestrel perched on a telephone wire above a roadside and open field is a familiar summer sight. ▪ Despite its robin-like size, this fierce predator routinely captures small rodents and birds, although large insects tend to make up the majority of its summer diet. ▪ The American Kestrel's scientific name, *sparverius*, is Latin for 'pertaining to sparrows,' even though sparrows are only an occasional prey item. Old field guides and old-time birders refer to this small falcon as the Sparrow Hawk.

I.D.: *General:* small falcon; 2 distinctive facial stripes. *Male:* rusty back; blue-gray wings; blue-gray crown with a rusty cap; lightly spotted underparts. *Female:* rusty back and wings. *In flight:* frequently hovers; long, rusty tail.
Size: L 7½–8 in. (19–20 cm); W 20–24 in. (51–61 cm).
Range: common summer breeder throughout the Rockies; uncommon to common winter visitor in the U.S. Rockies.
Habitat: open fields, forests, forest edges, grasslands, roadsides and agricultural areas with hunting perches.
Nesting: in a natural cavity or an abandoned woodpecker cavity (usually a flicker's); occa-

sionally uses an old magpie or crow nest; eggs are incubated for 29–30 days.
Feeding: swoops from a perch (often a power line or utility pole) or a hovering position; mainly eats insects, including grasshoppers, crickets, dragonflies and beetles; also eats mice, small birds, reptiles and amphibians.
Voice: a loud, often repeated, shrill *killy-killy-killy* when excited; female's voice is lower pitched.
Similar Species: *Merlin* (p. 84): lacks the distinctive facial stripes; far less common; does not hover. *Sharp-shinned Hawk* (p. 74): short, rounded wings; flap-and-glide flight.

MERLIN
Falco columbarius

Like the sorcerer of King Arthur's court, the male Merlin wears a dapper blue cape on his back. The main weapons of this small falcon—like all its falcon relatives—are speed, topography and surprise. Their sleek body design, long, narrow tail and pointed wings maximize speed. ■ Merlins tend to hunt small songbirds, and individual Merlins are known to concentrate their activities on one or two species. Through the fall migration, Merlins may follow larks and pipits south through high alpine meadows. ■ The scientific name *columbarius* is from the Latin for 'dove' or 'pigeon,' which the Merlin resembles in flight—it was formerly known as the Pigeon Hawk.

I.D.: *General:* heavily banded tail; heavily streaked underparts; no distinctive facial stripes; long, narrow tail. *Male:* blue-gray back and crown; rusty leg feathers. *Female:* brown back and crown. *In flight:* rapid wing beats; banded tail; pointed wings.
Size: *L* 10–12 in. (25–30 cm); *W* 23–26 in. (58–66 cm).
Range: uncommon migrant and winter visitor in the U.S. Rockies; rare migrant and summer breeder in the Canadian Rockies.
Habitat: *Breeding:* mainly coniferous forests; hunts along forest edges. *In migration:* open fields, alpine meadows, grasslands and along lakeshores.
Nesting: in either coniferous or deciduous trees, or in crevices and on cliffs; might reuse the abandoned nest of another raptor, crow, jay or magpie; might line nest with sprigs of green vegetation; either parent incubates the 4 or 5 eggs for 28–31 days.
Feeding: opportunistic; dives at, or overtakes in flight, small songbirds, such as waxwings, starlings, larks and sparrows; also eats large insects and nestlings.
Voice: loud, noisy, cackling cry: *kek-kek-kek-kek-kek or ki-ki-ki-ki*; calls in flight or while perched.
Similar Species: *American Kestrel* (p. 83): 2 facial stripes. *Peregrine Falcon* (p. 86): much larger; distinctive, dark hood. *Prairie Falcon* (p. 85): much larger; dark 'wing pits.' *Sharp-shinned Hawk* (p. 74) and *Cooper's Hawk* (p. 75): short, round wings; vertical breast streaks.

PRAIRIE FALCON

Falco mexicanus

Although it is most commonly encountered on the Great Plains, the Prairie Falcon is the most abundant large falcon in the Rockies, where it hunts in open country during migration in late summer and fall.

■ During their time in the Rockies, Prairie Falcons often concentrate around ground squirrel colonies in summer and around flocks of migrating songbirds in fall, when they routinely hunt in alpine meadows.

■ When young falcons first learn to fly, they tend to make many crash landings. Equipped for speed, their training flights are similar to sitting a 12-year-old child in the cockpit of a fighter jet and letting him or her fly the plane.

I.D.: *Sexes similar:* medium-sized; brown upperparts; light face with 2 dark brown, narrow facial stripes; underparts are white with brown spotting. *In flight:* black 'wing pits'; pointed wings; long, narrow, banded tail; quick wing beats.

Size: *Male:* L 14–15 in. (36–38 cm); W 37–39 in. (94–99 cm). *Female:* L 17–18 in. (43–46 cm); W 41–43 in. (104–109 cm).

Range: uncommon winter resident in the southern U.S. Rockies; locally uncommon summer visitor breeder in the central U.S. Rockies; uncommon late summer to fall transient through the Canadian front ranges.

Habitat: *In migration:* open, treeless country, such as alpine meadows, open fields, grasslands and sagebrush flats, in the montane and the subalpine. *Breeding:* river canyons and valleys in the foothills.

Nesting: typically on the Great Plains; on cliff ledges or crevices; sometimes in trees; rarely in abandoned nests of other raptors or crows; usually without nesting material.

Feeding: high-speed strike and kill by diving swoops; eats ground squirrels, chipmunks, waterfowl, grouse, songbirds, pigeons, shorebirds and other small vertebrates.

Voice: alarm call is a rapid, shrill *kik-kik-kik-kik*.

Similar Species: *Peregrine Falcon* (p. 86): lacks the dark 'wing pits' and the narrow mustache; dark hood. *Gyrfalcon* (p. 87): much larger; lacks the dark 'wing pits.' *Merlin* (p. 84): much smaller; light 'wing pits.' *Swainson's Hawk* (p. 78): fan-like tail; rounded wings in flight; lacks the dark 'wing pits.'

PEREGRINE FALCON
Falco peregrinus

The Peregrine Falcon's awesome speed and superior hunting skills were little defense against the chemical DDT from the 1940s to 1970s. Although banned in North America in 1972, DDT had so ravaged the Peregrine's population that the birds have yet to recover their former abundance. Despite intensive management in both the U.S. and Canada, southern populations of these birds have been painfully slow to recover. Wildlife managers erect open nest boxes and release captive-bred birds in hopes of boosting the wild population. ■ Peregrines now nest within the city limits of many urban centers. ■ The scientific name *peregrinus* is Latin for 'wandering,' reflecting this species' once-great range over much of the globe.

I.D.: *Sexes similar. Adult:* blue-gray back; dark, broad mustache; dark hood; light underparts with dark spots. *Immature:* similar patterning as an adult, but brown where the adult is blue-gray; heavier breast streaks. *In flight:* pointed wings; long, narrow, dark-banded tail.

Size: *Male: L* 15–17 in. (38–43 cm); *W* 37–43 in. (94–109 cm). *Female: L* 17–19 in. (43–48 cm); *W* 43–46 in. (109–117 cm).

Range: rare year-round in the southern U.S. Rockies; rare migrant and summer resident in the Canadian and northern U.S. Rockies; reintroduced at various locations just outside the Rockies in Canada and the U.S.

Habitat: lakeshores, river valleys, alpine meadows, rivermouths and open fields; open areas during migration.

Nesting: usually on rocky cliffs or cutbanks; no material is added, but the nest is littered with prey remains, leaves and grass; nest sites

are traditionally reused; female (mainly) incubates the 3 or 4 eggs for 32–34 days.

Feeding: high-speed, diving swoops; strikes birds in mid-air and guides them to a perch for consumption; pigeons, waterfowl, grebes, shorebirds, jays, flickers, swallows, ptarmigan and larger songbirds are the primary prey.

Voice: loud, harsh, continuous *cack-cack-cack-cack-cack* near nest site.

Similar Species: *Prairie Falcon* (p. 85): dark 'wing pits'; lacks the dark hood. *Gyrfalcon* (p. 87): seen only in winter in the Rockies; lacks the dark hood. *Merlin* (p. 84): lacks the broad mustache stripe; smaller.

GYRFALCON
Falco rusticolus

The Gyrfalcon is the largest of all falcons, and it is one of the world's most powerful avian hunters. Whether swooping down on prey from above or simply overtaking a bird in direct flight, a Gyrfalcon is an awesome hunter. To escape its deceptive speed and relentless pursuit, swift-flying ducks might plunge from the air into the water headfirst.
■ Once a Gyrfalcon or any other raptor catches its prey, one of its first instincts is to fan out its wings. This shielding is thought to hide the catch from other birds and mammals who would be happy to steal the prize. ■ The gray phase of the Gyrfalcon is the most commonly seen color phase in southern Canada and the northern U.S. The white phase— prized by falconers and birders alike—occurs mainly in the Arctic.

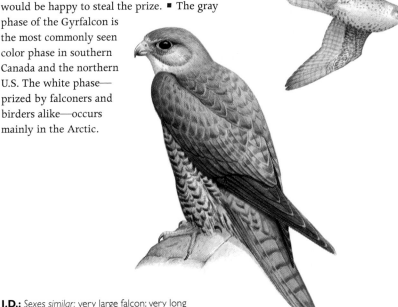

I.D.: *Sexes similar:* very large falcon; very long tail extends beyond the wing tips. *Adult:* usually gray-brown plumage; dark upperparts; light, heavily streaked underparts. *Immature:* darker and more heavily patterned than an adult.
Size: *Male:* L 20–22 in. (51–56 cm); W 48–51 in. (122–130 cm). *Female:* L 22–25 in. (56–64 cm); W 51–54 in. (130–137 cm).
Range: rare to uncommon winter visitor throughout the Rockies.
Habitat: open and semi-open areas, including marshes, fields and open wetlands, where there are prey concentrations.
Nesting: in the Arctic; usually on a high cliff ledge; also uses abandoned Rough-legged Hawk and raven nests; lines nesting site with sticks and twigs; pair incubates 4 eggs for up to 36 days; young fledge in 55 days.
Feeding: strikes prey in mid-air, follows it to the ground and consumes it there; locates prey from an elevated perch, by coursing low over the ground or by soaring; eats mainly birds, especially upland gamebirds, shorebirds, waterfowl and Rock Doves.
Voice: loud, harsh *kak-kak-kak.*
Similar Species: *Prairie Falcon* (p. 85): dark 'wing pits'; smaller. *Peregrine Falcon* (p. 86): dark hood; smaller. *Northern Goshawk* (p. 76): dark cap; light eyebrow; rounded wings in flight.

GRAY PARTRIDGE
Perdix perdix

Gray Partridges are perhaps most regularly seen in the early morning hours along quiet gravel roads, where they 'gravel up.' Like other seed-eating birds, partridges swallow small stones and sand to help crush the hard seeds they eat. The stones accumulate in the bird's gizzard (a muscular section of the stomach that is lined with hard plates) and help in digestion. ▪ Introduced from Eurasia in the early 1900s, the Gray Partridge is now the most abundant grouse over most of the agricultural areas of the Great Plains. While most native grouse have suffered at the conversion of the Plains, this partridge has benefited from the changes. ▪ Gray Partridges were formerly known as Hungarian Partridges, and they are still referred to as 'Huns' by many hunters.

I.D.: *General:* chestnut barring on the flank; gray breast; mottled brown back; rusty outer tail feathers; unfeathered, yellowish legs. *Male:* dark brown belly patch; dark chestnut face and throat. *Female:* white belly; pale chestnut marks on the face and throat.
Size: *L* 11–14 in. (28–36 cm).
Range: locally common in grasslands throughout Montana; locally uncommon in the Jackson Hole area.
Habitat: grasslands and agricultural fields, especially grain; occasionally in sagebrush flats.
Nesting: on the ground, in hayfields or pastures; scratches out a depression and lines the nest with coarse and fine grasses; female incubates 15–17 olive-colored eggs for 21–26 days.
Feeding: at dawn and dusk during summer; throughout the day during winter; gleans the ground for waste agricultural grain and seeds; also eats leaves and large terrestrial insects.
Voice: at dawn and dusk; sounds like a rusty gate hinge: *kee-uck*; call when excited is *kuta-kut-kut-kut*.
Similar Species: *Chukar* (p. 89): white throat; black barring on the flanks; red legs.

CHUKAR
Alectoris chukar

The Chukar is an Eastern European and Middle Eastern species that was introduced to North America as a gamebird. Most of the established populations are west of the Continental Divide, especially in the Great Basin. It seems to occupy an ecological niche left vacant by grouse and quails and competes little with native species. ▪ In fall and winter, Chukars feed in coveys of 5 to 40 birds, and they use their typical *chuck* or *chuck-or* call to reassemble scattered coveys. During summer, the call may help disperse breeding pairs.

I.D.: *Sexes similar. Adult:* grayish upperparts and breast; white cheeks and throat are bordered completely by black, forming a mask and 'necklace'; black barring on the flanks; reddish-pink bill, eye ring and legs; rufous outer tail feathers.
Size: *L* 13 in. (33 cm).
Range: uncommon to rare in the arid lands of Colorado, Utah, Idaho and Wyoming.
Habitat: rocky hillsides, dry sagebrush and grasslands in the foothills.

Nesting: on the ground; in a shallow scrape lined with grass and feathers; female incubates 9–16 eggs for about 23 days.
Feeding: gleans the ground for weed seeds, plucks leaves and fruits from shrubs and occasionally takes insects, especially grasshoppers.
Voice: rapid, laughing *chuck-chuck-chuck*.
Similar Species: *Gray Partridge* (p. 88): chestnut face; brown belly; no barring on the sides.

RING-NECKED PHEASANT

Phasianus colchicus

The spectacular Ring-necked Pheasant was introduced into North America from Asia in the mid-1800s. Many other gamebirds have also been introduced, but few have become as widespread, successful and tolerant of climatic conditions as this familiar bird. ▪ In winter, pheasants often segregate into small groups of males and larger flocks of females. ▪ Pheasants are not strong long-distance flyers, but they are powerful over short distances. They use their explosive bursts to fly over short open areas or quickly escape from predators, not outdistance them. ▪ The flight muscles of many gamebirds have few oxygen-carrying compounds and are not well developed for sustained flight. Because of the lack of these compounds, the breast muscles of pheasants are light in color, compared to the dark color of the continually working muscles in their legs.

I.D.: *General:* long tail; unfeathered legs. *Male:* green head; white collar; bronze underparts; naked red face patch. *Female:* mottled brown overall; light underparts.
Size: *Male:* L 30–36 in. (76–91 cm). *Female:* L 20–26 in. (51–66 cm).
Range: uncommon to common resident in valleys in the northern U.S. Rockies; rare to uncommon elsewhere in the Rockies.
Habitat: grasslands, pastures, ditches, agricultural lands, fields and occasionally croplands; rarely into the foothills.
Nesting: typically on the Great Plains; on the ground, among grass or sparse vegetation or next to a log or other natural debris; in a slight depression lined with grass and leaves; female incubates 10–12 eggs for up to 25 days.
Feeding: *Summer:* gleans the ground and vegetation for weed seeds and terrestrial insects. *Winter:* eats mainly buds and seeds.
Voice: loud, raspy, rooster-like *caw-caak* or *ca-ca,* mostly by the male.
Similar Species: male is distinctive. *Sharp-tailed Grouse* (p. 97): female is smaller and has a shorter tail. *Ruffed Grouse* (p. 91): female is smaller and has a fan-shaped tail. *Blue Grouse* (p. 94): female has a shorter tail, feathered legs and is grayer in color.

RUFFED GROUSE
Bonasa umbellus

The low drumming of the male Ruffed Grouse is a common spring sound in mountain woods. From atop an elevated site, the grouse arches back and beats the air with his cupped wings, producing deep, hollow booms. The sound is often felt before it's heard. The bird accelerates the beat during the display, in much the same rhythm as a starting lawnmower. The drumming is primarily restricted to the spring courting season, but, strangely, Ruffed Grouse also drum for a few weeks in fall. ▪ The Ruffed Grouse is named for the black ruffs on the sides of its neck. Displaying males erect these black patches to incite females.

♂

gray phase

I.D.: *Sexes similar:* small crest; mottled rusty-orange or gray-brown overall; black shoulder patches (or ruffs); banded tail with a dark terminal band. *Female:* incomplete terminal band.
Size: L 15–19 in. (38–48 cm).
Range: common in the Canadian Rockies and south through Glacier NP; uncommon in Yellowstone NP; rare south of Wyoming.
Habitat: aspen, cottonwood and poplar forests; spruce and pine woods.
Nesting: in a shallow depression among leaf litter; often beside logs, boulders and trees;

female incubates 9–12 eggs for 23–25 days.
Feeding: gleans the ground and vegetation; eats aspens buds, willow catkins and terrestrial insects.
Voice: *Male:* uses his wings to produce a hollow, drumming courtship sound of accelerating, deep booms. *Female:* may 'cluck' and 'hiss' when rearing chicks.
Similar Species: *Sharp-tailed Grouse* (p. 97): lacks the fan-shaped tail and the black shoulder patches. *Spruce Grouse* (p. 93): female lacks the small crest.

91

SAGE GROUSE

Centrocercus urophasianus

At dawn on early spring days, hundreds of Sage Grouse collect at breeding leks. Males enter the prairie arena, inflate their chests, spread their pointed tail feathers and strut to intimidate their peers and to attract females. The primary purpose of the dancing is to form pair bonding. Although leks are generally found in prime Sage Grouse habitat, males are not competing for territory. The most experienced and fittest males are always found at the center of the lek; immature males are inexperienced, poor strutters, and they are restricted to the periphery. The females are very selective, and one impressive male may mate with up to 75 percent of the nearby females.

I.D.: *Male:* large size; white breast; black bib and belly; long, pointed tail; mottled brown back; yellow comb. *Female:* mottled brown plumage; black belly.
Size: *Male: L* 27–34 in. (69–86 cm). *Female: L* 18–24 in. (46–61 cm).
Range: locally common in north central Colorado and the Wyoming Rockies.
Habitat: sagebrush flats in the plains, foothills or intermountain valleys.
Nesting: typically on the Great Plains; on the ground, usually under a sagebrush; in a shallow depression sparsely lined with leaves and

grass; female incubates 6–9 eggs for up to 27 days.
Feeding: mostly sagebrush leaves; flowers, buds and terrestrial insects during summer.
Voice: generally silent. *Male:* on breeding grounds, gurgles or makes a hollow *plop-plop* sound as air is released from the air sacs. *Female:* on breeding grounds, *quak-quak*.
Similar Species: *Ring-necked Pheasant* (p. 90): female lacks the black belly and has unfeathered legs. *Blue Grouse* (p. 94): fan-shaped tail; lacks the black belly; generally more blue-gray than a female Sage Grouse.

SPRUCE GROUSE

Falcipennis canadensis

The Spruce Grouse is almost exclusively a Canadian bird. Its range extends from coast to coast in Canada and all the way up through Alaska. Following the cool climate south through the Rockies, the range of the Spruce Grouse stops just short of Yellowstone National Park. ▪ Strutting grouse often display on trails or roads without regard for humans. Their display call could be the lowest pitched of any North American bird—it is nearly undetectable to the human ear.
▪ Spruce Grouse are often referred to as 'fool's hens' because they appear so trusting of humans—they are in fact relying on camouflage for protection.

'Franklin's Grouse'

I.D.: *Adult:* dark gray plumage; white-tipped undertail feathers; light specks on the belly; chestnut-tipped tail. *Male:* black upper breast and throat; red comb over the eye. *Female:* heavy barring on the underparts; grayish and reddish color phases. *'Franklin's Grouse':* white spots on the uppertail coverts; male has an all-dark tail; female has a white-tipped tail. *Immature:* heavily barred body.
Size: L 13–16 in. (33–41 cm).
Range: uncommon year-round throughout the Canadian and northern U.S. Rockies.
Habitat: conifer-dominated forests;

sometimes disperses into deciduous forests in migratory movements.
Nesting: on the forest floor; in a very well-hidden, shallow scrape lined with a few grasses and needles; female incubates 4–7 eggs for up to 21 days.
Feeding: live buds and needles of spruce, pine and fir trees; also eats berries, seeds and a few insects in summer.
Voice: very low, guttural *krrrk krrrk krrrk*.
Similar Species: *Blue Grouse* (p. 94): larger; male lacks the black front and the chestnut-tipped tail. *Ruffed Grouse* (p. 91): small crest; lacks the black front.

BLUE GROUSE
Dendragapus obscurus

In dense, montane forests, the owl-like hooting of the male Blue Grouse is one of the earliest signs of spring. His deep courting notes carry across the valleys while patches of snow still remain. The male's voice is so deep that the human ear can only hear a fraction of the sounds. The low frequencies travel well through forests, however, and they can carry hundreds of yards. ■ Hormonal changes cause these birds to make seasonal migrations, but rather than moving north-south, Blue Grouse simply move up and down mountain slopes.

■ *Dendragapus* is Greek for 'tree-loving,' but these birds are not strictly arboreal.

I.D.: *General:* white undertail covers; feathered legs. *Male:* gray-blue body; orange-yellow combs above the eyes; purple throat patches surrounded by white feathers. *Female:* mottled brownish gray overall. *Northern Rockies:* unbanded tail. *Southern Rockies:* gray band at the tail tip.
Size: *Male:* L 17–19 in. (43–48 cm). *Female:* L 18–22 in. (46–56 cm).
Range: common to uncommon resident throughout the Rockies.
Habitat: *Winter:* open coniferous forests in the montane. *Summer:* open coniferous forest; shrub meadows, avalanche slopes and shrubby ridges in the montane and the subalpine.

Nesting: on the ground, often near a fallen log or under a shrub; in a shallow depression lined with dead vegetation, such as leaves, twigs and needles; female incubates 7–10 buff-colored eggs for 25–28 days.
Feeding: leaves, berries, seeds and flowers; conifer needles and buds in winter; young birds eat grasshoppers and beetles.
Voice: deep, low hoots.
Similar Species: *Spruce Grouse* (p. 93): much smaller; banded tail. *Ruffed Grouse* (p. 91): much smaller; small crest; black shoulder patch; banded tail.

WILLOW PTARMIGAN
Lagopus lagopus

The Willow Ptarmigan is the largest North American ptarmigan. It is the same species that is called the Red Grouse in Great Britain, where it does not have a white winter molt. In North America, however, the Willow Ptarmigan molts three times a year, like the other ptarmigans, matching the seasonal changes in habitat. They are dark reddish brown and mottled in summer, more finely mottled in early fall and completely white in winter (except for the black tail feathers). ▪ All ptarmigans have red eye combs that can be inflated for courtship and aggression displays.

♀

♂

summer

I.D.: *Year-round:* black outer tail feathers; short, rounded wings; black bill. *Summer male:* chestnut brown head and neck; otherwise predominantly white splashed with brown on the upperparts. *Summer female:* mottled brown overall; white belly, legs and undertail coverts. *Winter:* all-white, except for the black outer tail feathers.
Size: *L* 13–14 in. (33–36 cm).
Range: uncommon year-round resident in Jasper NP; accidental elsewhere in the Rockies.
Habitat: open forests and shrub meadows in the upper subalpine and the alpine.

Nesting: in the Arctic or in alpine tundra; in a shallow scrape lined with grass and feathers; female incubates 7 eggs for 3 weeks.
Feeding: gleans vegetation and foliage for buds, flowers, leaves and small branches of willows and birch shrubs; occasionally eats some insects during summer.
Voice: loud, crackling *go-back go-back go-back.*
Similar Species: *White-tailed Ptarmigan* (p. 96): white tail; never has a reddish head and neck. *Spruce Grouse* (p. 93): female is larger and has an all-dark tail with a terminal band.

95

WHITE-TAILED PTARMIGAN
Lagopus leucurus

This bird is so well camouflaged throughout the year that it often flushes explosively from around the feet of hikers. It is grayish-brown in summer and transforms to pure white in winter.
- The White-tailed Ptarmigan is the smallest of the North American grouse. It mostly lives above treeline, in some of the coldest parts of the Rockies. To avoid the worst temperatures, ptarmigans huddle in close groups and often dig into snow burrows. - A ptarmigan's feet are fully feathered, partly to maintain body heat during winter, and partly because the feathered toes also act as snowshoes. A winter ptarmigan's foot has up to four times the surface area as that of a summer bird.

summer

I.D.: *Sexes similar:* white outer tail feathers; fully feathered feet. *Summer male:* mottled brown overall; white on the wings and belly; red comb during courtship. *Summer female:* mottled brown overall; black barring on the belly. *Winter:* white plumage; black eyes and bill. *Spring and fall:* intermediate plumages.
Size: L 12–14 in. (31–36 cm).
Range: common year-round resident in the Canadian and northern U.S. Rockies; local in the southern and central U.S. Rockies.
Habitat: moss, lichen and heather communities, rocky outcrops and willow and alder thickets in alpine areas at or above treeline; may move into the subalpine during harsh winters.

Nesting: on the ground; in a slight depression among rocks in snow-free alpine tundra; nest is lined with fine grass, leaves and lichens; female incubates 4–8 eggs for 24–26 days; parents guard their young for up to 2 months.
Feeding: gleans and picks the buds, stems, seeds, fruits and flowers of willows and other alpine plants; occasionally eats insects.
Voice: *Male:* high-pitched *ku-kriii kriii;* low *kuk-kuk-kuk. Female:* low 'clucks' around the chicks.
Similar Species: *Willow Ptarmigan* (p. 95): uncommon in the Canadian Rockies; lacks the white outer tail feathers. *Blue Grouse* (p. 94): female is much larger and lacks the white outer tail feathers.

SHARP-TAILED GROUSE
Tympanuchus phasianellus

The courtship dance of the male Sharp-tailed Grouse has been emulated in traditional dances of many aboriginal cultures. Courting grouse gather at traditional dancing grounds called 'leks.' With their wings drooping at their sides, their tails pointed skyward and their purple air sacs inflated, the males furiously stamp the ground. Each male has his own small stage that he defends against rival males. ▪ Locally, some populations of Sharp-tailed Grouse have begun to decline over the last few decades, causing concern to many wildlife managers. ▪ The Sharp-tailed Grouse is often mistakenly called a Prairie Chicken, but that name properly belongs to two species of grouse found on the Great Plains (*T. cupido* and *T. pallidicinctus*). ▪ 'Lek' is derived from the Swedish word for 'play.'

♂

I.D.: *Sexes similar:* mottled upperparts; spotted underparts; long central tail feathers; light outer trail feathers. *Male:* purple air sacs on the neck.

Size: *L* 15–20 in. (38–51 cm).

Range: common in the eastern foothills in Montana; locally common in southeastern Idaho and central Colorado; local at Waterton Lakes NP.

Habitat: open habitats, mostly grasslands, sagebrush flats, intermountain valleys.

Nesting: typically on the Great Plains up though the NWT; on the ground, occasionally under a shrub; usually not far from a lek; in a shallow depression lined with grass and feathers; female incubates 10–14 eggs for up to 24 days.

Feeding: gleans the ground and vegetation for buds, seeds and flowers; also eats insects and seeds.

Voice: rarely heard. *Male:* on breeding grounds, a mournful, cooing *hoo* or *hoo hoo*.

Similar Species: *Ruffed Grouse* (p. 91): slight crest; rounded tail. *Ring-necked Pheasant* (p. 90): female has a longer tail, unfeathered legs and less barring on the belly.

97

WILD TURKEY
Meleagris gallopavo

Wild Turkeys are wary birds with refined senses and a highly developed social system, so predators can seldom sneak up on a foraging, but attentive, flock.
■ Although turkeys prefer to stay on the ground, they can fly short distances, and they often roost in trees for the night. ■ The turkey is the only native North American animal that has been widely domesticated. The wild ancestors of chickens, pigs, cows, sheep and other most other domestic animals all came from Europe, Asia and Africa. ■ The Wild Turkey was Benjamin Franklin's choice for America's national emblem. It lost to the Bald Eagle by one ballot in a congressional vote. ■ The genus is named for *Meleager*, a character in Greek mythology who was a hero in a Caledonian boar hunt.

I.D.: *General:* very large; naked red-blue head; dark, glossy, iridescent body plumage; copper tail is tipped in dirty white; unfeathered legs. *Male:* long central breast feather; more colorful on the head and body; red wattles. *Female:* blue-gray head; less iridescent body.
Size: *Male: L* 48–50 in. (122–127 cm). *Female: L* 35–37 in. (89–94 cm).
Range: local resident in the foothills north to the Canadian border; absent from high elevations.
Habitat: mixed woodlands and agricultural areas in the foothills.

Nesting: on the ground in open woods or along the edge of a field; in a slight depression lined with grass and leaves; female incubates 10–12 eggs for up to 28 days.
Feeding: forages on the ground for various plant items, including seeds, fruits, bulbs and sedges; also eats insects, such as ground beetles and grasshoppers, and less frequently amphibians.
Voice: wide array of sounds: courting male gives a loud *gobble*; alarm call is a loud *pert*; gathering call is a *cluck*; contact call is a loud *keouk-keouk-keouk*.
Similar Species: none.

VIRGINIA RAIL
Rallus limicola

The best way to experience a Virginia Rail is to sit alongside a wetland marsh, clap your hands three or four times and wait patiently. At best, this slim bird may reveal itself for an instant to a determined observer, but most often, the bird's voice is all that betrays its presence. ▪ When pursued by an intruder or predator, a rail will scurry away through dense, protective vegetation, rather than risk a getaway flight. ▪ Rails are very narrow birds that have modified feather tips and flexible vertebrae, all of which allow them to squeeze through the narrow confines of their marshy homes—it almost makes you think that 'as thin as a rail' refers to these birds.

I.D.: *Sexes similar. Adult:* rusty breast; barred flanks; gray cheeks; long, downcurved, reddish bill; very short tail. *Immature:* much darker overall; light bill. *In flight:* chestnut wing patch.
Size: *L* 9–11 in. (23–28 cm).
Range: uncommon summer breeder in the central and southern U.S. Rockies; very uncommon migrant elsewhere in the Rockies.
Habitat: freshwater wetlands, especially in cattail and bulrush marshes. *In migration:* wetlands near lakes and marshes.
Nesting: concealed in emergent vegetation, usually suspended just over the water; loose

basket nest is made of coarse grass, cattail stems or sedges; pair incubates the spotted eggs for up to 20 days.
Feeding: probes into soft substrates for soft-bodied invertebrates, such as earthworms, beetles, snails, spiders, insect larvae and nymphs; gleans vegetation for snails and beetles; also eats pondweeds and seeds.
Voice: call is an often repeated, telegraph-like *tick-tick-tick-tick-queea;* also grunts and croaks.
Similar Species: *Sora* (p. 100): short, yellow bill; black mask.

SORA
Porzana carolina

The Sora is the most common and widespread rail in North America, but it is seldom seen by birdwatchers. Instead, it is usually identified by its characteristic call. ▪ The Sora habitually flicks its short, stubby tail. This odd gesture is thought to distract prey into believing that the Sora's tail is in fact the bird's head. ▪ This inhabitant of marshy areas swims quite well over short distances, despite the fact that its feet are not webbed. ▪ Although some Soras may overwinter in the southern U.S., most spend the winter in the West Indies.

breeding

I.D.: *Sexes similar. Adult:* short, yellow bill; front of the face is black; gray neck and breast; long, greenish legs. *Immature:* brown overall; dark bill; yellow legs.
Size: *L* 8–10 in. (20–25 cm).
Range: locally common summer breeder throughout the Rockies.
Habitat: wetlands with abundant emergent cattails, bulrushes, sedges and grasses.
Nesting: usually over water, but occasionally in a wet meadow, under concealing vegetation; well-built basket nest is made of grass and aquatic vegetation; pair incubates 10–12 eggs for up to 20 days.
Feeding: gleans and probes vegetation and substrates for seeds, plants, aquatic insects and mollusks.
Voice: alarm call is a sharp *keek*; courtship song begins *or-Ah or-Ah*, descending quickly in a series of *weee-weee-weees*.
Similar Species: *Virginia Rail* (p. 99): long, reddish, downcurved bill.

AMERICAN COOT
Fulica americana

The American Coot is a delightful blend of comedy and confusion. This member of the rail family appears to have been made from leftover pieces of other birds: it has the bill of a chicken, the feet of a grebe and the body of a duck. ▪ When coots swim, their heads rock back and forth in direct synchrony with their swimming speed. ▪ American Coots are constantly squabbling with one another. They can often be seen running across the surface of the water, charging rivals and attempting to intimidate them. ▪ The distinctive calls of American Coots can be heard echoing across wetlands throughout the warmest months. ▪ Coots are also colloquially known as Mud Hens.

Babies are dark like momma, but with red feathers on head.

I.D.: *Sexes similar. Adult:* gray-black, duck-like bird; white, chicken-like bill; long, green-yellow legs with lobed toes; white undertail coverts. *Immature:* lighter body color; darker bill and legs.

Size: *L* 13–16 in. (33–41 cm).

Range: fairly common summer breeder throughout the Rockies; uncommon winter resident on open water in the U.S. Rockies.

Habitat: shallow marshes, ponds and wetlands with open water and emergent vegetation, such as cattail and bulrush marshes.

Nesting: in emergent vegetation; floating nest, built by the pair, is usually made of cattails and grass; pair incubates 8–12 eggs for 21–25 days.

Feeding: often gleans the water surface for algae, aquatic vegetation and invertebrates; also eats submerged water plants; sometimes dives for tadpoles and fish.

Voice: in summer, calls frequently through the day and night: *kuk-kuk-kuk-kuk-kuk.*

Similar Species: *Ducks* (pp. 47–69): all lack the chicken-like, white bill and uniform, black body color. *Grebes* (pp. 31–35): swim without pumping their heads back and forth; rarely seen on land.

101

SANDHILL CRANE
Grus canadensis

A deep, resonant rattling announces the approach of a flock of migrating Sandhill Cranes long before the birds can be seen. These migrations can entertain a birder for an entire fall morning as flock after flock glides effortlessly overhead. The large, V-shaped flocks look very similar to flocks of Canada Geese, but the cranes' rattling calls are distinctly different from the honking of geese. ▪ Sandhill Cranes nest in Idaho, western Wyoming, Montana and in the Canadian boreal forest. It is unlikely that a birder would unknowing stumble across a crane nest—the ever-vigilant parents noisily announce the presence of all threats.

I.D.: *Sexes similar:* very large bird with long legs and a long neck; pale gray plumage (often becomes stained a rusty color from iron oxides in the water); naked red crown; long, straight bill. *Immature:* lacks the red crown; reddish-brown plumage that at times appears patchy. *In flight:* neck is fully extended; legs are extended; slow downbeat; quick upstroke.
Size: L 40–50 in. (102–127 cm); W 6–7 ft. (1.8–2.1 m).
Range: locally common breeder through Wyoming and Idaho north to Glacier NP; rare elsewhere in the Rockies.
Habitat: *In migration:* agricultural fields, mudflats and shorelines. *Breeding:* isolated, open marshes, and bogs surrounded by forests and shrubs.
Nesting: on a large mound of aquatic vegetation in the water or along a shoreline; pair incubates 2 olive-splotched eggs for 29–32 days; young hatch at different times, because the incubation begins with first egg; young first fly at about 50 days.

Feeding: probes and gleans the ground for insects, soft-bodied invertebrates, waste grain, shoots and tubers; frequently takes amphibians, reptiles, small mammals and nesting birds.
Voice: loud, resonant rattling: *gu-rrroo gu-rrroo gurrroo.*
Similar Species: *Great Blue Heron* (p. 39): flies with its neck folded back over its shoulders; lacks the red forehead patch. *Whooping Crane* (p. 316): exceedingly rare throughout North America; all-white plumage with black flight feathers.

SEMIPALMATED PLOVER
Charadrius semipalmatus

Small flocks of Semipalmated Plovers touch down on shorelines in the mountains while passing through on their marathon migrations. During their brief stay in the Rockies, these stocky birds do wind sprints across the flats, intermixed with teetering probes. ■ Shorebird plumage is generally categorized into two forms: cryptic and disruptive coloration. Most sandpipers have cryptic coloration, which blends into the background of these birds' typical habitat. Disruptive coloration is the patterning featured in most plovers. The heavy, distinctive banding breaks the form of the bird into unrecognizable pieces. Like the banding on a zebra, the contrast between dark and light bands in plovers makes it difficult for predators to pinpoint the bird's form. ■ The scientific name *semipalmatus* refers to the slight webbing between the toes of this plover.

breeding

I.D.: *Sexes similar. Adult:* dark brown back; white breast with 1 black, horizontal band; long, orange legs; stubby, orange, black-tipped bill; white face patch above the bill; white throat and collar; brown head; black band across the forehead; small white eyebrow. *Immature:* dark legs and bill; brown banding.
Size: *L* 7 in. (18 cm).
Range: uncommon migrant throughout the Rockies.
Habitat: sandy beaches, lakeshores, river edges and mudflats in the montane.

Nesting: on the tundra; often colonial; in a slight depression in sand or gravel, sparsely lined with vegetation; pair incubates 4 eggs for up to 25 days.
Feeding: run-and-snatch feeding, usually on shorelines and beaches; eats crustaceans, worms and insects.
Voice: crisp, high-pitched, 2-part, rising whistle: *tu-wee.*
Similar Species: *Killdeer* (p. 104): 2 black bands across the breast; larger.

KILLDEER
Charadrius vociferus

The ubiquitous Killdeer is usually the first shorebird a beginning birdwatcher identifies. Its loud calls seize the attention of those visiting this bird's varied environments. ▪ If anyone approaches a Killdeer's nest, this bird will feign injury and fan its bright rusty tail to lure the intruder away from its eggs or young. Although the Killdeer may be the master of deception, several species of ducks and other shorebirds also practice this defense strategy. ▪ The common name is an imitation of this bird's call. The scientific name *vociferus* means 'vocal.'

I.D.: *Sexes similar. Adult:* long, dark yellow legs; white breast with 2 black bands; brown back; white underparts; brown head; white eyebrow; tail projects beyond the wing tips; white face patch above the bill; black forehead band; rusty rump. *Immature:* downy; only 1 breast band.

Size: *L* 9–11 in. (23–28 cm).

Range: uncommon to common migrant and summer breeder throughout the Rockies.

Habitat: open environments, fields, lakeshores, sandy beaches, mudflats, gravel streambeds, wet meadows and grasslands from the foothills to the subalpine.

Nesting: usually on any piece of open ground, including shorelines, beaches, fields and gravel roads; in shallow depression, usually unlined; pair incubates 4 eggs for 28 days; occasionally has 2 broods per season.

Feeding: run-stop-and-snatch feeder; mainly eats insects.

Voice: loud and distinctive *kill-dee kill-dee kill-deer* and variations, including *deer-deer*.

Similar Species: *Semipalmated Plover* (p. 103): adult is smaller and has only 1 breast band; present only in migration, so it is unlikely to be seen during summer.

BLACK-NECKED STILT
Himantopus mexicanus

Black-necked Stilts stride daintily around wetlands on their long, gangly legs. Although they are very vocal in the Rocky Mountains, Black-necked Stilts rarely nest here; they typically breed on either side of the mountain ranges near prairie wetlands. ■ Whether it is along a smelly sewage lagoon or an alkaline pond, the Stilt's dignity adds a sense of subtle glory to the landscape. It is rather odd that one of North America's most beautiful birds associates with such bleak and dreary environments. ■ In the battle for the title of most beautiful North American shorebird, it is quite convenient that Black-necked Stilts and American Avocets can often be observed beside one another. ■ With proportionately the longest legs of any North American bird, this shorebird deserves the name 'stilt.'

I.D.: *Sexes similar:* very long, orange legs; dark upperparts; clean white underparts; long, straight, needle-like bill; small, white eyebrow; male is blacker above than the female.

Size: L 14–15 in. (36–38 cm).

Range: rare spring and fall migrant in the southern Rockies; local breeder in the Montana and Idaho Rockies.

Habitat: breeds along marshy lakes and ponds; forages lake edges and exposed mudflats.

Nesting: typically on the Great Plains and Great Basin; in a shallow depression on the ground; often in dense colonies near alkaline or open shorelines; nest is sparsely lined with vegetation; pair incubates the eggs for about 25 days.

Feeding: picks prey from the water's surface or from the bottom in brackish ponds and alkaline lakes; primarily eats small flies and other aquatic invertebrates; rarely eats seeds.

Voice: not vocal during migration; loud, sharp *yip-yip-yip-yip* in summer; *kek-kek-kek-kek* in flight.

Similar Species: *American Avocet* (p. 106): upturned bill; lacks the black on the head.

AMERICAN AVOCET
Recurvirostra americana

An American Avocet in full breeding plumage may be the most elegant bird in North America. To some birders, its graceful features and striking colors are unmatched. ▪ During courtship, the female avocet extends her dainty bill forward and lowers her chin until it just clears the water's surface. The male struts around his statuesque mate until conditions are perfect; then the male jumps atop the still female and the pair quickly mates. After the male dismounts, the pair cross their slender bills and walk away in unison, reinforcing their bond.

breeding

I.D.: *Sexes similar:* long, upturned, black bill; long, pale blue legs; black wings with wide, white patches; white underparts; female's bill is more upturned and shorter than the male's. *Breeding:* peachy-red head, neck and breast. *Non-breeding:* gray head, neck and breast. *In flight:* like a flying stick; long skinny legs and neck; black-and-white wings.
Size: L 17–18 in. (43–46 cm).
Range: uncommon migrant in the southern and central U.S. Rockies; uncommon to rare migrant north of Wyoming.
Habitat: lakeshores, alkaline wetlands and exposed mudflats.
Nesting: typically on the Great Plains and Great Basin; semi-colonial; in a shallow depression along a dried mudflat, exposed shoreline or open area, always near water; nest is sparsely lined with vegetation; pair incubates 4 eggs for up to 29 days.
Feeding: sweeps its bill from side to side through the water's surface; picks up minute crustaceans, aquatic insects and, occasionally, seeds; males sweep lower in the water column than females; occasionally swims and 'tips up' duck-like.
Voice: harsh, shrill *plee-eek plee-eek* near the nest.
Similar Species: *Black-necked Stilt* (p. 105): straight bill; mostly black head. *Willet* (p. 110): grayish overall; straight bill.

GREATER YELLOWLEGS

Tringa melanoleuca

The Greater Yellowlegs is usually one of the birds that performs the lookout role among mixed flocks of shorebirds. At the first sign of danger, these large sandpipers begin calling, bobbing their heads and moving slowly away from the threat. The Greater Yellowlegs usually retreats into deeper water before becoming airborne. ▪ Many shorebirds, including the Greater Yellowlegs, hop around beach flats on one leg. True amputees can be hard to separate from birds that are just stubborn one-leggers, most of which can take off and land while keeping one leg tucked away. ▪ The scientific name *melanoleuca* is Greek for 'black and white,' in reference to this bird's plumage.

breeding

I.D.: *Sexes similar:* medium-sized; long, bright yellow legs; dark bill is longer than the head width. *Breeding:* brown-black back and wing covers; fine, dense, dark streaking on the head, neck and breast; subtle, dark eye line; light lores. *Non-breeding:* gray overall; slight streaks on the head.

Size: *L* 13–15 in. (33–38 cm).

Range: common migrant and uncommon summer breeder in the Canadian and northern U.S. Rockies; uncommon south of Montana.

Habitat: almost all types of wetlands, including beaver ponds, bogs, alluvial wetlands, sedge meadows and lakeshores.

Nesting: well hidden in a depression on the ground, usually in open bogs or natural openings in muskeg, and never far from water; nest is built on a dry mound and is sparsely lined with leaves, moss and grass; female incubates 4 eggs for 23 days.

Feeding: usually wades in water up over its knees; occasionally snatches prey from the water's surface; commonly sweeps its bill from side to side; primarily eats aquatic invertebrates, but will also eat small fish.

Voice: quick, whistled series of *tew-tew-tew-tew-tew*, usually 3–5 notes.

Similar Species: *Lesser Yellowlegs* (p. 108): smaller; shorter bill; generally calls in pairs of *tews*. *Willet* (p. 110): black-and-white wings; heavier bill.

LESSER YELLOWLEGS
Tringa flavipes

With a series of continuous, rapid-fire calls, Lesser Yellowlegs streak across the surface of wetlands during spring migration. They stop over in the mountains to forage in shallow pools. These shorebirds prefer to stride along soaked substrates in 1–2 in. (2.5–5.1 cm) of water. ▪ Occasionally, when they are disturbed, Lesser Yellowlegs retreat to the tops of spruce trees, using this uneasy perch to scan the surroundings. ▪ Lesser and Greater yellowlegs are very similar birds, and both occur in migration through the Rockies. The Lesser's bill is shorter than the length of its head and thinner than the Greater's longer bill. The Greater's bill is also slightly upturned—so slightly that it can be observed one minute and not the next. Even if the exact identity of the bird is not easily found, it is still quite respectable to simply write 'yellowlegs' in your field notes.

breeding

I.D.: *Sexes similar:* medium-sized; bright yellow legs; dark bill is shorter than the head width; brown-black back and wing covers; fine, dense, dark streaking on the head, neck and breast; subtle, dark eye line; light lore.

Size: *L* 10–11 in. (25–28 cm).

Range: uncommon migrant throughout the Rockies.

Habitat: sedge meadows, lakeshores, ponds, mudflats and beaver ponds up to the subalpine.

Nesting: in the boreal forest; usually in open bogs or natural openings in muskeg; in a depression on a dry mound; nest is sparsely lined with leaves and grass; pair incubates 4 blotched eggs for 22–23 days.

Feeding: snatches prey from the water's surface; frequently wades in shallow water; primarily eats aquatic invertebrates, but will also take small fish and tadpoles.

Voice: high-pitched *tew-tew*.

Similar Species: *Greater Yellowlegs* (p. 107): larger; slightly longer, upturned bill; more heavily streaked underparts in breeding plumage. *Solitary Sandpiper* (p. 109): white eye ring; greenish legs.

SOLITARY SANDPIPER
Tringa solitaria

No other shorebird has such an unusual nesting site—a tree! The Solitary Sandpiper's nesting strategy remained undiscovered by early ornithologists because they never thought to look for this bird's nest in abandoned songbird nests in trees. ▪ Shorebirds lay very large eggs and incubate them for long periods of time. By developing in the egg rather than in the nest, a chick's chance of survival is increased. By the time sandpiper chicks break out of their eggs, they are ready for the world. Such highly developed hatchlings, known as precocial young, fend for themselves soon after leaving the nest. (The hatchlings of many songbirds are born naked and helpless; they are called altricial young.) ▪ True to its name, the Solitary Sandpiper is frequently seen alone or in small groups, bobbing its body like a Latin dancer.

breeding

I.D.: *Sexes similar:* white eye ring; short green legs; brown-gray spotted back; white lore; brown-gray head, neck and breast have fine white streaks; dark uppertail feathers have black and white barring on the sides.
Size: *L* 7¹/₂–9 in. (19–23 cm).
Range: uncommon migrant and summer resident in Alberta and British Columbia; uncommon migrant in the U.S. Rockies.
Habitat: wet meadows, sewage lagoons, muddy ponds, sedge wetlands and beaver ponds in migration; breeds in heavily forested wetlands.
Nesting: typically in the boreal forest; in a spruce tree in a bog or muskeg; will use the abandoned nest of a thrush, blackbird or other songbird; pair incubates 4 eggs for 23–24 days; young jump from the nest to the ground shortly after hatching.

Feeding: stalks shorelines, picking up aquatic invertebrates, such as waterboatmen and damselfly nymphs; also gleans for terrestrial invertebrates; occasionally stirs the water with a foot to spook out prey.
Voice: high, thin *peet-wheet* or *wheet wheet wheet* during summer.
Similar Species: *Lesser Yellowlegs* (p. 108): no eye ring; bright yellow legs. *Spotted Sandpiper* (p. 111): incomplete eye ring; very spotted breast; orange, black-tipped bill.

WILLET
Catoptrophorus semipalmatus

If you spot a Willet slowly walking along the shore of a wetland, there is little to alert you to this bird's spirited character. At the instant it takes flight, however, its wondrous black-and-white wings flash in harmony with its rhythmic call—a dominant performance at the wetland theater. ▪ It is thought that the bright, bold flashes of the Willet's wings may serve as danger warnings to other shorebirds. They may also intimidate predators during a Willet's dive-bombing defense of its young. ▪ 'Willet' is an onomatopoeic description of this bird's common call. The genus name *Catoptrophorus* is a Latinized form of 'mirror-bearing,' a reference to its black-and-white wings.

breeding

I.D.: *Sexes similar:* plump; heavy, straight, black bill; lightly mottled, gray-brown plumage; light throat and belly. *In flight:* black-and-white wing pattern.

Size: L 14–16 in. (36–41 cm).

Range: local breeder in the southern and central U.S. Rockies and north to eastern Montana; extremely rare vagrant in the Canadian Rockies.

Habitat: *In migration:* shores of marshes, wet fields and lakes. *Nesting:* drier areas.

Nesting: typically on the Great Plains and Great Basin; in open, dry areas and sandy flats, occasionally far from water; in a shallow depression lined with grass and other vegetation; occasionally builds a cup nest; pair incubates 4 eggs for 22–29 days.

Feeding: feeds by probing muddy areas; also gleans the ground for insects; occasionally eats shoots and seeds.

Voice: generally silent in migration; loud, rolling *will-will willet*, *will-willet* on breeding grounds.

Similar Species: *Marbled Godwit* (p. 114): much longer bill; larger body. *Greater Yellowlegs* (p. 107): long, yellow legs; lacks the bold wing pattern.

SPOTTED SANDPIPER
Actitis macularia

The Spotted Sandpiper is the most commonly encountered sandpiper in the Rocky Mountains, as well as throughout North America. Its stiff-winged, arthritic flight is commonly seen low over riverbanks, lakeshores, ponds and most wetlands. ▪ It wasn't until 1972 that the unexpected truths about the Spotted Sandpiper's breeding activities were realized. Similar to the phalaropes, female Spotted Sandpipers were defending territories and leaving the males to tend the nests and eggs. This unusual nesting behavior—polyandry (from the Greek for 'many men')—is found in only about one percent of all bird species. ▪ The scientific name *macularia* is Latin for 'spotted.'

breeding

I.D.: *Sexes similar:* teeters continuously. *Breeding:* white underparts are heavily spotted with black (slightly more so in the female); yellow-orange legs; yellow-orange, black-tipped bill; white eyebrow. *Non-breeding* and *Juvenile:* pure white breast; brown bill; dull yellow legs.
Size: *L* 7–8 in. (18–20 cm).
Range: common migrant and summer breeder throughout the Rockies.
Habitat: shorelines, gravel beaches, ponds, rivers, marshes, alluvial wetlands and streams up to 6000 ft. (1800 m).
Nesting: usually near water; often under overhanging vegetation, among logs or under bushes; in a shallow depression lined with grass; male almost exclusively incubates and raises the 4 young.
Feeding: picks and gleans along shorelines for terrestrial and aquatic invertebrates; also snatches flying insects from the air.
Voice: sharp, crisp *eat-wheat, eat-wheat, wheat-wheat-wheat-wheat.*
Similar Species: *Solitary Sandpiper* (p. 109), *Lesser Yellowlegs* (p. 108) and *other sandpipers:* all lack the spotted breast. *Baird's Sandpiper* (p. 118): doesn't teeter; lacks the obvious spotting on the underparts; present only in migration.

111

UPLAND SANDPIPER
Bartramia longicauda

Every May, in an open field nestled deep within the Rocky Mountains, an Upland Sandpiper lands upon a fence post and gracefully folds its long wings. Having just completed its migration from the Argentinian grasslands, the ever-graceful shorebird scans its frosty surroundings and then begins instinctive rituals that will serve as a foundation for the breeding season. For the next several months, the male will maintain a steady vigil over his chosen territory, while his look-alike mate remains concealed nearby. For this short period, Upland Sandpipers reflect the pulse of their temporary home, reacting quickly and loudly to the presence of an intruder and embracing the peaceful times with calm and stoic dignity. ■ *Bartramia* honors the ground-breaking and enthusiastic early American botanist William Bartram. A credible ornithologist in his own right, Bartram's energy and passion for wild things is beautifully eternalized in the habits of the Upland Sandpiper.

Range: local breeder in the Montana Rockies; uncommon vagrant in most of the Rockies.

Habitat: hayfields, ungrazed pastures, natural grasslands and open areas.

Nesting: typically on the Great Plains; in a depression in dense grass clusters or along marshes; pair incubates 4 eggs for 21–27 days.

Feeding: gleans the ground for insects, especially grasshoppers, crickets and weevils.

I.D.: *Sexes similar:* small, rounded head; long, thin neck; mottled upperparts; lightly streaked underparts; dark beady eyes; very light belly and undertail coverts; yellow legs; bill is about the same length as the head.

Size: *L* 11–12½ in. (28–32 cm).

Voice: courtship song is an airy, whistled *whip-whee-ee you*; alarm call is *quip-ip-ip*.

Similar Species: *Mountain Plover* (p. 317): shorter neck; no breast streaking. *Willet* (p. 110): heavier bill; wings flash black and white in flight.

LONG-BILLED CURLEW
Numenius americanus

Armed with a bill that is more than 7 in. (18 cm) long, the Long-billed Curlew is the deepest prober on inland mudflats. The largest of North America's shorebirds, it forages in terrestrial, grassy environments during the summer months and in migration. Its long, downcurved bill is a wonderfully dexterous tool for picking up grasshoppers—while keeping its watchful eyes above the undulating prairie grass. ■ The Long-billed Curlew breeds mainly on undisturbed prairie grasslands, which are very restricted in the Rocky Mountains, occurring only in Yellowstone National Park. Male curlews put on spectacular displays over their nesting territory: they give loud, ringing calls while fluttering higher and then gliding lower in an undulating flight.

I.D.: *Sexes similar:* very long, downcurved bill (slightly longer in the female); buff-brown underparts; brown upperparts; mottled back; unstriped head; long legs.
Size: *L* 20–26 in. (51–66 cm).
Range: historical breeder, now rare in valleys in the central and northern U.S. Rockies; vagrant elsewhere in the Rockies.
Habitat: short-grass prairie, occasionally in grainfields and pastures; often near water during migration.
Nesting: usually on dry prairie on the Great Plains; in a slight depression sparsely lined with grass and other debris; pair incubates

4 eggs for 27–30 days; when danger approaches, they lay their heads flat on the ground.
Feeding: *In migration:* probes shorelines and mudflats for soft-bodied invertebrates. *During breeding:* picks grasshoppers and other invertebrates from grass and from along sloughs.
Voice: most common call in summer is a loud whistle: *cur-lee cur-lee cur-lee*; also a melodious, rolling *cuurrleeeuuu.*
Similar Species: *Marbled Godwit* (p. 114): straight, bicolored bill.

113

MARBLED GODWIT
Limosa fedoa

The Marbled Godwit's bill may look plenty long enough to reach buried prey, but the godwit doesn't seem content with its reach: it is frequently seen with its head submerged beneath the water's surface or with its face pressed up against a mudflat. These deep probes appear to satisfy this large shorebird, and a godwit looks genuinely pleased with a face full of mud. ■ The godwit's bill has a dark tip that may give it extra strength, because black pigments are stronger than light-colored pigments. ■ Some birdwatchers playfully call this species the 'Garbled Modwit.'

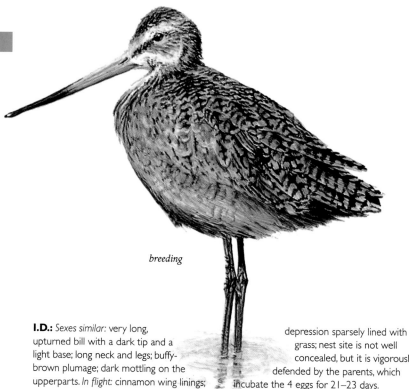

breeding

I.D.: *Sexes similar:* very long, upturned bill with a dark tip and a light base; long neck and legs; buffy-brown plumage; dark mottling on the upperparts. *In flight:* cinnamon wing linings; distinctive, long, upturned bill.

Size: L 16–20 in. (41–51 cm).

Range: uncommon migrant in the southern U.S. Rockies; rare breeder in the central U.S. Rockies; extremely rare in the Canadian Rockies.

Habitat: muddy shorelines of lakes and reservoirs, wet meadows, moist grasslands and open areas.

Nesting: on short-grass prairie; in a shallow depression sparsely lined with grass; nest site is not well concealed, but it is vigorously defended by the parents, which incubate the 4 eggs for 21–23 days.

Feeding: probes deeply in soft substrates for worms and invertebrate larvae; picks grasshoppers and beetles from long grass; may also eat the tubers and seeds of aquatic vegetation.

Voice: loud, duck-like (2-syllable) squawks: *co-rect co-rect;* or *god-wit god-wit.*

Similar Species: *Long-billed Curlew* (p. 113): downcurved bill. *Hudsonian Godwit* (p. 317): very rare migrant; white base to its tail.

SEMIPALMATED SANDPIPER
Calidris pusilla

While most of the North American continent feasts twice yearly on the great migrations of 'wind birds,' the passage of shorebirds through the Rockies amounts to little more than table scraps. Rocky Mountain shorelines are visited yearly by small numbers of Semipalmated Sandpipers, which peck and probe in mechanized fury, replenishing their body fat for the remainder of their long trip. ▪ Although the mountains may not host the abundance of Semis found elsewhere, our wetlands are just as vital to individual birds. Semipalmated Sandpipers migrate almost the entire length of the Americas, and they require that their migratory pit stops provide ample food resources.
▪ 'Semipalmated' refers to the slight webbing between this bird's front toes. The scientific name *pusilla* is Latin for 'petty' or 'small.'

non-breeding

I.D.: *Sexes similar:* all-dark, short, straight bill; dark legs. *Breeding:* mottled upperparts; rufous ear patch; faint streaks on the upper breast and flanks. *Non-breeding:* gray-brown upperparts; white underparts; faint, white eyebrow. *In flight:* narrow, white wing stripe; white rump is split by a black line.
Size: L 5½–7 in. (14–18 cm).
Range: uncommon fall migrant along the eastern slopes of the Rockies; uncommon spring and fall migrant west of the Rockies.
Habitat: mudflats and shorelines of ponds and lakes up to the subalpine.

Nesting: in the Arctic; on a small mound or tussock; in a slight depression lined with grass, moss and leaves; pair incubates 4 eggs for 18–22 days.
Feeding: probes soft substrates and gleans the surface for aquatic insects and crustaceans.
Voice: flight call is a harsh *cherk*.
Similar Species: *Western Sandpiper* (p. 116): longer, slightly downcurved bill. *Least Sandpiper* (p. 117): pale legs. *Dunlin* (p. 318): downcurved bill.

115

WESTERN SANDPIPER
Calidris mauri

Migrant Western Sandpipers are found in the same areas as Semipalmated and Least sandpipers, and they frequently mingle with both these species. The Western Sandpiper's arctic breeding grounds are farther west than those of the Semipalmated and Least sandpipers, however, and it is more likely to migrate through the western Rockies. ■ The challenge of identifying 'peeps' awaits the interested birder at a variety of moist habitats during the spring and fall migrations. Even if the subtleties of plumage are not your primary interest, a morning spent with shuffling sandpipers will prove to be enjoyable.

non-breeding

I.D.: *Sexes similar:* long, black, slightly down-curved bill; black legs. *Breeding:* rusty crown, ear and wing patches; V-shaped streaking on the upper breast and flanks; light underparts. *Non-breeding:* gray-brown upperparts; white underparts; white eyebrow. *In flight:* narrow, white wing stripe; white rump is split by a black line.

Size: *L* 6–7 in. (15–18 cm).

Range: common fall migrant and uncommon spring migrant in the Colorado Rockies; rare to uncommon migrant elsewhere in the Rockies.

Habitat: mudflats and shorelines of ponds and lakes up to the montane.

Nesting: in the Arctic; on a small mound or tussock; in a slight depression lined with grass, moss and leaves, occasionally domed by surrounding, arching vegetation; pair incubates 4 eggs for 20–22 days.

Feeding: gleans the substrate and probes quickly into soft mud and shallow water; occasionally submerges its head while probing; eats primarily aquatic insects, worms and crustaceans.

Voice: flight call is a high-pitched *cheep*.

Similar Species: *Semipalmated Sandpiper* (p. 115): shorter, straight bill. *Dunlin* (p. 318): black belly, darker upper breast and wider, white wing stripe in breeding plumage. *Least Sandpiper* (p. 117): smaller; light-colored legs.

LEAST SANDPIPER
Calidris minutilla

The Least Sandpiper is the smallest of the shorebirds, but its size is not a deterrent to its migratory feats. Like most other North American 'peeps'—a term used to group the nearly indistinguishable *Calidris* sandpipers—the yellow-legged Least Sandpiper migrates between the Arctic and the southern tip of South America. ▪ Because arctic summers are so short, shorebirds must maximize their breeding time. One way shorebirds ensure quick reproduction is to lay comparatively large eggs: the entire clutch may weigh over half the weight of the female! These large eggs allow the shorebird's young to hatch in an advanced state of development and get an early jump on life.

non-breeding

I.D.: *Sexes similar. Adult:* black bill; yellow legs; dark, mottled back; buff-brown breast, head and nape; light breast streaking. *Immature:* like an adult, but with a faintly streaked breast.
Size: L 5–6¹/₂ in. (13–17 cm).
Range: rare spring migrant and common fall migrant in the Canadian Rockies; locally common migrant in the northern U.S. Rockies; uncommon migrant in the Colorado Rockies.
Habitat: sandy beaches, lakeshores, ditches, sewage lagoons, mudflats and the edges of wetlands in the montane and the subalpine.

Nesting: in the arctic taiga and tundra; on a dry site near a raised mound; in a small depression built of grass and leaves; pair incubates 4 eggs for about 21 days.
Feeding: probes or pecks the substrate in short grass, on mudflats or in shallow pools; eats mosquitoes, beach fleas, amphipods, gastropods, flies, other aquatic invertebrates and occasionally seeds.
Voice: high-pitched *kreee.*
Similar Species: *Other 'peeps'* (pp. 115–19 & 317–18): all tend to have dark legs and are generally larger.

117

BAIRD'S SANDPIPER
Calidris bairdii

This sandpiper is a modest-looking shorebird with extraordinary migratory habits. Like many shorebirds, the Baird's Sandpiper only remains on its breeding grounds in the tundra for a very short period of time. Soon after the chicks hatch, the adult birds flock together and begin their southern migration, usually in July. The parents abandon their young in the Arctic. A few weeks after the parents have left, the young flock together in a second wave of southern migrants.
■ Spencer Fullerton Baird, a director of the Smithsonian Institution, organized several natural history expeditions across North America. For his efforts, Elliott Coues chose to name this bird in Baird's honor.

non-breeding

I.D.: *Sexes similar:* black legs and bill; wings extend beyond the tail; faint, buff-brown breast speckling; large black patterns on the back and wing covers.
Size: L 7–7¹/₂ in. (18–19 cm).
Range: common fall migrant in Jasper NP; uncommon migrant in Colorado; locally common fall migrant in the northern U.S. Rockies; rare spring migrant throughout the Rockies.
Habitat: sandy beaches, grassy areas, mud-flats and the edges of wetlands up to the alpine.

Nesting: on the arctic tundra; on a dry hummock; in a slight depression lined with grass and leaves; young begin to fly 20 days after hatching.
Feeding: gleans and picks aquatic invertebrates, especially larval mosquitoes and flies; also eats terrestrial beetles and grasshoppers; rarely probes.
Voice: soft, rolling *kriit kriit.*
Similar Species: *Pectoral Sandpiper* (p. 119): sharply delineated pectoral markings. *Least Sandpiper* (p. 117): light-colored legs; smaller.

PECTORAL SANDPIPER
Calidris melanotos

Moving northward through the Rockies in May, individual Pectoral Sandpipers commonly associate with groups of other shorebirds on our wetlands. ■ The Pectoral Sandpiper is one of the few sandpiper species that shows sexual dimorphism: the females are only two-thirds the size of the males. ■ When a predator approaches, this sandpiper frequently inflates the air sacks in its neck in alarm, raising its feathers. ■ The common name 'pectoral' refers to the location of the male's prominent air sacs on the breast. The males inflate these sacs as part of their courtship ritual. The scientific name *melanotos* is Greek for 'black back.'

non-breeding

I.D.: *Sexes similar:* brown breast streaks contrast with the light belly and undertail coverts; black, slightly downcurved bill; long, yellow legs; mottled upperparts; dark crown; wing tips extend beyond the tail.
Size: *L* 9 in. (23 cm).
Range: rare spring migrant and uncommon to common fall migrant throughout the Rockies.
Habitat: along lakeshores, marshes and mudflats.

Nesting: on the arctic tundra; in a small depression, often near water; well-built cup nest is lined with grass, moss and lichens; female incubates 4 eggs.
Feeding: probes and pecks the ground, primarily for small insects (mainly flies), beetles and occasionally grasshoppers.
Voice: sharp, short, low *krrick krrick.*
Similar Species: *Other 'peeps'* (pp. 115–18 & 317–18): all lack the well-defined light belly and dark pectoral region.

119

LONG-BILLED DOWITCHER
Limnodromus scolopaceus

Mudflats and marshes in the Rockies occasionally host these enthusiastic shore-birds during their spring and fall migrations. Long-billed Dowitchers can be easily identified: they forage in tight flocks, each probing repeatedly into mudflats in motions similar to a sewing machine. ▪ Long-billed Dowitchers often migrate with the closely related, but slightly less common, Short-billed Dowitcher, and the two are almost impossible to tell apart when they are silent. ▪ Mixed flocks of shorebirds demonstrate a variety of foraging styles. Some species probe deeply, while others pick at the water's surface or glean the shorelines. It is thought that large numbers of shorebirds can coexist because their different foraging styles reduce competition for the food sources.

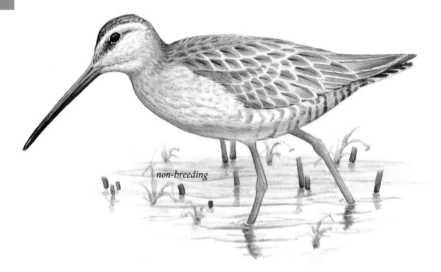

non-breeding

I.D.: *Sexes similar:* very long, straight, dark bill (longer in the female); very stocky body; short neck. *Breeding:* reddish underparts; lightly barred flanks; dark, mottled upperparts; dark eye line; light eyebrow; long, dark yellow legs; white lower back. *Immature:* gray overall; white belly.
Size: L 11–12½ in. (28–32 cm).
Range: uncommon to common fall migrant and rare spring migrant throughout the Rockies.
Habitat: along lakeshores, shallow marshes and mudflats in the montane and the subalpine.
Nesting: on the arctic tundra; often near

water; in a shallow, elevated scrape lined with grass and moss; pair incubates the eggs for 21 days.
Feeding: probes in shallow water and on mudflats with a quickly repeated up-down motion of bill; frequently plunges its head below the water; eats larval flies, worms and other soft-bodied invertebrates.
Voice: alarm call is a single, loud *keek*.
Similar Species: *Short-billed Dowitcher* (p. 318): call is *tu*; faint barring on the flanks; bill is slightly shorter. *Common Snipe* (p. 121): heavily streaked upperparts; longer legs; different foraging techniques; lacks the white wedge on the lower back.

COMMON SNIPE
Gallinago gallinago

The eerie, hollow sound produced by a Common Snipe's specialized outer tail feathers vibrating in the wind is a characteristic night sound of the marsh. To produce these winnowing sounds, snipes fly high above their marshland habitats and then dive steeply. During the dive, they spread their outer tail feathers, producing the haunting notes. ■ The Common Snipe's bill is a wonderfully dexterous tool. The tip of the bill is hardened, but it is extremely sensitive, and it is capable of feeling earthworms and larval insects. Also, the upper mandible can move upward—an extremely practical adaptation for an animal feeding in mudflats.

non-breeding

I.D.: *Sexes similar:* long, sturdy, dark grayish bill; short legs (for a shorebird); heavily striped head and back; white belly; streaked breast; dark eye stripe; otherwise mottled brown. *In flight:* quick zig-zags as it takes off.
Size: *L* 10¹/₂–11¹/₂ in. (27–29 cm).
Range: locally common migrant and summer breeder throughout the Rockies; uncommon winter resident in the southern Rockies; rare winter resident in the Canadian Rockies.
Habitat: cattail and bulrush marshes, sedge meadows, poorly drained floodplains, willow wetlands, bogs and fens throughout the montane and the subalpine.

Nesting: usually in dry grass, often under vegetation; nest is made of grass, moss and leaves; female incubates 4 eggs for about 20 days; both parents raise the young.
Feeding: probes soft substrates for soft-bodied invertebrates, mostly larvae and earthworms.
Voice: eerie, accelerating courtship 'song': *woo-woo-woo-woo-woo-woo*; alarm call is a nasal *wheat wheat wheat*.
Similar Species: *Long-billed Dowitcher* (p. 120): lacks the heavy striping on the head and back; usually seen in flocks. *Marbled Godwit* (p. 114): much larger; bicolored bill; much longer legs.

121

WILSON'S PHALAROPE
Phalaropus tricolor

Not only are phalaropes the most colorful of the shorebirds, they also are the most unusual. These intriguing birds practice a mating strategy known as polyandry—each female mates with several males—which is extremely rare throughout the animal kingdom. The brightly colored female phalarope defends the nest site from other females and leaves her mates to tend the eggs. This breeding strategy is unusual because it takes a massive amount of energy for a female to produce eggs, and most female birds want to protect their investment. Even Audubon was fooled by the phalarope's breeding habits; he mislabeled the female and male birds in all of his illustrations. ■ This bird bears the name of Alexander Wilson, one of the fathers of North American ornithology.

breeding

I.D.: *General:* dark, needle-like bill; chestnut throat; black eye line; white eyebrow; light gray underparts; black legs. *Breeding female:* gray cap; very sharp colors. *Breeding male:* dark cap; dull colors.

Size: L 8¹/₂–9¹/₂ in. (22–24 cm).

Range: common migrant and local summer breeder in the Rockies; uncommon migrant north of Wyoming.

Habitat: *Breeding:* beaver ponds, sedge meadows and cattail marshes. *In migration:* open water of lakes and reservoirs.

Nesting: typically on the Great Plains and in the western mountains; often near water; in a

depression lined with grass and other vegetation; nest is often well concealed; male incubates the 4 eggs and rears the young.

Feeding: whirls in tight circles in shallow or deep water, picking invertebrates from the water's surface or just below it; on land, makes short jabs to pick up food in open areas.

Voice: deep nasal *work work* on the breeding grounds.

Similar Species: *Red-necked Phalarope* (p. 123): dark head and back; migrant through the Rockies. *Lesser Yellowlegs* (p. 108): yellow legs; streaked underparts.

RED-NECKED PHALAROPE

Phalaropus lobatus

Red-necked Phalaropes spin and whirl in shallow water during their migratory stopovers in the Rockies, displaying an unexpected foraging technique for a shorebird. Phalaropes swim in tight circles, stirring up tiny crustaceans and picking daintily at the water's surface with their needle-like bills. ■ The Red-necked Phalaropes migrating through the Rockies in fall have come a long way from their arctic nesting grounds, but they still have even farther to go: most of them winter south of the Equator, at sea off western South America ■ Phalaropes have individually webbed toes, like those of grebes, and they are good swimmers. ■ 'Phalarope' is a translation of the Greek words for 'coot's foot'; the coot is another bird with lobed toes.

breeding

I.D.: *General:* thin, black bill; long, black legs; long neck. *Breeding female:* chestnut neck and throat; white chin; blue-black head; incomplete, white eye ring; white belly; buff stripes on the upper wings. *Breeding male:* white eyebrow; less intense colors than the female. *Non-breeding:* white underparts; black mask.
Size: *L* 7 in. (18 cm).
Range: uncommon fall migrant and rare spring migrant throughout the Rockies; local spring migrant at Freezeout Lake, Montana.
Habitat: *In migration:* open waterbodies, including ponds, lakes, large sloughs and sewage ponds.

Nesting: on the tundra; often near water; on a hummock lined with grass and lichens; male incubates the eggs and rears the young.
Feeding: whirls in tight circles in shallow or deep water, picking invertebrates from the water's surface or just below it; on land, makes short jabs to pick up food in open areas.
Voice: often noisy in migration; soft *krit krit krit*.
Similar Species: *Wilson's Phalarope* (p. 122): breeds in the Rockies; female has a lighter head and back.

123

FRANKLIN'S GULL
Larus pipixcan

Drifting in from their prairie stronghold, Franklin's Gulls are most frequently seen in the Rockies during migration, often in the company of look-alike Bonaparte's Gulls. Also called the Prairie Dove, this bird is best known to farmers on the Great Plains; Franklin's Gulls often follow tractors to opportunistically snatch up invertebrates. ▪ The Franklin's Gull is unique among gulls, because it undergoes a complete molt in spring and fall. ▪ The scientific name *pipixcan* is from the Aztec word for Mexico, where this bird was initially collected. ▪ Sir John Franklin, a polar explorer, is best known, perhaps, for leading the ill-fated expedition of 1845.

breeding

I.D.: *Sexes similar:* gray mantle; white eye ring; black wing tips with white spots; white underparts. *Breeding:* black head; white eye ring; orange bill; breast often has a pinkish tinge; red-orange legs. *Non-breeding:* white head; dark patch on the back of the head.
Size: L 13–15 in. (33–38 cm); W 37 in. (94 cm).
Range: local breeder in Montana and Idaho; rare migrant and summer visitor elsewhere in the Rockies.
Habitat: agricultural fields, marshlands, inland lakes, flooded rivermouths, fields, meadows and landfills in the montane.

Nesting: colonial; usually in dense emergent vegetation; floating platform is built above water and lined with fine grass and plant down; pair incubates 3 eggs for 25 days.
Feeding: very opportunistic; gleans agricultural fields and meadows for grasshoppers and cutworms; catches dragonflies, mayflies and other flying invertebrates in mid-air.
Voice: mewing, shrill *weeeh-ah weeeh-ah* while feeding and in migration.
Similar Species: *Bonaparte's Gull* (p. 125): adult has a black bill and shows more white in its wings.

BONAPARTE'S GULL
Larus philadelphia

This small, graceful gull migrates through our area in small, reserved flocks that stop over without drawing attention to themselves. When they reach their summer nesting grounds just north of the Rockies, Bonaparte's Gulls choose to nest in trees, quite unlike other gulls. ▪ These gulls seem reserved in comparison to other gulls, and they more closely resemble terns in behavior. Like terns, Bonaparte's Gulls tend not to forage in landfills, preferring to dine on the surface of lakes and marshes. ▪ This small gull was not named for the French emperor, but rather for his nephew, zoologist Charles Lucien Bonaparte. The first specimen described was a winter bird found near Philadelphia, hence its scientific name.

breeding

I.D.: *Sexes similar:* black bill; gray mantle; white eye ring; white underparts. *Breeding:* black head; orange legs. *Non-breeding:* white head; dark ear patch. *In flight:* white leading edge to the wings.
Size: *L* 12–14 in. (30–36 cm); *W* 33 in. (84 cm).
Range: rare migrant in the U.S. Rockies; uncommon to common summer visitor and migrant in the Canadian Rockies.
Habitat: large lakes, rivers and marshlands in the montane.

Nesting: in the boreal forest; occasionally in a colony; in coniferous trees; occupies abandoned stick nests of crows, jays or raptors.
Feeding: dabbles and tips up for aquatic invertebrates, small fish and tadpoles; gleans the ground for terrestrial invertebrates; also captures insects in the air.
Voice: scratchy, soft *eer eer* while feeding.
Similar Species: *Franklin's Gull* (p. 124): adult has an orange bill and shows a lot less white in the wings.

125

RING-BILLED GULL
Larus delawarensis

Although gulls are never numerous in the Rockies, the Ring-billed Gull is the odds-on favorite to be seen. This gull's largest mountain nesting colonies are in the Yellowstone area, but they are occasionally seen throughout the mountains, taking advantage of free meals around landfills and day-use areas. ■ The Ring-bill's population is steadily increasing, along with the northern and western expansion of its range. ■ When Ring-billed Gulls arrive in the Rockies in early spring, their heads are snowy white, but before their fall departure, molting stains their purity with browns. ■ 'Gull' appears to be derived from a Celtic word describing the wailing cry of these birds. The scientific name *delawarensis* indicates the origin of the first scientifically described specimen—the Delaware River.

breeding

I.D.: *Sexes similar. Adult:* medium-sized; white head; yellow bill and legs; black ring around the bill tip; pale gray back; yellow eyes; black wing tips; black primaries with small white spots; white underparts. *Immature:* gray back; brown wings and breast.
Size: *L* 18–20 in. (46–51 cm); *W* 48 in. (122 cm); male is slightly larger.
Range: common migrant and local breeder from Rocky Mountain NP north to Montana; uncommon migrant and summer visitor in the Canadian Rockies.
Habitat: large lakes, reservoirs, wetlands, rivers, landfills, golf courses, agricultural fields and public areas, mostly through the montane.

Nesting: in the northern prairies and around the Great Lakes; colonial; often on open beaches, islands or shorelines; on the ground in a shallow scrape lined with plants, nearby debris, grass and sticks; pair incubates 3–6 eggs for 23–28 days.
Feeding: gleans the ground for garbage, arthropods, rodents and earthworms; scavenges; surface tips for aquatic invertebrates and fish.
Voice: high-pitched *kakakaka-akakaka*; also a low, laughing *yook-yook-yook.*
Similar Species: *California Gull* (p. 127): much larger; no bill ring; dark eyes. *Herring Gull* (p. 128): larger; pink legs; no bill ring.

CALIFORNIA GULL
Larus californicus

In 1848 and 1855, Utah's harvests were threatened by swarms of grasshoppers until large numbers of California Gulls mercifully appeared, ate the pests and saved the crops. A monument in Salt Lake City commemorates those events, and the California Gull is the state bird of Utah. ■ California Gulls tend to nest on islands with very little protective cover—the open water keeps them safe from terrestrial predators—where concentrations of gulls can soar. The nests are generally placed no closer than the distance two gulls can bridge with aggressive bill jabs from atop their nests. ■ In the Rockies, California Gull populations seem to have declined with the closure of many landfills in the mountain parks, but their breeding range is expanding to the north.

breeding

I.D.: *Sexes similar. Adult:* white head; yellow bill and legs; dark eyes; red spot on the lower mandible tip; dark gray back; black wing tips; black primaries with small white spots; white underparts. *Immature:* mottled brown.
Size: L 18–20 in. (46–51 cm); W 48–54 in. (122–137 cm).
Range: common migrant and local breeder in the U.S. Rockies; uncommon migrant and summer visitor in the Canadian Rockies.
Habitat: large lakes, wetlands, rivers, landfills and public areas, mostly through the montane.
Nesting: on the Great Plains and in the Pacific Northwest; colonial; often on open beaches or shorelines; usually on the ground

in a shallow scrape lined with plants, grass, feathers and small sticks; pair incubates 2–3 eggs for 23–27 days.
Feeding: gleans the ground for terrestrial invertebrates, especially grasshoppers, earthworms and cutworms; scavenges; surface tips for aquatic invertebrates.
Voice: high-pitched, nasal *kiarr-kiarr,* most often heard at breeding colonies.
Similar Species: *Herring Gull* (p. 128): adult is much larger and has light eyes and pink legs. *Ring-billed Gull* (p. 126): adult has light eyes and a black ring around its bill. *Mew Gull* (p. 319): adult is much smaller and shows more white in its primaries.

127

HERRING GULL
Larus argentatus

Although the Herring Gull is one of the most commonly seen gulls over most of North America, it is not easy to find in the Rockies. As a bird of ocean coasts and large lakes, the large Herring Gull finds little suitable habitat in the mountains. ▪ The Herring Gull is a wonderfully adaptive species over most of its range, and its population has increased as a result of human development. Herring Gulls also occur in Europe and parts of coastal Asia. ▪ The Herring Gull, like many gulls, has a small red spot on its lower mandible that serves as a target for the young. When a downy chick pecks at the lower mandible, the parent instinctively feeds it by regurgitation. ▪ Prior to obtaining their full adult plumage and color, Herring Gulls go through no less than seven changes of brownish plumage. ▪ The scientific name *argentatus* is Latin for 'silvery,' probably in reference to this bird's back or underwing.

breeding

I.D.: *Sexes similar:* large gull; yellow bill; red spot on the lower mandible tip; light eyes; light gray back; black wing tips; pink legs. *Breeding:* white head; white underparts. *Non-breeding:* white head and nape is washed with brown. *Immature:* mottled brown.
Size: *L* 23–26 in. (58–66 cm); *W* 58 in. (147 cm).
Range: rare, but regular, migrant throughout the Rockies.
Habitat: *In migration:* large lakes, wetlands, rivers, landfills and public areas throughout the montane.
Nesting: in Canada and Alaska; colonial, often with other gulls, pelicans and cormorants; usually on the ground on open beaches, islands or shorelines; in a shallow scrape lined with plants and sticks; pair incubates 3 eggs for 31–32 days.
Feeding: very opportunistic, generalist feeder; surface tips for aquatic invertebrates and small fish; gleans the ground for insects and worms; scavenges dead fish and garbage at landfills; also eats other birds' eggs and young.
Voice: loud, bugle-like *kleew-kleew;* also an alarmed *kak-kak-kak.*
Similar Species: *California Gull* (p. 127): much smaller; dark eyes; green legs. *Ring-billed Gull* (p. 126): black ring around the bill; smaller.

CASPIAN TERN
Sterna caspia

In size and habits, the mighty Caspian Tern bridges the gulf between smaller terns and raucous gulls. It is the largest tern in North America, and its wing beats are slower and more purposeful than those of small terns; in flight, the Caspian Tern can be confused with gulls. These blood red–billed terns are often seen in association with gulls on exposed sandbars or mudflats. ▪ As Ring-billed Gulls expand their range to the north and west in North America, the Caspian Tern follows these pioneers to establish breeding colonies. ▪ There is perhaps no other bird that possesses such an odd North American breeding distribution as the Caspian Tern. Isolated pockets of these terns breed sparsely in Utah and Wyoming, along the Pacific Coast, in the Mackenzie district in the Northwest Territories, around the Great Lakes and in Newfoundland. ▪ This species was first collected on the Caspian Sea in Asia, hence its name.

breeding

I.D.: *Sexes similar:* black cap; heavy, blood red bill; light gray wing covers; black legs; shallowly forked tail; white underparts; long, frosty, pointed wings.
Size: *L* 19–23 in. (48–58 cm); *W* 50–55 in. (127–140 cm).
Range: rare migrant in the U.S. Rockies; local breeder in the central and northern U.S. Rockies.
Habitat: *In migration:* shorelines and over large lakes, wetlands and rivers up to the montane.
Nesting: in the Rockies, only on Molly Island on Yellowstone Lake; in a shallow scrape on bare sand, dirt or rocks; nest is sparsely lined with vegetation, rocks or twigs; pair incubates 1–3 eggs for 20–22 days.
Feeding: hovers over water and plunges headfirst after small fish, tadpoles and aquatic invertebrates; also feeds by swimming and gleaning at the water's surface.
Voice: low, harsh *ca-arr;* also a loud *kraa-uh.*
Similar Species: *Common Tern* (p. 130) and *Forster's Tern* (p. 131): much smaller; lack the heavy, red bill.

COMMON TERN
Sterna hirundo

Wheeling about in mid-air to a stationary hover, the Common Tern quickly dives headfirst into the water, often bouncing up to the surface with a small fish in its thin bill. ■ Terns are effortless fliers and some of the greatest migrants. The Arctic Tern, which passes the eastern toe of the Rockies, migrates more than 11,000 mi. (17,700 km) in its yearly round-trip journey from the Arctic to the Antarctic. Recently, a Common Tern banded in Great Britain was recovered in Australia— a record distance. ■ Common Tern colonies are loud and noisy. If an intruder approaches a nest, the parent will dive repeatedly, often defecating quite accurately during the lowest point of the dive.

breeding

I.D.: *Sexes similar. Breeding:* black cap; thin, red, black-tipped bill; light gray wing covers; red legs; white rump; mostly white tail; white underparts. *Non-breeding:* lacks the black cap; black nape. *In flight:* shallowly forked tail; long, pointed wings.
Size: *L* 13–16 in. (33–41 cm); *W* 30 in. (76 cm).
Range: rare migrant in the southern Rockies; uncommon migrant north of Glacier NP and through the Canadian Rockies.
Habitat: large lakes, open wetlands and slow-moving rivers, primarily up to the montane.
Nesting: typically east of the Rockies; usually colonial; usually on a beach or other open area without vegetation; in a small scrape lined sparsely with pebbles, vegetation or shells; pair incubates 3 eggs for up to 27 days.
Feeding: hovers over the water and plunges headfirst after small fish and aquatic invertebrates.
Voice: high-pitched, drawn-out *keee-are*, most commonly heard at colonies, but also in foraging flights.
Similar Species: *Forster's Tern* (p. 131): yellow-orange bill and legs; mostly gray tail; silver-tipped primaries; black mask in winter. *Arctic Tern:* rare in migration; all–deep red bill; deeply forked tail; light primaries. *Caspian Tern* (p. 129): much larger; heavy, all-red bill.

FORSTER'S TERN
Sterna forsteri

The Forster's is the only tern in the Rockies that has an exclusively North American breeding distribution, but it bears the name of a man who never visited this continent. Johann Forster, who lived and worked in England, examined several tern specimens from the Hudson Bay region. He suggested that there was an additional species aside from the very similar Common Tern. Thomas Nuttall agreed, and in 1832 he named the species the Forster's Tern in his classic *Manual of Ornithology*. Forster's greatest naturalist experience may have been on board the famous Cook voyage to the south Pacific. On that trip, both his natural history observations and his quarrels with the captain are legendary. ▪ Terns are not named for their aerial maneuverability: 'tern' comes from their Old Norse name *therna*.

breeding

I.D.: *Sexes similar. Breeding:* black cap and nape; thin, orange, black-tipped bill; light gray back; red legs; white underparts; white rump; mostly gray tail. *Non-breeding:* lacks the black cap; black mask over the eyes. *In flight:* shallowly forked tail; long, pointed wings.
Size: *L* 14–16 in. (36–41 cm); *W* 31 in. (79 cm).
Range: rare migrant and uncommon summer visitor in the southern U.S. Rockies; rare migrant and summer visitor in the Canadian Rockies.
Habitat: *Summer:* cattail marshes and backwaters. *In migration:* lakes.
Nesting: typically on the Great Plains and in the Northwest; occasionally colonial; atop floating vegetation in freshwater marshes, occasionally on muskrat lodges or on a grebe's nest; both parents incubate the eggs and raise the young.
Feeding: hovers above the water and plunges headfirst after small fish and aquatic invertebrates.
Voice: call when flying is a nasal, short *keer keer;* also a grating *tzaap.*
Similar Species: *Common Tern* (p. 130): darker red bill and legs; mostly white tail; dark-tipped primaries; call is longer and drawn out. *Caspian Tern* (p. 129): much larger; all-red bill.

BLACK TERN
Chlidonias niger

Black Terns dip, dive, swoop and spin in dizzying foraging flights, picking insects neatly off the water's surface or catching them in mid-air. Even in stiff winds, these dark terns knife through the air with ease. Synchronous foraging flocks of Black Terns occasionally number in the hundreds. Unfortunately, these dizzying displays are less commonly encountered now, because populations of this bird have declined since the 1960s. ▪ Black Terns also occur in Europe, Africa and Asia. ▪ In order to spell this tern's genus name correctly, one must misspell *chelidonias*, the Greek word for 'swallow.' When the Black Tern was initially described and named, the author accidentally left out the 'e,' a mistake that must now be perpetuated.

breeding

I.D.: *Sexes similar. Breeding:* black head and underparts; gray back, tail and wings; white undertail coverts; black bill; reddish-black legs. *Non-breeding:* white underparts. *In flight:* long, pointed wings; shallowly forked tail.
Size: L 9–10 in. (23–25 cm); W 24 in. (61 cm).
Range: uncommon migrant and local breeder north to the southern Canadian Rockies; increasingly rare northward.
Habitat: shallow, freshwater cattail marshes, sloughs and lake edges with emergent vegetation.

Nesting: typically at lower elevations throughout Canada and the northern U.S.; usually in colonies; on matted vegetation on the surface of the water among emergent vegetation; builds a small platform of loose, dead vegetation; incubates 3 eggs for up to 3 weeks.
Feeding: snatches insects from the air, from tall grass and from the water's surface; also eats freshwater fish.
Voice: greeting call is a shrill, metallic *kik-kik-kik-kik-kik*; typical alarm call is *kreea*.
Similar Species: none.

ROCK DOVE
Columba livia

The Rock Dove is the familiar pigeon of our cities and farms. It only occurs in heavily developed or modified areas of the Rockies, such as towns, cities, agricultural areas and railway yards, where it can be extremely common. ▪ The Rock Dove was introduced to North America in the 17th century. It was likely initially domesticated from Eurasian birds in about 4500 BC, as a source of meat. Since that time, Rock Doves have also been used by humans as message couriers—both Caesar and Napoleon used them—and as scientific subjects. Much of our understanding of bird migration, endocrinology, sensory perception, flight and other avian traits, is derived from experiments involving Rock Doves. ▪ No other 'wild' bird varies as much in coloration as the Rock Dove—possibly a result of semi-domestication and inbreeding.

I.D.: *Sexes similar:* color is highly variable (iridescent blue-gray, red, white or tan); usually has a white rump and orange feet; dark-tipped tail. *In flight:* holds its wings in a deep V while gliding.
Size: *L* 12–13 in. (31–33 cm); male is usually larger.
Range: locally very common throughout the Rockies.
Habitat: urban areas, railway yards, agricultural areas and grain terminals up to the montane.

Nesting: on ledges of barns, cliffs, bridges, buildings and towers; flimsy nest is made of sticks, grass and assorted vegetation; pair incubates 2 eggs for about 18 days.
Feeding: gleans the ground for waste grain, seeds and fruits; occasionally eats insects.
Voice: soft, cooing *coorrr-coorrr-coorrr.*
Similar Species: *Band-tailed Pigeon* (p. 134): dark rump; gray band on the tail; yellow feet; white band on the nape.

133

BAND-TAILED PIGEON
Columba fasciata

Band-tailed Pigeons feed in flocks, clinging clumsily to branches that bend under their weight. As the pigeons yo-yo up and down, they carefully pluck acorns, berries and seeds from neighboring limbs. ■ The Band-tailed Pigeon primarily occurs west of the Rockies and is most likely to be encountered in the Pacific Northwest. This forest-dwelling pigeon very nearly suffered the same fate as the Passenger Pigeon of eastern North America.

■ Flocks of Band-tailed Pigeons regularly visit mineral springs throughout their range, attracted by the dissolved calcium in the water—not unlike the way that deer and other hoofed mammals are attracted to salt licks.

I.D.: *Sexes similar:* purple head and breast; white band on the back of the head; grayish band on the tail; dark rump; iridescent green nape; yellow, black-tipped bill; grayish wings.
Size: L 13–15 in. (33–38 cm).
Range: local breeder in the southern Colorado and Utah Rockies; extremely rare in the Rockies north of Colorado.
Habitat: agricultural areas, open ponderosa pine forests and hillsides covered in fruit-bearing shrubs in the foothills and the lower montane.
Nesting: typically west of the Rockies and south into New Mexico; near the crotch of a

tree; fragile stick platform nest has very little lining; pair incubates the usually single egg for up to 20 days.
Feeding: gleans vegetation for nuts, especially acorns; also eats other seeds and frequently berries and invertebrates during migration.
Voice: owl-like, deep, hollow *whoo-whoo-whoo.*
Similar Species: *Rock Dove* (p. 133): white rump; dark bill; lacks the gray band on the tail. *Mourning Dove* (p. 135): longer, white-edged tail; lacks the purple head and the glossy green nape.

MOURNING DOVE

Zenaida macroura

When Mourning Doves burst into flight, their wings clap above and below their bodies for the first few wing beats. These birds are swift, direct fliers, and their wings can be heard whistling through the wind.
▪ The soft cooing of Mourning Doves filters through forests and shrublands and can be heard from great distances. ▪ All members of the pigeon family (including doves), feed 'milk' to their young. Since birds lack mammary glands, this isn't true milk but a nutritious liquid produced by glands in the bird's crop. The chicks insert their bills down the adult's throat to eat the thick liquid. ▪ The common name reflects this bird's sad song; the genus name *Zenaida* honors Zénaïde, Princess of Naples, the wife of Charles Lucien Bonaparte (the zoologist nephew of the French emperor).

I.D.: *Sexes similar:* olive-brown plumage; small head; long, white-trimmed, tapering tail; sleek body; dark, shiny patch below the ear; dull red legs; dark bill; pale-rosy underparts.
Size: L 11–13 in. (28–33 cm).
Range: common breeder in Glacier NP and in the Colorado Rockies; uncommon breeder in the Canadian and central U.S. Rockies.
Habitat: open woodlands, forest edges, agricultural areas and riparian forests; has benefited from human-induced habitat change.

Nesting: in the fork of a shrub or tree, or occasionally on the ground; female builds a fragile, shallow nest from twigs supplied by the male; pair incubates 2 eggs for 14 days.
Feeding: gleans the ground and vegetation for the seeds of agricultural crops, weeds and native vegetation; visits feeders; produces crop milk for its newly hatched young.
Voice: mournful, soft *coooo-coooo-ah coooo-coooo-ah.*
Similar Species: *Black-billed Cuckoo* (p. 136): lighter underparts; darker upperparts; shorter neck. *Rock Dove* (p. 133): stockier; white rump; shorter tail. *Band-tailed Pigeon* (p. 134): shorter tail; white band on the nape; plumage tends not to be olive-brown.

BLACK-BILLED CUCKOO
Coccyzus erythropthalmus

Most birds are silenced by the arrival of storm systems, but when storms darken spring skies, the Black-billed Cuckoo abandons its normally quiet and shy behavior to vocalize with loud bursts from a shrubby thicket. ▪ In their dense, tangled habitat, cuckoos are heard more often than they are seen; one can only hope for a glimpse of a cuckoo as it flies hurriedly from one thicket to the next. ▪ In spite of their seeming reluctance to fly in their breeding territories, these cuckoos migrate great distances to the tropics for winter. ▪ The Black-billed Cuckoo does not sing like a cuckoo clock; that voice is from the Common Cuckoo of Europe and Asia.

I.D.: *Sexes similar:* brown upperparts; white underparts; long, white-spotted tail; down-curved, dark bill; reddish eye ring.
Size: *L* 12 in. (30 cm).
Range: uncommon to rare summer resident and migrant in Grand Teton NP; rare migrant and summer resident elsewhere in the Rockies.
Habitat: densely vegetated woodlands, shrubs and thickets; often associated with riparian regions; in lower elevations.
Nesting: typically northeast of the Rockies; in a shrub or small tree; nest is made of twigs and lined with grass and other vegetation;

occasionally lays its eggs in other birds' nests; pair normally incubates 2–3 eggs for up to 13 days.
Feeding: gleans hairy caterpillars from leaves, branches and trunks; also eats other insects and occasionally berries.
Voice: a fast *cu-cu-cu* or *cu-cu-cu-cu-cu* in summer.
Similar Species: *Mourning Dove* (p. 135): slender neck; peach-colored underparts. *Yellow-billed Cuckoo* (p. 137): very rare in the Rockies; yellow bill; prominent white spots on the undertail; lacks the red eye ring.

YELLOW-BILLED CUCKOO

Coccyzus americanus

The North American populations of the Yellow-billed Cuckoo are declining significantly. The range of the western subspecies, in particular, has declined dramatically, although it was never common in the Rockies. The declines have been attributed to the loss of mature, closed-canopy riparian forests. ▪ The Yellow-billed Cuckoo's call is composed of rather strange-sounding *kaw* or *kawp* notes. It sounds like the bird is pounding on a hollow wood drum. Cuckoos often call on dark, cloudy days, and they are called 'Rain Crows' in some parts of their range. ▪ Some Yellow-billed Cuckoos migrate as far south as Argentina for the winter.

I.D.: *Sexes similar:* olive-brown upperparts; white underparts; slightly downcurved bill; black upper mandible; yellow lower mandible; long tail with large white spots on the underside; rufous in the wings.

Size: L 11–13 in. (28–33 cm).

Range: rare migrant and local summer breeder in Colorado and western Idaho; accidental elsewhere in the Rockies.

Habitat: riparian thickets and woodlands, second-growth woodlands and overgrown farmlands; also in city parks and orchards.

Nesting: on a horizontal branch in a thorn-bush, shrub or small evergreen tree; nest is a messy structure loosely built of twigs and lined with roots and grass; pair incubates 4 eggs for 9–11 days.

Feeding: gleans vegetation for insect larvae, especially hairy caterpillars; also eats berries, amphibians and other birds' eggs.

Voice: long series of deep, hollow *koks*, slowing near the end: *kuk-kuk-kuk-kuk kuk kop kow kowlp kowlp.*

Similar Species: *Black-billed Cuckoo* (p. 136): all-black bill; red eye ring; more muted undertail patterning.

FLAMMULATED OWL
Otus flammeolus

The Flammulated Owl is a highly migratory owl—it usually winters in Mexico or Central America—probably because its diet is composed largely of insects, which are scarce in winter in North America. ■ A quick field identification for the Flammulated Owl is that it is the only small owl with dark eyes. Otherwise, it is very similar to a screech-owl, although the Flammulated Owl has shorter 'ears' and a reddish facial disk. ■ The Flammulated Owl is a strictly nocturnal bird, and its apparent rarity might be due more to its secretive nature than to actual scarcity.

gray phase

I.D.: *Sexes similar:* small owl; small ear tufts; dark eyes; rufous facial disk; dark bill; vertical breast streaks; gray-brown overall; white eyebrow.
Size: L 6–7 in. (15–18 cm).
Range: uncommon to common resident in the southern and central U.S. Rockies; migrates in the southern Rockies.
Habitat: mature to old-growth ponderosa pine and Douglas-fir forests; occasionally in mixed woods of aspen.
Nesting: usually in an abandoned woodpecker cavity, often lined with a few wood chips; female incubates 3–4 eggs for about 2 days.
Feeding: swoops from a perch for moths and beetles in flight and gleans for grasshoppers, spiders, scorpions and small mammals.
Voice: low series of *hoo-hoops* given at 3–4-second intervals.
Similar Species: *Western Screech-Owl* (p. 139): larger; light-colored eyes; larger ear tufts; lacks the rufous in the plumage.

WESTERN SCREECH-OWL
Otus kennicottii

Despite its small size, the Western Screech-Owl is a mighty hunter. It has the most varied diet of any North American owl: it preys on everything from insects that it catches in mid-air to doves and pigeons that nearly outweigh it. ▪ Western Screech-Owls are silent and reclusive by day; they roost tucked up on limbs or within dense shrubs in a maze of branches. ▪ Where Western Screech-Owls are present, they are year-round residents. It is only from May to March, however, that they are most often encountered. This owl's whistle curls through both natural and suburban woodlots at this time, revealing this small, nocturnal bird. ▪ Robert Kennicott, for whom this species is scientifically named, traveled and collected through northern Canada and Alaska. Like so many of the early field naturalists, his life was short: he died at the age of 30.

I.D.: *Sexes similar:* ear tufts; heavy, vertical breast streaks; yellow eyes; dark bill.
Size: L 7–11 in. (18–28 cm);
W 18–24 in. (46–61 cm).
Range: uncommon resident in Glacier and Waterton Lakes NPs; uncommon to common in the western Rockies in Utah, Idaho and B.C.; locally common in western Montana; rare elsewhere in the Rockies.
Habitat: open deciduous woodlands and riparian forests with a dense understorey, mostly in the foothills.
Nesting: in abandoned woodpecker cavities, magpie nests, nest boxes and natural cavities; adds no nesting materials; female incubates 2–5 white eggs for up to 34 days.

Feeding: hunts at night; swoops from a perch, often in a forest; eats invertebrates, mice, voles, amphibians, earthworms and songbirds; can capture animals larger than itself.
Voice: series of soft, accelerating, evenly pitched whistles and notes, with a rhythm like that of a bouncing ball coming to a stop.
Similar Species: *Great Horned Owl* (p. 140): much larger; horizontal breast banding. *Long-eared Owl* (p. 147): ear tufts are very close together; body is compressed. *Northern Saw-whet Owl* (p. 150) and *Boreal Owl* (p. 149): no ear tufts.

139

GREAT HORNED OWL

Bubo virginianus

This common nocturnal hunter is among the most formidable of mountain predators. Great Horned Owls use their special-ized hearing and human-sized eyes to hunt mice, rabbits, grouse and occasionally fish. They have a poorly developed sense of smell, however, which might be why these owls are the only consistent predator of skunks—worn-out and discarded Great Horned Owl feathers are often identifiable by a simple sniff.

- The Great Horned Owl, the provincial bird of Alberta, is frequently seen in the Rockies, and it breeds throughout the forested areas of North America.

I.D.: *Sexes similar:* ear tufts; fine, horizontal breast streaking; facial disc has a dark outline; white chin; heavily mottled upperparts; plumage varies from light gray to dark brown.
Size: L 18–25 in. (46–64 cm);
W 36–60 in. (91–152 cm).
Range: uncommon to common year-round resident throughout the Rockies.
Habitat: mixed forests, agricultural areas, shrublands and riparian woodlands from the foothills to the subalpine.
Nesting: in the abandoned stick nest of a Red-tailed Hawk, crow, raven, eagle or heron; also nests on cliffs; adds little material to the nest ; pair incubates the eggs for about 33 days.

Feeding: mostly nocturnal, but during winter it also hunts in the day; usually swoops from a perch; detects prey with ears and eyes; eats voles, mice, hares, squirrels, skunks, pocket gophers, grebes, geese, grouse and even fish.
Voice: 6 deep hoots during the breeding season: *hoo-hoo-hoo hoo-hoo hooo* or *eat-my-food I'll-eat you!*
Similar Species: *Western Screech-Owl* (p. 139): much smaller; vertical breast streaks. *Long-eared Owl* (p. 147): vertical breast streaks; ear tufts are very close together; compressed body. *Great Gray Owl* (p. 146) and *Barred Owl* (p. 145): no tufts.

SNOWY OWL
Nyctea scandiaca

When thermometers freeze and the landscape moans in winter's grip, Snowy Owls can be seen defiantly atop a high perch. Even in the worst winter weather, this arctic visitor is shielded from the cold by a thick feather coat that almost hides its black bill and talons. ▪ Feathers are excellent insulators: a simple ruffle creates many air pockets, which shield the bird's warm body temperature from freezing conditions. ▪ As Snowy Owls age, their plumage becomes lighter, and old males are the most characteristic in their near-white dress. ▪ Snowy Owls are erratic visitors to the Rockies; they can be numerous, especially when arctic lemming and vole populations are exceedingly low.

I.D.: *General:* predominantly white plumage; yellow eyes; black bill and talons; no ear tufts. *Adult male:* almost entirely white body with very little dark flecking. *Adult female:* dark barring on the breast and upperparts. *Immature:* heavy barring on the white body.
Size: *L* 20–27 in. (51–69 cm); *W* 54–66 in. (137–168 cm); female is noticeably larger.
Range: sporadic winter visitor throughout the Rockies.
Habitat: open environments, such as agricultural areas, open fields, pastures and shorelines at low elevations; often perches on human-made structures, such as fenceposts, buildings and telephone poles.

Nesting: on the arctic tundra; in a slight depression on a raised hummock or gravel bank; very little lining is added; female incubates 3–4 elongated eggs for 32–34 days.
Feeding: swoops from a perch, often punching through the snow, to take mice, voles, rats, grouse, hares, weasels and, infrequently, songbirds.
Voice: quiet during winter.
Similar Species: *Great Gray Owl* (p. 146): gray plumage. *Great Horned Owl* (p. 140): brown plumage; ear tufts.

NORTHERN HAWK OWL
Surnia ulula

True to its name, the Northern Hawk Owl lives as far north as the treeline. Even in severe winters, hawk owls undergo only slight migrations down into the northern U.S. ▪ All owls, as well as many other birds, such as herons, gulls, crows and hawks, regurgitate 'pellets'—the indigestible parts of prey compressed into an elongated ball. The feathers, fur and bones that make up the pellets are interesting to analyze, because they reveal which species the owl has recently eaten. Although these pellets may look disgusting, they are generally quite clean and dry. Owl pellets can be found under frequently used roost sites.

▪ In our region, hawk owls are best observed during winter; look for them perched over roadsides and open fields. They are generally quite 'tame' and are easily approached.

I.D.: *Sexes similar:* long tail; no ear tufts; fine horizontal barring on the underparts; light-colored face is bordered with black; light bill; yellow eyes; white-spotted forehead.
Size: *L* 15–17 in. (38–43 cm);
W 33 in. (84 cm).
Range: rare year-round resident in Jasper and Banff NPs; winter resident elsewhere in the Canadian Rockies.
Habitat: black-spruce bogs and muskegs, old burns and roadside trees in the montane; forages in the lower subalpine.
Nesting: typically in the boreal forest and taiga; in the abandoned nests of crows, ravens and jays, abandoned woodpecker cavities and broken-off treetops; adds no lining; incubates 5–7 eggs for 25–30 days.

Feeding: swoops from a perch; mainly eats voles, mice and birds; also eats insects in summer.
Voice: usually quiet; whistled breeding trill; call is an accipiter-like *kee-kee-kee*.
Similar Species: *Northern Pygmy-Owl* (p. 143): much smaller; 2 false 'eyes' on the back of the head. *Northern Saw-whet Owl* (p. 150) and *Boreal Owl* (p. 149): short tail; vertical breast streaks.

NORTHERN PYGMY-OWL

Glaucidium gnoma

Even when the Northern Pygmy-Owl is looking the other way, two dark, false 'eyes' on the back of its head stare blankly toward you. Because larger birds and mammals are less likely to attack a bird that is looking in their direction, the pygmy owl is able to 'guard' its own back. ■ The appropriately named pygmy-owl is our smallest owl, but it regularly catches prey that outweigh it. In fierce battles, the owl is often dragged some distance before it kills its prey. ■ By imitating this owl's whistled call, birders are frequently mobbed by chickadees, which do not discriminate when they hear the simple notes. ■ The scientific name *gnoma* is Greek for 'knowledge and wisdom.'

red phase

I.D.: *Sexes similar:* long tail; dark breast; 2 false 'eyes' on the nape; dark belly streaks on light underparts; no ear tufts; dark face; light bill; yellow eyes; white chin; gray and red color phases.
Size: *L* 7 in. (18 cm); *W* 15 in. (38 cm).
Range: uncommon year-round resident in Jasper and Banff NPs; and in the U.S. Rockies.
Habitat: coniferous, deciduous or mixed forests, often in riparian regions, in the foothills and the montane; occasionally in townsites in winter.

Nesting: typically west of the Rockies; in abandoned woodpecker cavities and natural tree hollows; nest is usually unlined; female incubates 3–4 eggs for about 28 days.
Feeding: usually between dusk and dawn; swoops from a perch; eats small rodents, large insects, small birds, reptiles and amphibians.
Voice: single, evenly spaced (about 3 every 2 seconds), whistled *whew-whew-whew-whew*; continuous and easily imitated.
Similar Species: *Northern Hawk Owl* (p. 142): much larger; no false 'eyes.'

BURROWING OWL
Athene cunicularia

Only where the Great Plains meet the mountains will you see these endangered, prairie-nesting ground owls in the Rockies. Burrowing Owls require open, treeless areas of short-grass prairie to live. ▪ The conversion of native grasslands to cropland has reduced the breeding range of these birds, and certain chemicals used in agriculture have been known to decrease breeding success. ▪ When they perch at the entrance of their burrows, these long-legged owls look very similar to ground squirrels or prairie dogs, with which this owl closely associates.

I.D.: *Sexes similar. Adult:* long legs; rounded head; no ear tufts; yellow bill; short wings; white spotting on the breast; brown upper-parts are flecked with white. *Immature:* buff-brown breast is unspotted.
Size: L 8–9 in. (20–23 cm); W 20–24 in. (51–61 cm).
Range: uncommon local breeder in appropriate habitat east of the Rockies in Montana; historical breeder in Yellowstone NP.
Habitat: open grasslands and semi-desert shrublands in treeless country in the prairies and the foothills.

Nesting: typically on the Great Plains; often colonial; in abandoned ground squirrel, badger, hare or prairie dog earth burrows; enlarges the burrow up to 7 ft. (2.1 m) deep with claws; might add grass, sticks or other debris, such as dried cow dung, to the nest site; female incubates 7–9 eggs for up to 30 days.
Feeding: opportunistic; stalks prey or pounces from flight or from a mound or a fencepost perch; eats mostly ground insects, such as grasshoppers, beetles and crickets; also eats small rodents, birds, amphibians and reptiles.
Voice: call is a harsh *chuk*; rasping, rattle-snake-like warning call when inside burrows. *Male:* mournful *coo-coo-roo* in courtship.
Similar Species: *Short-eared Owl* (p. 148): heavily streaked breast; short legs; long wings; doesn't nest in burrows.

BARRED OWL
Strix varia

The madhouse chorus of courting Barred Owls is one of the most memorable sounds of North American forests. The escalating laughs, hoots and howls reinforce the bond between a pair. Bold birdwatchers can join in the frenzied activity by imitating the courtship calls. But take care—your voice will be perceived as a threat and might provoke a spirited attack from these easily stressed and highly territorial owls. ▪ The Barred Owl is very adaptable, and it has been less affected by the loss of old-growth forests than some other species; it has expanded its range westward and northward in North America. ▪ This owl has relatively weak talons; it mainly preys on smaller animals.

I.D.: *Sexes similar:* dark eyes; horizontal streaking around the neck and upper breast; vertical streaking on the belly; light bill; no ear tufts; dark gray-brown, mottled plumage.
Size: L 17–24 in.(43–61 cm); W 40–50 in. (102–127 cm); female is slightly larger.
Range: uncommon year-round resident in the Canadian and northern U.S. Rockies.
Habitat: mature coniferous and mixedwood forests, often along riparian regions, up to the montane.
Nesting: typically in the boreal forest and eastern hardwood forests; in natural tree cavities, broken-off treetops or the abandoned stick nests of other birds; adds

very little to the nest; female incubates 2 or 3 eggs for up to 33 days.
Feeding: nocturnal; swoops from a perch to pounce on its prey; mainly eats mice, voles and squirrels; also eats amphibians and smaller birds.
Voice: most characteristic of all the owls; loud, hooting, rhythmic, laughing call, heard mostly in spring, but also throughout the year: *Who cooks for you? Who cooks for you all?*
Similar Species: *Great Gray Owl* (p. 146) and *Northern Hawk Owl* (p. 142): light-colored eyes; heavy vertical barring on the underparts. *Great Horned Owl* (p. 140): ear tufts; light-colored eyes.

145

GREAT GRAY OWL

Strix nebulosa

With a face in the shape of a satellite dish, the Great Gray Owl lets scarcely a scurry or twitch escape its attention. This magnificent sensory structure swivels smoothly, focusing instantly on sounds and movement in the owl's often bleak environment. Once a vole is detected, the Great Gray launches itself from its perch, glides in on fixed wings and often punches through deep snow to acquire its meal.

■ This most regal and impressive owl is one of the most sought-after birding experiences in the Rocky Mountains. ■ Although the magnificent Great Gray Owl is the largest of all North American owls, it is outweighed by as much as 15 percent by the Snowy Owl and the Great Horned Owl. ■ The Great Gray Owl lives throughout the northern hemisphere.

I.D.: *Sexes similar:* gray plumage; large, rounded head; no ear tufts; yellow eyes; well-defined, ringed facial disk; white throat; long tail.
Size: *L* 24–33 in. (61–84 cm); *W* 54–60 in. (137–152 cm); female is a little larger.
Range: uncommon resident in the central and northern U.S. Rockies and the Canadian Rockies.
Habitat: forest clearings, roadsides and open meadows in the montane and the subalpine.

Nesting: typically in the boreal forest, usually near spruce bogs or muskeg; in abandoned hawk, raven or eagle nests; occasionally nests atop a tall stump; adds little nest material; female incubates 2–4 eggs for up to 36 days.
Feeding: listens and watches from a perch; then swoops to catch voles, mice, shrews, gophers, squirrels and small hares.
Voice: slow, deep, almost inaudible *hoot hoot.*
Similar Species: *Great Horned Owl* (p. 140): ear tufts. *Snowy Owl* (p. 141): white plumage.

LONG-EARED OWL
Asio otus

Long-eared Owls will either inflate or compress their bodies in response to certain situations. To scare an intruder, the owl expands its air sacs, puffs its feathers and spreads its wings to double its size in a threat display. When hiding from an intruder or predator, it compresses itself into a long, thin, vertical form. By slimming down, the owl is trying to blend into the stumps and branches where it frequently roosts. ▪ This nocturnal predator hunts in open areas, but it returns to dense, wooded environments to roost out the day. ▪ Despite the common use of 'eared' in many owl names, the tufts on top of these birds' heads are made only of feathers.

I.D.: *Sexes similar:* long ear tufts are relatively close together; slim body; vertical belly markings; light brown facial disk; mottled brown plumage; yellow eyes; white around the bill.
Size: L 13–16 in. (33–41 cm); W 36–47 in. (91–119 cm).
Range: locally uncommon year-round resident throughout the Rockies; rare winter resident in the Canadian Rockies.
Habitat: dense, mixed forests and tall shrublands, usually next to open spaces, such as grasslands and meadows, in the foothills.
Nesting: often in abandoned crow, magpie or hawk nests; occasionally in natural tree cavities; female incubates 4–5 eggs for up to 25–30 days.
Feeding: nocturnal; flies low, pouncing on prey from the air; eats mainly voles and mice, occasionally shrews, pocket-gophers and small rabbits, and also small birds and amphibians.

Voice: breeding call is a low, soft *quoo-quoo*; alarm call is *weck-weck-weck*.
Similar Species: *Western Screech-Owl* (p. 139): ear tufts are farther apart; body is less compressed. *Great Horned Owl* (p. 140): much larger; ear tufts are farther apart; body is less compressed.

SHORT-EARED OWL
Asio flammeus

Short-eared Owls have the ability to strike their wing tips together below them, producing a courtship clap to prospective mates. These birds typically inhabit open country, where visual aerial displays—called the sky dance—are more effective than the elaborate hooting of owls living in deep woods. ▪ The evening foraging flights of this owl are very distinctive. It beats its long wings slowly, similar in many ways to a butterfly, as it courses low over wet meadows. ▪ This owl's life revolves around the population levels of voles, leading to nomadic movements in response to prey availability.

I.D.: *Sexes similar:* yellow eyes in black sockets; heavy, vertical streaking on the buffy belly; straw-colored upperparts; short ear tufts are rarely seen. *In flight:* dark elbow patches; deep wing beats; long wings.
Size: *L* 13–17 in. (33–43 cm); female is slightly larger.
Range: rare to uncommon year-round resident throughout the Rockies; populations can fluctuate greatly from year to year; most likely to be seen in migration.

Habitat: open country, including grasslands, wet meadows and cleared forests. *In migration:* frequently in alpine meadows.
Nesting: on the ground; in a slight depression sparsely lined with grass; female incubates 4–7 eggs for 26–37 days.
Feeding: uses hearing, vision and flight adaptations to forage low over marshes, wet meadows and tall vegetation; pounces from the air; eats mainly voles and other small rodents, as well as insects, small birds and amphibians.
Voice: generally quiet; produces a soft *toot-toot-toot* during the breeding season; also 'barks' like a small dog and squeals.
Similar Species: *Burrowing Owl* (p. 144): much longer legs; shorter tail; shorter wings. *Long-eared Owl* (p. 147): long ear tufts; shorter wings; rarely hunts during the day.

BOREAL OWL
Aegolius funereus

The Boreal Owl routinely ranks in the top five of the most desired species to see, according to birdwatcher surveys; it rarely ventures into populated areas, and its remote northern breeding grounds are hard for birders to reach. During winters of heavy snowfall or prey scarcity, however, Boreal Owls migrate southward and into lower elevations, resulting in a few rare sightings of these mysterious birds. ▪ Because of the Boreal Owl's remote habitat and nocturnal activity patterns, science has yet to discover many aspects of its ecology and behavior. This small owl is known to be very well adapted to snowy forest environments: it is quite capable of locating and catching prey that live underneath the snow! ▪ This approachable owl was named the 'Blind One' by aboriginal peoples, because it was easily captured by hand. (Like all owls, it actually has excellent vision.)

I.D.: *Sexes similar. Adult:* small body; large, rounded head; light facial disk with a dark border; light bill; vertical, rusty streaks on the underparts; brown, white-spotted upperparts; heavily spotted forehead; black, vertical eyebrow; short tail. *Immature:* brown underparts; brown face with white between the eyes.

Size: L 9–12 in. (23–31 cm.).

Range: uncommon in the Canadian and northern U.S. Rockies; locally rare year-round resident in the U.S. Rockies.

Habitat: mature coniferous and mixed forests at lower latitudes, often adjacent to open meadows up to lower subalpine.

Nesting: typically in the boreal forest; in abandoned woodpecker cavities and natural hollows in trees; lines the cavity with a few feathers; female incubates 4–6 white eggs for 26–32 days.

Feeding: swoops from a perch for voles, mice, shrews and insects; caches food; might plunge through snow for food.

Voice: rapid, accelerating, continuous whistle: *whew-whew-whew-whew*; easily imitated.

Similar Species: *Northern Saw-whet Owl* (p. 150): adult has a dark bill and lacks the heavy forehead spotting and the vertical eyebrow; immature has reddish underparts. *Western Screech-Owl* (p. 139): ear tufts; dark bill; dark face.

NORTHERN SAW-WHET OWL
Aegolius acadicus

Saw-whets are opportunistic hunters, taking whatever they can, whenever they can. These small owls often catch more than they can eat, and they are known to store their food, usually in trees. The stored food freezes quickly in winter, and it has recently been discovered that the owls 'incubate' the frozen prey to thaw it out. ■ This small owl delivers its slow, whistling notes through the nights from mid-winter through early spring. The common name 'saw-whet' comes from one of this owl's calls, which was thought to be similar to the sound of a large mill saw being sharpened. ■ The scientific name *acadicus* is Latin for 'from Acadia' (New Brunswick, Nova Scotia and Maine), the region from which this bird was first collected.

Nesting: in abandoned woodpecker cavities and natural hollows in trees; female incubates 5–6 white eggs for 27–29 days.

Feeding: swoops from a perch; eats mainly mice and voles, also larger insects, songbirds and shrews, and occasionally amphibians; caches food.

I.D.: *Sexes similar. Adult:* small body; large, rounded head; light, unbordered facial disk; dark bill; vertical, rusty streaks on the underparts; brown, white-spotted upperparts; lightly streaked forehead; short tail. *Immature:* white between the eyes; rich brown upperparts; buff-brown underparts.

Size: L 7–9 in. (18–23 cm).

Range: uncommon spring migrant and summer breeder in the Canadian Rockies; uncommon resident in the U.S. Rockies.

Habitat: pure and mixed coniferous and deciduous forests in the foothills and the montane.

Voice: single, evenly spaced (about 1 per second) whistled *whew-whew-whew-whew*; continuous and easily imitated.

Similar Species: *Boreal Owl* (p. 149): adult has a light-colored bill; heavy spotting on its forehead; a dark, vertical eyebrow and a dark border to the facial disk; immature has a brown breast. *Northern Pygmy-Owl* (p. 143): light-colored bill; proportionately longer tail; patches on the nape; lacks the white streaking on the forehead.

COMMON NIGHTHAWK
Chordeiles minor

Frequently, warm summer and cool spring evenings are filled with the night-hawk's continual courtship calls and erratic flights. The male flies high above dry forests and forest clearings, gaining elevation for the courtship climax. From a great height, he dives swiftly to the ground, finally thrusting his wings forward in a braking action as he pulls out of the dive. The quick thrust of the wings produces a deep, hollow *vroom*. ▪ The nighthawk has a very wide gape fringed with feather shafts that effectively increase the size of the mouth for catching insects. ▪ Nighthawks are generally less nocturnal than other members of their family, but they still spend most daylight hours resting on a tree limb or on the ground. They have very short legs and small feet, and they sit lengthwise, not across the branch like most birds.

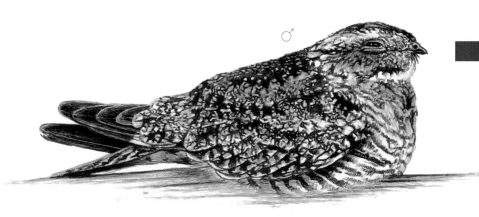

I.D.: *Sexes similar:* cryptic, light to dark brown plumage; barred underparts. *Male:* white throat. *Female:* buff throat. *In flight:* white wrist patches; long, pointed wings; shallowly forked tail; flight is erratic.
Size: *L* 8¹/₂–10 in. (22–25 cm).
Range: fairly common migrant and breeder throughout the Rockies.
Habitat: dry coniferous forests, open woodlands, meadows, larger lakes and grasslands in the foothills.

Nesting: on bare ground, in a spot chosen by the female; female incubates 2 eggs for about 19 days.
Feeding: catches insects in flight; eats mosquitoes, beetles, flying ants, moths and other insects.
Voice: frequently repeated, nasal *peent peent*; also makes a deep, hollow *vrooom* with its wings.
Similar Species: *Common Poorwill* (p. 152): much less common; lacks the white wrist patches; shorter, rounder wings.

COMMON POORWILL
Phalaenoptilus nuttallii

In 1946, the scientific community was shocked by the discovery of a Common Poorwill that was cold to the touch and appeared not to be breathing or to have a heartbeat. Although poorwills do not enter true hibernation like some mammals, they use short-term 'torpor'—their body temperature drops as low as 43° F (6° C) for a few days at a time—to survive cold periods when their prey (flying insects) are unavailable. Not all poorwills use torpor; many of them migrate to tropical climates for winter. ■ The 1946 discovery was clearly not the first suggestion of this strange habit in poorwills. In 1804, Meriwether Lewis found a mysterious 'goatsucker ... to be passing into the dormant state.' Perhaps the scientific community's amazement was needless: the Hopi could have told them their name for the bird was *Hölchoko*, 'the sleeping one.'

I.D.: *Sexes similar:* cryptic, light to dark brown plumage; pale throat; finely barred underparts. *Male:* white corners on the tail feathers. *Female:* buff corners on the tail feathers. *In flight:* rounded wings and tail.
Size: L 7¹/₂–8¹/₂ in. (19–22 cm).
Range: locally common in drier mountain habitats in Montana, Idaho and western Colorado.
Habitat: dry, open, grassy environments, rocky canyons, ponderosa pine forests and open shrublands in the foothills.

Nesting: typically on the Great Plains and in the Southwest; on bare ground; pair incubates 2 white eggs for 20–21 days.
Feeding: on the wing; eats mainly moths, beetles and other flying insects.
Voice: frequently heard at dusk and through the night: *poor-will poor-will*; at close range, a hiccup-like sound can be heard at the end of the phrase.
Similar Species: *Common Nighthawk* (p. 151): long, pointed wings; white wrist patches.

BLACK SWIFT

Cypseloides niger

The fast-flying Black Swift, the largest of the North American swifts, is very restricted in its mountain breeding range. Only along the steep vertical walls of canyons do small, semi-colonial groups of Black Swifts nest. ■ During pleasant weather, Black Swifts forage very high in the air, while bad weather brings them closer to the ground. Black Swifts might leave their young for many hours while foraging, only returning to their nests with any reliability at dusk. ■ Swifts cast a characteristic boomerang silhouette in flight. They are shaped much like swallows—long, tapering wings, small bills, wide gape and long, sleek bodies—but they are not closely related. ■ The wing beat of swifts only appears to alternate, and it looks uncomfortable because of their stiff, rigid wings.

I.D.: *Sexes similar:* black overall; slender, sleek body; white-tipped feathers around the forehead; very small legs. *In flight:* long, tapering wings angle backward; short, slightly forked tail; rapid wing beat.

Size: *L* 7 in. (18 cm).

Range: locally common summer breeder in the Canadian Rockies; locally uncommon breeder in the U.S. Rockies.

Habitat: canyons and wet cliffs in the montane.

Nesting: semi-colonial; on a canyon ledge, often near a waterfall; nest is made of moss, mud and algae; pair incubates 1 egg for up to 27 days.

Feeding: on the wing; eats flying insects, especially stoneflies, caddisflies and mayflies.

Voice: high-pitched *plik-plik-plik-plik.*

Similar Species: *Vaux's Swift* (p. 154): smaller; lighter overall color. *White-throated Swift* (p. 155): smaller overall; light patterns on the underparts.

VAUX'S SWIFT
Chaetura vauxi

The Vaux's Swift is the most common swift west of the Rockies. In late summer and early fall, large flocks may be seen circling in tight groups, prior to plunging collectively into roosting trees or chimneys.
■ Swifts, when not in flight, use their small but strong claws to cling to vertical surfaces. While many swifts in eastern areas choose chimneys and other structures to nest and to roost in, the Vaux's Swift continues to prefer decaying trees for its rest areas in the West.
■ John Kirk Townsend named this bird after William Sansom Vaux, an eminent mineralogist. Although Vaux well deserved the honor, it is somewhat ironic that one of the West's most aerial birds is named for a man whose passion was for earth-bound treasures.

Habitat: forages in forest openings, river valleys and lakeshores and breeds in mature coniferous and deciduous forests in the foothills and the montane.

Nesting: typically west of the Rockies; in a hollow tree cavity or chimney; nest is made of sticks, twigs and conifer needles and glued to the inner wall of the cavity with saliva; pair incubates 4–5 white eggs for 18–19 days.

Feeding: on the wing, often just above the treetops; feeds almost entirely on flying insects, including flies, moths, ants and aphids.

Voice: courtship call is a fast, twittering *chip-chip-chip-cheweet-cheweet.*

Similar Species: *Black Swift* (p. 153): black; much larger overall. *White-throated Swift* (p. 155): light and dark patterning on the underparts. *Bank Swallow* (p. 201): dark breast band on white underparts. *Northern Rough-winged Swallow* (p. 200): dirty white underparts; heavier wings; larger tail.

I.D.: *Sexes similar:* brownish-gray overall. *In flight:* brown upperparts; lighter underparts with a very pale throat; squared-off tail; long wings taper backward.

Size: *L* 5 in. (13 cm).

Range: locally common summer breeder in the Montana Rockies; rare breeder south of Wyoming.

WHITE-THROATED SWIFT

Aeronautes saxatalis

The White-throated Swift is one of the frequent fliers of the bird world; only incubation and rest keep this bird out of the air. White-throated Swifts feed, drink, bathe and even mate while flying. During their lifespan, it is likely that many of these birds travel more than a million miles; their body form is one of the most highly evolved for flight. ▪ The White-throated Swift is the fastest North American swift; it's possible that it is among the fastest birds in the world. White-throated Swifts have been observed flying at an estimated 200 m.p.h. (320 km/h). ▪ The genus name *Aeronautes* is Greek for 'air sailor.'

I.D.: *Sexes similar:* black upperparts; white throat tapering to the belly; black flanks with white patches; slender, sleek body. *In flight:* long, tapering wings angle backward; slightly forked tail.

Size: *L* 6–7 in. (15–18 cm).

Range: locally uncommon summer breeder in the U.S. Rockies; very rare in the Canadian Rockies.

Habitat: forages in open habitat and breeds on cliffs and large, rocky outcroppings in the foothills.

Nesting: colonial; in a crack or crevice on a cliff face; shallow saucer of twigs and conifer needles is glued together with saliva; pair incubates 4–5 eggs for 18–19 days.

Feeding: on the wing; feeds almost entirely on flying insects.

Voice: shrill, descending laugh: *skee-e-e-e.*

Similar Species: *Vaux's Swift* (p. 154) and *Black Swift* (p. 153): lack the white and dark underparts. *Bank Swallow* (p. 201) and *Violet-green Swallow* (p. 199): lack the dark flanks with white patches and the wing 'pits.'

BLACK-CHINNED HUMMINGBIRD
Archilochus alexandri

Hikers in the mountains and foothills might have the good fortune of watching a Black-chinned Hummingbird forage at one of the hundreds of flowers it normally visits in a single day. ▪ The Black-chinned Hummingbird is the western counterpart of the Ruby-throated Hummingbird, the most wide-ranging hummer in North America. ▪ Naturalist H.G.L. Reichenbach was obviously deeply influenced by Greek mythology. He named several hummingbird genera after Greeks—*Archilochus* was one of the first Greek poets. The species name *alexandri* is from the name of its discoverer, a doctor who collected specimens in Mexico.

I.D.: *General:* iridescent green upperparts; white collar; long, narrow bill; small white spot behind the eye. *Male:* black throat with a violet band below it; white underparts; green 'vest'. *Female:* all-white underparts; buff sides; light green forehead.
Size: *L* 3–3¹/₂ in. (7.6–9 cm).
Range: rare summer breeder in the U.S. Rockies; vagrant north into the southern Canadian Rockies.
Habitat: riparian forests and deciduous shrubs in the foothills.

Nesting: tiny cup nest of plant down and spider webs is saddled on a branch; female incubates 2 eggs for up to 16 days.
Feeding: hovers in the air and probes flowers for nectar; also eats small insects.
Voice: soft, high-pitched, warbling courtship songs; buzz and chip alarm calls; wings buzz in flight.
Similar Species: *Ruby-throated Hummingbird*: female has a shorter bill and a more greenish crown. *Broad-tailed Hummingbird* (p. 158): male has a lighter, red throat.

CALLIOPE HUMMINGBIRD

Stellula calliope

The male Calliope Hummingbird's sparkling rose-purple throat rays are unmistakable. As they flit about in the montane, their dainty colors complement the vivid complexion of the landscape. ■ The Calliope is the smallest North American hummingbird and the smallest long-distance migrant in the bird world, traveling up to 5500 mi. (8900 km) in a year. Contrary to some popular myths, hummingbirds never hitch-hike on the backs of geese or eagles. ■ Hummingbirds and swifts belong to the order Apodiformes, which means 'without legs,' an allusion to the very small legs of these birds. ■ Novice birdwatchers often ponder the pronunciation of this bird's name. It is generally accepted as 'ca-lie-o-pee,' but variations are plentiful (and often amusing).

I.D.: *General:* iridescent green upperparts; long, narrow bill; short tail. *Male:* light purple streaks running down the throat from the bill; white underparts; light green flanks. *Female:* white underparts; peach-colored flanks; dark green spots on the throat.

Size: L 3¹/₄ in. (8 cm).

Range: common migrant and summer breeder in the greater Yellowstone area; uncommon breeder in the Canadian and northern U.S. Rockies; uncommon fall migrant in the Colorado Rockies.

Habitat: disturbed areas; avalanche slopes, burns and shrubby meadows in the montane and the subalpine.

Nesting: tiny cup nest of plant down, moss, scales and spider webs is saddled on a branch under an overhanging branch or foliage; often builds over previously used nests; female incubates 2 eggs for up to 16 days.

Feeding: probes flowers for nectar while hovering; also eats small insects.

Voice: high-pitched chattering *tsew* note.

Similar Species: *Rufous Hummingbird* (p. 159): longer tail and bill; female often has red spotting on the throat. *Broad-tailed Hummingbird* (p. 158): longer tail and bill; female shows rufous in the tail.

BROAD-TAILED HUMMINGBIRD
Selasphorus platycercus

During the last week of May, the southern Rocky Mountains are the site of a most unusual daily migration. Male Broad-tailed Hummingbirds make daily reconnaissance flights between their alpine breeding grounds and the lower foothills. Although the males stake out and defend their territories in the alpine, the lack of flowering plants there forces them to feed at lower elevations, where they find flowers, gardens and feeders. ▪ During courtship displays and aggressive flights, the males use their tapered primary feathers to produce an eerie, buzzing, insect-like trill. ▪ *Selasphorus* is Greek for 'light-bearing,' and it refers to this bird's bright plumage; *platycercus* is Greek for 'broad-tailed.'

♂

I.D.: *General:* iridescent green upperparts; long, narrow bill; broad tail. *Male:* red throat; white underparts; green flanks. *Female:* pale underparts; peach-colored flanks; white throat.
Size: *L* 4 in. (10 cm).
Range: common summer breeder in the Colorado Rockies; rare in the central and northern U.S. Rockies.
Habitat: ponderosa pine, Douglas-fir and other coniferous forests, disturbed areas, avalanche slopes and burns in the montane and the subalpine up to 10,000 ft. (3000 m).

Nesting: often over a stream; tiny cup nest of plant down and spider webs, covered with lichen or leaves, is saddled on a branch; female incubates 2 eggs for up to 16 days.
Feeding: probes flowers for nectar while hovering; eats many small insects.
Voice: call is a harsh *tew*; male's wings produce a cricket-like buzz when displaying.
Similar Species: *Rufous Hummingbird* (p. 159): male is rusty-red overall. *Black-chinned Hummingbird* (p. 156): male has a very dark throat. *Calliope Hummingbird* (p. 157): shorter bill; female lacks the rufous in the tail.

RUFOUS HUMMINGBIRD

Selasphorus rufus

The Rufous Hummingbird's annual migration through the Rocky Mountains co-incides with the blooming of the flowers. The only commonly seen copper-colored hummers in the Rockies, Rufous Hummingbirds migrate north in spring along the temperate West Coast en route to their breeding grounds in the northern Rockies. Once the females are done rearing their young, the birds follow the late-blooming alpine meadows south through the Rockies. The alpine flowers provide the food they need for their migration to Central and South America. ▪ To attract pollinators (insects and hummingbirds), plants produce colorful flowers with sweet, energy-rich nectar. As hummingbirds visit flowers for the food, they spread pollen from one flower to another, ensuring the plants' survival.

I.D.: *General:* long, thin, black bill; mostly rufous tail. *Male:* red back, tail and flanks; scarlet, scaled throat; green crown; white breast and belly. *Female:* green back; red-spotted throat; rufous flanks; light underparts.
Size: L 3¹/₄–3¹/₂ in. (8–9 cm).
Range: common migrant and summer breeder in the Canadian Rockies; common fall migrant in the U.S. Rockies.
Habitat: Douglas-fir forests, forest edges, meadows and willow shrubs in the montane and the subalpine.

Nesting: tiny cup nest of plant down and spider webs, covered with lichens and leaves, is saddled on a drooping conifer branch; female incubates 2 eggs for up to 14 days.
Feeding: probes mostly red flowers for nectar while hovering; also eats small insects and sap.
Voice: call is a gentle *chewp chewp*; also makes a fast buzz: *zeee-chuppity-chup*.
Similar Species: *Calliope Hummingbird* (p. 157) and *Broad-tailed Hummingbird* (p. 158): females have much less rufous in their tails.

BELTED KINGFISHER
Ceryle alcyon

The Belted Kingfisher's distinctive rattle and shaggy mane announce areas of shallow, calm waters. With a precise headfirst dive, it can catch fish at depths of up to 2 ft. (61 cm). This bird's large head and bill might help it penetrate the water's surface while foraging. ▪ Female kingfishers have the traditional female reproductive role, but, like phalaropes, they are more colorful than their mates. ▪ A breeding pair of kingfishers alternates in excavating their nest burrow. They use their bills to chip away at the dirt and then kick the dirt out of the tunnel with their small feet. ▪ *Alcyon* (Halcyone) was the daughter of the wind god in Greek mythology; she and her husband were transformed into kingfishers.

I.D.: *General:* blue upperparts; shaggy blue crest; blue breast band; white collar; long, straight bill; short legs; white underwings; small, white patch near the eye. *Female:* rust-colored 'belt' (occasionally incomplete). *Male:* no 'belt.'
Size: *L* 11–14 in. (28–36 cm).
Range: uncommon to common spring, summer and fall breeder throughout the Rockies; uncommon winter resident in the U.S. Rockies; rare winter resident in the Canadian Rockies.
Habitat: *Summer:* large rivers, lakes and beaver ponds, adjacent to earth banks. *Winter:* open rivers.

Nesting: in a cavity at the end of an earth burrow, often up to 7 ft. (2.1 m) deep, dug by the pair with their bills and claws; pair incubates 6–7 eggs for up to 24 days.
Feeding: dives headfirst, either from a perch or from a hover above the water; eats mostly small fish, aquatic invertebrates and tadpoles.
Voice: fast, repetitive rattle—*crrrr-crrrr-crrrr-crrrr*—like a tea cup shaking on a saucer.
Similar Species: none.

LEWIS'S WOODPECKER
Melanerpes lewis

The Lewis's Woodpecker forgoes many traditional woodpecker habits. Rather than clinging to tree trunks and chipping away for grubs, the Lewis's Woodpecker does much of its foraging as flycatchers do, catching insects on the wing. It is frequently seen perched on wires, and it often soars and flies directly, without undulating. ■ This dark woodpecker is named in honor of Meriwether Lewis, one of the co-leaders of the famous Lewis and Clark expedition. Lewis was chosen to lead this trip to the Pacific by his long-time acquaintance, President Thomas Jefferson. Although Lewis was not trained as a naturalist, his diary entries include many concise observations of natural history.

I.D.: *Sexes similar. Adult:* dark green upperparts; dark red face; light gray breast and collar; pinkish belly; dark undertail coverts; sharp, stout bill. *Immature:* brown head and face; brown breast; lacks the red in the face and the light gray collar.
Size: *L* 11 in. (28 cm).
Range: uncommon resident in the Colorado Rockies; summer resident in the western Montana Rockies; rare in the greater Yellowstone area; rare breeder north into the Canadian Rockies.
Habitat: open riparian cottonwood, ponderosa pine and Douglas-fir forests in the montane.

Nesting: excavates a cavity in a dead or dying tree; pair incubates 6–7 white eggs for about 15 days.
Feeding: flycatches for flying invertebrates; probes into cracks and crevices for invertebrates.
Voice: harsh series of *churr-churr-churr-churr-churr.*
Similar Species: *Williamson's Sapsucker* (p. 164): male has a large, white wing patch and lacks the red face.

161

YELLOW-BELLIED SAPSUCKER
Sphyrapicus varius

This sapsucker is typically an eastern bird, and it only enters the Rockies through the low passes in Jasper National Park. ▪ Yellow-bellied Sapsuckers can be closely approached around their nest sites, which are almost exclusively in aspen-dominated stands. ▪ Like most woodpeckers, they feed their young almost constantly—both parents must return to the nest site with food every 5 to 10 minutes. ▪ Loony Toons cartoons have long had fun at the expense of the Yellow-bellied Sapsucker, but contrary to rumor, these woodpeckers are no more cowardly than other birds. ▪ The scientific name *varius* refers to the variability once thought to exist within the species. It is no longer as variable, however, because the Red-naped Sapsucker and the Red-breasted Sapsucker, which were once regarded as subspecies of the Yellow-bellied Sapsucker, are now considered separate species.

I.D.: *General:* black bib; red forecrown; black-and-white face, back, wings and tail; yellow wash on the belly. *Male:* red chin. *Female:* whitish chin.

Size: L 7–8 in. (18–20 cm).

Range: uncommon migrant and summer resident in Banff and Jasper NPs; rare elsewhere in the Rockies.

Habitat: deciduous and mixed woods in the foothills and the lower montane.

Nesting: in a cavity, usually in a live birch or aspen with heart-rot; usually lines the cavity with wood chips; pair incubates 5–6 eggs for 12–13 days.

Feeding: hammers trees for insects; creates 'wells' and collects sap and trapped insects; also flycatches for insects.

Voice: nasal, cat-like *meow*; territorial/courtship hammering has a Morse-code quality and rhythm.

Similar Species: *Red-naped Sapsucker* (p. 163): adult is extremely similar but has a small red patch on the back of the head; range is very useful in separating the species.

RED-NAPED SAPSUCKER
Sphyrapicus nuchalis

Red-naped Sapsuckers arrive in the Rockies in May and immediately begin foraging. Sapsuckers have adopted a variation on the woodpecker theme: they drill lines of parallel 'wells' in tree bark. As the wells fill with sap, they attract insects, and Red-naped Sapsuckers make their rounds, collecting the trapped bugs and pooled sap. Some people think that the damaging effect on ornamental and harvestable trees overshadows the bird's resourcefulness, but most healthy trees can withstand a series of sapsucker wells. This foraging behavior has convinced some people that some birds are capable of advance planning.

- The Red-naped Sapsucker was formerly considered a subspecies of the Yellow-bellied Sapsucker, a species of eastern North America.

♂

I.D.: *General:* red forehead; red patch behind the ear; black-and-white–striped head; black bib; yellow wash on the breast; black-and-white wings and back; white rump; light yellow upper back with fine black streaking. *Male:* red chin and throat. *Female:* white chin; red throat.
Size: *L* 8¹/₂ in. (22 cm).
Range: fairly common migrant and summer breeder south of Waterton Lakes and Glacier NPs; rare north to Jasper NP.
Habitat: aspen and birch woodlands and alder shrubs in the foothills.
Nesting: excavates a cavity in a living aspen or other deciduous tree; occasionally uses the same tree for 2 years, making a new hole; lines cavity with wood chips; pair incubates 4–5 eggs for 13 days.

Feeding: hammers a series of small, square wells in living trees; eats the sap and insects from the wells; frequently flycatches insects.
Voice: call is a cat-like *meow*; tapping is irregular and Morse code–like.
Similar Species: *Hairy Woodpecker* (p. 166) and *Downy Woodpecker* (p. 165): lack the red forehead and the black bib. *Williamson's Sapsucker* (p. 164): male is darker overall and has a large, white wing patch.

163

WILLIAMSON'S SAPSUCKER

Sphyrapicus thyroideus

While the male and female of most woodpeckers look very much alike, in the Williamson's Sapsucker they are very different. This difference in plumage so confused early naturalists that for 20 years after being discovered, males were known as the Williamson's Sapsucker, while females were thought to be a completely separate species, which was called the Black-breasted Woodpecker. ■ This sapsucker is named in honor of Robert Williamson, a topographical engineer who led surveying expeditions through the western U.S. ■ The feet of woodpeckers allow them to move vertically. Two toes face forward, one toe points off to the side at a 90° angle, and the small hind toe generally points backward.

I.D.: *Male:* black overall; white 'mustache,' trailing eyebrow and wing patch; yellow belly; red chin; white rump; black-and-white flanks. *Female:* brown head; brown and white barring on the back and wings; white rump; black bib; yellow wash on the belly. *In flight:* both sexes show a white rump.
Size: L 9 in. (23 cm).
Range: uncommon summer breeder in the U.S. Rockies north from Colorado.
Habitat: open Douglas-fir and other coniferous forests and mixed woods in the foothills and the montane.
Nesting: typically west of the Rockies; excavates a cavity in a tree trunk or dead limb; often uses the same tree, but a different cavity, the following year; pair incubates 5–6 eggs for 13 days.
Feeding: hammers a series of small, square wells in living trees; eats the sap and insects from the wells; occasionally eats berries and also flycatches for insects.
Voice: loud, shrill *chur-cheeur-cheeur;* tapping is irregular, slow and Morse code–like.
Similar Species: *Three-toed* (p. 167), *Hairy* (p. 166) and *Downy* (p. 165) woodpeckers: lack the bold, white wing patch, the red chin and the yellow wash on the belly. *Northern Flicker* (p. 169): spotted underparts; more patterning on the head than a female Williamson's.

DOWNY WOODPECKER
Picoides pubescens

This woodland bird's soft taps filter through aspen forests, betraying its presence. ■ The Downy Woodpecker is the smallest and most familiar woodpecker in North America; it is often the first woodpecker that novice birdwatchers discover. Like many other small birds, Downies are generally more approachable and more tolerant of humans than larger species. ■ Woodpeckers have feathered nostrils to filter out the sawdust they produce by hammering. To cushion the shock of banging the head, woodpeckers have evolved a thick skull, large bill, neck and skull muscles and a narrow space between the brain and the inner skull.

I.D.: *General:* clear white belly and back; black wings are barred with white; black eye line and crown; short, stubby bill; mostly black tail; white outer tail feathers are spotted with black. *Male:* small red patch on the back of the head. *Female:* no red patch.
Size: L 6–7 in. (15–18 cm).
Range: uncommon to locally common resident throughout the Rockies.
Habitat: all wooded environments, including aspen forests and tall deciduous shrubs, up to the subalpine.
Nesting: excavates a cavity in a dying or decaying trunk or limb; pair shares in the excavation, which lasts more than 2 weeks; lines cavity with wood chips; incubates 4–5 eggs for 11–13 days.
Feeding: forages on trunks and branches; chips and probes for insect eggs, cocoons, larvae and adults; also eats nuts and seeds; attracted to feeders.

Voice: long, unbroken trill: *trrrrrrrrr*; call is either a sharp *pik* or *ki-ki-ki*.
Similar Species: *Hairy Woodpecker* (p. 166): larger; bill is as long as the head is wide; no spots on the white outer tail feathers.

HAIRY WOODPECKER
Picoides villosus

A second or third look is often required to confirm the identity of the Hairy Woodpecker, which is easily confused with its smaller cousin, the Downy Woodpecker. ▪ During courtship, Hairy Woodpeckers drum rhythmically on trees—the wood reverberates with the sound. In courtship flights, this bird's wings produce loud sounds when they are occasionally beaten against the bird's flanks. ▪ The secret to the woodpeckers' wood-boring ways is hidden in their bills: most woodpeckers have very long tongues—in some cases more than four times the length of the bill—and the tip of the tongue is sticky with saliva, and it is finely barbed to seize wood-boring insects. The length of the tongue is made possible by twin structures that wrap around the perimeter of the skull; these structures store the tongue in much the same way that measuring tape is stored in its case.

Nesting: excavates a nest site in a live or decaying trunk or limb; pair shares in the excavation, which lasts more than 2 weeks; lines cavity with wood chips; pair incubates 4–5 eggs for up to 12 days.

Feeding: forages on trunks and branches; chips, hammers and probes bark for insect eggs, cocoons, larvae and adults; also eats nuts, fruit and seeds; attracted to feeders.

Voice: loud, sharp call: *peek peek*; long, unbroken trill: *keek-ik-ik-ik-ik-ik.*

Similar Species: *Downy Woodpecker* (p. 165): smaller; shorter bill; dark spots on the white outer tail feathers.

I.D.: *General:* pure white belly; black wings are spotted with white; black cheek and crown; bill is about as long as the head is wide; black tail with white outer tail feathers. *Male:* small red patch on the back of the head. *Female:* no red patch.

Size: L 7½–9½ in. (19–24 cm).

Range: locally common year-round resident throughout the Rockies.

Habitat: aspen, spruce and mixed forests up to the montane.

THREE-TOED WOODPECKER

Picoides tridactylus

Within most mature coniferous forests, evidence of this woodpecker's foraging activities is seen more commonly than the bird itself. In their search for insect eggs and invertebrates, Three-toed Woodpeckers flake off bits of bark from old, dying coniferous trees, exposing the lower, red surface of the trunk. After years of serving as forage sites, the trees take on a reddish look and are skirted with bark chips. ▪ Most woodpeckers do not randomly forage for their meals; instead, they often listen for grubs under the bark and in the wood. ▪ The Rocky Mountain race of the Three-toed Woodpecker has a back that is nearly all white. ▪ The Three-toed Woodpecker and the Black-backed Woodpecker both have three toes rather than four.

I.D.: *General:* black-and-white barring down the center of the back; white underparts; black barring on the sides; predominantly black head with 2 white stripes; black tail with white outer tail feathers. *Male:* yellow crown. *Female:* black crown with occasional white spotting.
Size: *L* 8–9 in. (21–24 cm).
Range: uncommon in the Canadian Rockies and the northern and central U.S. Rockies; rare in Rocky Mountain NP.
Habitat: spruce and fir forests, disturbed areas, avalanche slopes and burns in the montane and the subalpine.
Nesting: excavates a cavity in a dead or dying conifer trunk; excavation may take up to 12 days; pair incubates 4 eggs for up to 2 weeks.

Feeding: gleans under bark flakes for larval and adult wood-boring insects; occasionally eats berries.
Voice: call is a low *pik*; drumming is a prolonged series of steady bursts.
Similar Species: *Black-backed Woodpecker* (p. 168): solid black back. *Hairy Woodpecker* (p. 166): clean white back; lacks the barring on the sides.

167

BLACK-BACKED WOODPECKER
Picoides arcticus

The Black-backed Wood-
pecker frequently
chooses the top of
a broken snag on
which to perch and
drum during the
spring courtship
season. The yellow-
capped males are so
focused on this activity
that they are easily ap-
proached. Black-backed
Woodpeckers are rarely
seen, unfortunately, so these
courtship displays are uncommon sights. For the best
chance of seeing a Black-backed
Woodpecker, enter a newly burned
forest (where wood-boring beetles
thrive), and follow your ears. ▪ Woodpeckers use their stiff tail feathers to prop
themselves up against trees. ▪ The scientific
name *arcticus* reflects this bird's northern
distribution.

Nesting: typically in the northern boreal
forest; excavates a cavity in a dead or dying
conifer trunk or limb; excavation may take up
to 12 days; pair incubates 4 eggs for up to
2 weeks.

Feeding: gleans under bark flakes for larval
and adult wood-boring insects; occasionally
eats berries.

Voice: call is a low *pik*; drumming is a
prolonged series of steady bursts.

Similar Species: *Three-toed Woodpecker*
(p. 167): white back with black, horizontal
barring. *Williamson's Sapsucker* (p. 164): male
has a black breast, a white rump and a white
wing patch.

I.D.: *General:* solid black back; white underparts; black barring on the sides; predominantly
black head with a black 'mustache' and a single
white line below the eye; 3 toes; black tail
with pure white outer tail feathers. *Male:*
yellow crown. *Female:* black crown.

Size: L 9–10 in. (23–25 cm).

Range: locally uncommon resident in the
Rockies north of Wyoming; locally common
in large burns throughout western Montana
and northern Idaho.

Habitat: coniferous forests, disturbed areas,
avalanche slopes and burns in the montane.

NORTHERN FLICKER
Colaptes auratus

The Northern Flicker is the most terrestrial of all North American woodpeckers. Feeding on ants and other land insects, flickers appear almost robin-like when they hop about in grassy meadows or forest clearings. ▪ Flickers are often seen bathing in dusty depressions or 'anting.' Dust particles absorb oils and bacteria harmful to the birds' feathers. To clean themselves more thoroughly, flickers (and other birds) squish ants and then preen themselves with the remains. Ants contain formic acid, which kills small parasites on the skin and feathers. ▪ The 'Red-shafted Flicker'—red wing and tail linings and a red 'mustache' in the male—occurs throughout most of the Rockies; the 'Yellow-shafted Flicker'—yellow wing and tail linings and a black 'mustache' in the male—breeds east of the Rockies. There is hybridization between the two forms in the eastern foothills.

♂

'Red-shafted Flicker'

♀

I.D.: *General:* brown, barred back and wings; spotted underparts; black bib; white rump; long bill; gray face; brown crown. *'Red-shafted' male:* red wing and tail linings; red 'mustache.' *'Red-shafted' female:* red wing and tail linings; no 'mustache.'
Size: *L* 13 in. (33 cm).
Range: uncommon to common migrant and breeder throughout the Rockies; less common in winter.
Habitat: open mixed woodlands, forest edges, fields and meadows from the foothills to the subalpine.
Nesting: male or female chooses the nest site; pair excavates the cavity in a dead or dying deciduous tree for about 2 weeks; builds a new cavity annually; uses nest boxes; lines the cavity with wood chips; pair incubates 5–8 eggs for up to 11 days.
Feeding: forages on the ground for ants and other terrestrial insects; also eats berries and nuts; probes bark; occasionally flycatches.
Voice: loud, laughing, rapid *wick-wick-wick-wick-wick-wick*.
Similar Species: none.

169

PILEATED WOODPECKER
Dryocopus pileatus

With its powerful bill and stubborn determination, the Pileated Woodpecker chisels out rectangular cavities in its unending search for grubs and ants. The telltale cavities are often the only evidence that a Pileated Woodpecker is in a forest community. A pair of breeding Pileated Woodpeckers generally requires more than 100 acres (40 ha) of mature forest to settle. ▪ Not surprisingly, a woodpecker's bill becomes shorter as the bird ages. In Audubon's historic painting of the Pileated Woodpecker, he correctly depicted the bills of the juveniles as slightly longer than those of their parents. ▪ There's no real consensus on whether this bird's name is pronounced 'pie-lee-ated' or 'pill-e-ated'—it's generally a matter of preference.

I.D.: *General:* predominantly black; white wing linings; flaming red crest; yellow eyes; stout, dark bill; white stripe running from the bill to the shoulder; white chin. *Male:* red 'mustache'; crest extends from the forehead. *Female:* no 'mustache'; crest starts on the crown.
Size: *L* 16–19 in. (41–48 cm).
Range: uncommon year-round resident in the Canadian Rockies; increasingly uncommon south through Yellowstone NP.
Habitat: mature coniferous or mixedwood forests in the montane; prefers areas with dead and dying trees.
Nesting: pair excavates a cavity in a dead or

dying tree trunk; excavation can take 3–6 weeks; lines the cavity with wood chips; pair incubates 4 eggs for 15–18 days.
Feeding: often hammers the base of rotting trees, creating fist-sized rectangular holes; eats carpenter ants, wood-boring beetle larvae, berries and nuts.
Voice: loud, fast, laughing, rolling *yucka-yucka-yucka-yucka* that carries great distances through the woods.
Similar Species: *American Crow* (p. 194): lacks the white underwings and the flaming red crest. *Other woodpeckers* (pp. 161–69): much smaller.

OLIVE-SIDED FLYCATCHER

Contopus cooperi

The Olive-sided Flycatcher dwells in the penthouse of the coniferous forest: it often nests more than 50 ft. (15 m) up in trees and forages high above all other flycatchers. ▪ The call of the Olive-sided Flycatcher is one of the most distinctive avian voices in the Rocky Mountains. For novice birdwatchers, its most common call is often paraphrased as the simple and easily remembered *quick-three-beers*. ▪ The Olive-sided Flycatcher also breeds in spruce bogs across the boreal forest. ▪ Flycatchers, phoebes and kingbirds belong to the suborder of perching birds known as the 'suboscines,' which are character-ized by their simple calls and drab plumage. ▪ The scientific name *borealis* is Latin for 'northern.'

Habitat: mature spruce-fir and riparian forests and burned over woodlands, often on steep slopes, in the montane and the subalpine.

Nesting: high in a conifer, usually on a horizontal branch far from the trunk; nest is made with twigs and plant fibers and bound with spider silk; female incubates 3 eggs for 14 days.

Feeding: flycatches insects from a perch.

I.D.: *Sexes similar:* 'open,' dark olive-gray 'vest'; light throat and belly; olive brown upperparts; white rump patches; dark bill; no eye ring.
Size: L 7¹/₂ in. (19 cm).
Range: locally common to uncommon migrant and breeder throughout the Rockies.

Voice: *Male:* chipper and lively *quick-three-beers*, with the second note highest in pitch; when excited, a descending *pip-pip-pip*.
Similar Species: *Western Wood-Pewee* (p. 172): smaller; lacks the white rump patches.

WESTERN WOOD-PEWEE
Contopus sordidulus

Following this bird's characteristic, down-slurred call normally leads to the mid-level of the forest, where the Western Wood-Pewee calls persistently throughout the day. It chooses a perch beneath the crown of a tree, on a snag or on a branch, from which to launch itself in long, looping foraging ventures. ■ The nest of the Western Wood-Pewee is well camouflaged by both its shape and color—the completed structure resembles a bump on a horizontal limb. Despite this concealing masterpiece, these small flycatchers vigorously defend their nests by chasing and vocalizing against hawks, jays and chipmunks. ■ *Contopus* is Latin for 'short foot,' a reference to the wood-pewee's small feet; *sordidulus* refers to this bird's dirty, dusky color.

I.D.: *Sexes similar:* dark olive-brown upperparts; light underparts; 2 faint white wing bars; no eye ring; light-colored lower mandible; light undertail coverts; light-colored throat.
Size: L 5–6 in. (13–15 cm).
Range: uncommon to common migrant and breeder in the Rockies.
Habitat: open woodlands and deciduous, ponderosa pine and riparian forests in the foothills and the montane.
Nesting: on a horizontal limb in a tree; small cup nest is made with plant fibers and bound with spider silk; female incubates 3 eggs for 12–13 days.
Feeding: flycatches insects.
Voice: plaintive whistle, *peee you*, that drops off at the end; song is *fee-rrr-eet*.

Similar Species: *Olive-sided Flycatcher* (p. 171): white rump patches; larger. *Dusky* (p. 176), *Hammond's* (p. 175) and *Least* (p. 174) flycatchers: white eye rings. *Willow Flycatcher* (p. 173): darker lower mandible; browner upperparts; lighter underparts.

WILLOW FLYCATCHER

Empidonax traillii

On its nesting grounds, the shy Willow Flycatcher is an inconspicuous bird that prefers to remain out of sight. Only when an avian intruder violates this small bird's territory, does the Willow Flycatcher aggressively reveal itself. When out foraging, this small flycatcher moves constantly from one perch to another in low, dense shrubs. ▪ The Willow Flycatcher and the Alder Flycatcher were once categorized as a single species called the Traill's Flycatcher. Thomas Stewart Traill was an Englishman who helped John James Audubon find a British publisher for his book *Ornithological Biography*.

I.D.: *Sexes similar:* olive-brown upperparts; 2 whitish wing bars; no eye ring; white throat; yellowish belly; pale olive breast.

Size: *L* 5³/₄ in. (15 cm).

Range: uncommon migrant and breeder in the Rockies; less common in Waterton and Glacier NPs.

Habitat: willow and dwarf-birch thickets from the foothills to the lower subalpine.

Nesting: small cup nest is built in a fork in a small shrub; female incubates 3–4 eggs for 13 days.

Feeding: flycatches for insects; also gleans vegetation for larval and adult invertebrates.

Voice: *Male:* quick, sneezy *fitz-bew* (up to 30 times a minute) that drops off at the end.

Similar Species: *Western Wood-Pewee* (p. 172): gray-olive upperparts; darker lower mandible. *Cordilleran* (p. 177), *Least* (p. 174), *Hammond's* (p. 175) and *Dusky* (p. 176) flycatchers: light-colored eye rings.

LEAST FLYCATCHER
Empidonax minimus

The Least Flycatcher is one of the boldest and most pugnacious songbirds in the aspen forests along the eastern front ranges of the Rockies. During the nesting season, it is noisy and aggressive, driving away all avian intruders. ▪ Male Least Flycatchers reach their peak of aggression during the courtship season, when they fight furiously with rival males. The victor wins the right to select and chase a female for considerable distances in the hope of mating. ▪ An incubating female Least Flycatcher remains on her nest with extreme vigilance, so much so that a toppled tree was once found with a female still on the nest.

I.D.: *Sexes similar:* olive-brown upperparts; 2 white wing bars; light-colored eye ring; long, narrow tail; dark bill; light throat; dark tail.
Size: *L* 5–6 in. (13–15 cm).
Range: common breeder in the Canadian Rockies south through Glacier NP; uncommon migrant in the central and southern U.S. Rockies.
Habitat: aspen forests and alder and willow thickets up to the lower subalpine.
Nesting: on a horizontal branch in a small tree or shrub; female builds the small cup nest with plant fibers and bark and lines it with grass, plant down and feathers; female incubates 4 eggs for up to 15 days.
Feeding: flycatches insects and gleans the foliage of trees and shrubs for insects; also eats fruit and seeds.

Voice: constantly repeated, whistled *che-bec che-bec.*
Similar Species: *Willow Flycatcher* (p. 173): no eye ring. *Hammond's Flycatcher* (p. 175): darker underparts and throat. *Dusky Flycatcher* (p. 176): outer tail feathers have whitish edges. *Cordilleran Flycatcher* (p. 177): yellow throat.

HAMMOND'S FLYCATCHER

Empidonax hammondii

The Hammond's Flycatcher lives higher in the mountains than other *Empidonax* flycatchers, commonly nesting up to 10,000 ft. (3000 m) in the Rockies. It tends to prefer conifer stands greater than 20 acres (8 ha) in size and at least 80 years of age. Because of modern forestry practices, logging might affect the stability of this species's populations, and it might become increasingly dependent on our national parks for habitat preservation. ▪ *Empidonax* is a wonderful name for these confusing, but endearing, birds—it means 'lord of the mosquitoes.' ▪ William Hammond, after whom this Empid is named, was an army surgeon who sent animal specimens from western North America to the Smithsonian Institution.

breeding

I.D.: *Sexes similar:* olive-brown upperparts; 2 white wing bars; distinct, light eye ring; gray face; dark lower mandible; light gray throat; dark tail with gray outer edge.

Size: *L* 5¹/₂ in. (14 cm).

Range: uncommon to common migrant and breeder in the Rockies.

Habitat: coniferous forests, especially stands of mature spruce-fir, in the montane and the subalpine.

Nesting: on a limb in a coniferous tree; small cup nest is made with plant fibers, leaves and grass and lined with feathers and grass; female incubates 3–4 eggs for up to 15 days.

Feeding: flycatches and hover-gleans vegetation for insects.

Voice: *Male:* quick, whistled *tse-beek, seweep sup seep* or *peek*.

Similar Species: *Willow Flycatcher* (p. 173): no eye ring. *Least Flycatcher* (p. 174): light lower mandible; call is *che-bec. Cordilleran Flycatcher* (p. 177): yellow underparts. *Dusky Flycatcher* (p. 176): practically indistinguishable in the field, except for its deciduous forest habitat.

DUSKY FLYCATCHER

Empidonax oberholseri

Late spring storms can be disastrous for entire populations of Dusky Flycatchers. In the past, snow and freezing rain in June has killed nearly all the Dusky Flycatchers in the affected regions. Fortunately, such weather is normally a local event, and the following year finds other Dusky Flycatchers returning to fill the void created by the unseasonable storms. ▪ The male Dusky Flycatcher stays around the nest after the eggs are laid to help the female raise the young birds. ▪ The Dusky Flycatcher was formerly considered a subspecies of the Gray Flycatcher, but it was split off in 1939. ▪ The scientific name *oberholseri* honors Dr. Harry Oberholser, one of the finest 20th-century ornithologists. He worked for the U.S. Fish and Wildlife Service and the Cleveland Natural History Museum.

breeding

I.D.: *Sexes similar:* olive-brown upperparts; 2 faint, white wing bars; light-colored eye ring; dark bill with orange at the base of the lower mandible; white throat; long, dark tail trimmed with white.

Size: L 5–6 in. (13–15 cm).

Range: common to uncommon breeder throughout the Rockies.

Habitat: deciduous forests, willow thickets, mixed coniferous forests and avalanche slopes in the montane.

Nesting: in the crotch of a small shrub; small cup nest is made of weeds, plant fibers, feathers, grass and fur; female incubates 3–4 eggs for 15–16 days.

Feeding: flycatches for aerial insects; also gleans and hover-gleans leaves, limbs and bark for larval and adult insects.

Voice: *Male:* quick, whistled *tse-beek preet,* rising at the end.

Similar Species: *Willow Flycatcher* (p. 173): no eye ring. *Least Flycatcher* (p. 174): light lower mandible; call is *che-bec. Cordilleran Flycatcher* (p. 177): yellow underparts. *Hammond's Flycatcher* (p. 175): practically indistinguishable in the field, except for its mature spruce-fir forest habitat and its call, *tse-beek.*

CORDILLERAN FLYCATCHER
Empidonax occidentalis

After launching from an exposed perch, a Cordilleran Flycatcher demonstrates the famed foraging technique characteristic of its family: snapping up a flying insect in mid-air, the flycatcher loops back to return to the same perch it vacated moments earlier. ■ Cordilleran Flycatchers arrive in the Rockies' still woods in April and begin nesting in the latter part of May. ■ 'Hawking' and 'sallying' are words used interchangeably with the term 'flycatching.' ■ The Cordilleran Flycatcher and the Pacific-slope Flycatcher were formerly lumped together in one species, called the Western Flycatcher. Although now regarded as distinct species, their similar field characteristics remain a troubling issue that perpetuates their uncertain status. ■ The scientific name *occidentalis* is Latin for 'western.'

I.D.: *Sexes similar:* olive-green upperparts; 2 white wing bars; yellowish throat; light-colored eye ring; orange lower mandible.
Size: L 5¹/₂ in. (14 cm).
Range: uncommon to common breeder in the southern U.S. Rockies; rare elsewhere in the Rockies.
Habitat: coniferous and riparian woodlands or shady deciduous forests, often near seepages and springs, in the montane.
Nesting: in a cavity in a small tree, bank, bridge or cliff face; lines the cavity with moss,

lichens, plant fibers, bark, fur and feathers; female incubates 3–4 eggs for 15 days.
Feeding: flycatches for insects.
Voice: *Male:* call is a chipper whistle: swee-deet.
Similar Species: *Willow Flycatcher* (p. 173) and *Western Wood-Pewee* (p. 172): no eye rings. *Least* (p. 174), *Hammond's* (p. 175) and *Dusky* (p. 176) flycatchers: lack the almond-shaped eye ring and the completely orange lower mandible; songs are very useful in field identification.

SAY'S PHOEBE
Sayornis saya

This large, handsome flycatcher is a very early spring migrant that frequently reuses its nesting sites. It often builds its nest under a ledge, where it is shielded from harsh weather. ▪ The Say's Phoebe is frequently encountered in the western foothills around ranch buildings and other structures. It flycatches insects from a low perch. ▪ This species is the only bird whose genus and species names are derived from the same person, Thomas Say, a versatile naturalist whose primary contributions were in the field of entomology. ▪ The name 'phoebe' comes from the call of a close relative, the Eastern Phoebe.

I.D.: *Sexes similar:* apricot belly and undertail coverts; dark tail; brown-gray breast and upperparts; dark head; no eye ring; very faint wing bars.
Size: *L* 7½ in. (19 cm).
Range: rare migrant and summer resident in the Canadian and northern U.S. Rockies; very rare in the southern U.S. Rockies; historical breeder in Yellowstone NP.
Habitat: open areas and shrublands, often near cliffs or buildings, in the montane and the subalpine.

Nesting: in a cavity on a cliff face, on beams, or under a bridge, eave or other structure; nest is made with grass, moss and fur; female incubates 4–5 eggs for up to 17 days.
Feeding: flycatches for aerial insects; also gleans buildings and vegetation for insects.
Voice: call is a softly whistled *pee-ter* or *pee-ur*; song is *pitseedar.*
Similar Species: *Flycatchers* (pp. 171–77): all lack the apricot belly. *Townsend's Solitaire* (p. 226): lacks the apricot belly; salmon color in the wings and tail.

WESTERN KINGBIRD
Tyrannus verticalis

The tumble-flight courtship display of the Western Kingbird is one of the West's most entertaining spring scenes. Twisting and turning, the male flies 60 ft. (18 m) up, suddenly stalls, and then tumbles, flips and twists as he falls toward the ground. ▪ This persistent species often chases flying insects for more than 40 ft. (12 m) and up to heights of 20–40 ft. (6–12 m) before snapping its bill upon its prey. ▪ The Western Kingbird is less of a tyrant than its eastern cousin; the two species occasionally nest near one another. ▪ Western Kingbirds are commonly seen perched on fenceposts, barbed wire and power lines, surveying for prey. ▪ The hidden red crown is flared in courtship displays and in combat with rivals. ▪ The scientific name *verticalis* refers to this bird's hidden crown.

I.D.: *Sexes similar:* gray head and breast; yellow belly and undertail coverts; dark brown tail; white outer tail feathers; white chin; black bill; ashy gray upperparts; dark gray mask; unforked tail; thin, orange-red crown.
Size: L 8–9 in. (20–23 cm).
Range: locally uncommon breeder and migrant throughout the U.S. Rockies; rare in the Canadian Rockies.
Habitat: open areas and willow and birch shrubs in agricultural, open and riparian areas up to the lower montane.

Nesting: near the trunk of a deciduous tree; frequently on human structures, such as barns, towers and telephone pole crossbeams; cup nest is lined with fur, twigs, roots and feathers; female incubates 4–5 eggs for 14 days.
Feeding: flycatches aerial insects, such as bees, wasps, butterflies and moths; occasionally eats berries.
Voice: chatty, twittering *whit-ker-whit*; also *pkit-pkit-pkeetle-dot*.
Similar Species: *Cassin's Kingbird* (p. 321): very rare in the southern U.S. Rockies; lacks the white outer tail feathers; darker breast and upperparts.

EASTERN KINGBIRD

Tyrannus tyrannus

Tyrannus (absolute ruler) is a fitting name for the Eastern Kingbird—no large bird is safe flying within the territory of this fearless tyrant. The Eastern Kingbird pursues large birds boldly, frequently pecking and plucking them until they no longer pose a threat, whether real or perceived. ■ During the kingbird's courtship, its hidden red crown is flared to complement the white-tipped tail feathers. ■ Like the flight of a butterfly, this bird flutters slowly—but noisily; it chatters continuously in courtship. ■ Eastern Kingbirds rarely walk or hop on the ground. They prefer to fly, even for very short distances. ■ The kingbird is known to bathe by flying low over water, so that its belly touches the surface. Once wet, the bird lands in a safe area to complete its bath.

I.D.: *Sexes similar:* black upperparts; white underparts; white-tipped tail; black bill; small crest; thin orange-red crown; no eye ring; black legs.

Size: L 8½ in. (22 cm).

Range: uncommon to locally common migrant and summer breeder throughout the Rockies.

Habitat: open areas with willow and birch shrubs, agricultural areas and riparian regions in the foothills and the montane.

Nesting: on a horizontal limb in a small tree or shrub; also in cavities and human-made structures; pair builds the cup nest with plant fibers, grass, roots, feathers and fur; female incubates 3–4 eggs for up to 14 days.

Feeding: flycatches aerial insects; infrequently eats berries.

Voice: call is a quick, loud, chattering *kit-kit-kitter-kitter,* also a buzzy *dzee-dzee-dzee.*

Similar Species: *Tree Swallow* (p. 198): lacks the black back and the white-tipped tail; more streamlined.

NORTHERN SHRIKE

Lanius excubitor

Northern Shrikes retreat from their northern breeding grounds to overwinter in southern Canada and the northern U.S. These predatory songbirds migrate through the mountains during spring and fall, and they are occasionally seen in semi-open areas, where they perch hawk-like on treetops. ▪ Despite its robin-like size, the Northern Shrike can quickly kill small birds and rodents. When this shrike strikes, it sometimes seizes its prey with its feet and pecks at the animal until it is restrained. ▪ The Northern Shrike's macabre behavior of impaling its kills on thorns and barbs has earned it the names 'butcher bird' and 'nine-killer.' ▪ This species ranges around the Northern Hemisphere: it is also found in Scandinavia and Asia, and it overwinters in Britain and Japan. ▪ *Lanius* is Latin for 'butcher,' and *excubitor* is Latin for 'watchman' or 'sentinel.' 'The Watchful Butcher' is an appropriate description of the Northern Shrike's foraging behavior.

I.D.: *Sexes similar. Adult:* black tail and wings; pale gray upperparts; finely barred, light underparts; black mask does not extend above the hooked bill. *Immature:* faint mask; light brown upperparts. *In flight:* white wing patches; white-edged tail.

Size: *L* 10 in. (25 cm)

Range: uncommon migrant and winter resident in the southern and central U.S. Rockies; rare winter resident in the Canadian and northern U.S. Rockies.

Habitat: shrublands, grasslands and road-sides, at low to high elevations, during winter and in migration.

Nesting: on the taiga; in spruce, willows or shrubs; loose, bulky nest is made with sticks, bark and moss.

Feeding: swoops down on prey from a perch or chases prey through the air; regularly eats small birds, shrews and rodents; commonly takes insects if they are available.

Voice: usually silent; infrequently calls a grating *shek shek* during migration.

Similar Species: *Loggerhead Shrike* (p. 182): summer resident; adult's mask extends above the bill; juvenile has brownish-gray, barred upperparts. *Northern Mockingbird* (p. 234): slim bill; no mask.

181

LOGGERHEAD SHRIKE

Lanius ludovicianus

Loggerhead Shrikes offer a refreshing splash of color in the grassland bird scene, which is dominated by brown and gray birds. ▪ The Loggerhead Shrike has very accurate vision, and, historically, they perched atop shrubs and short trees in open areas in the mountain parks. Unfortunately, Loggerhead Shrikes have declined over much of their range, owing to habitat destruction and the decline of their foods. ▪ Loggerhead Shrikes, like others in their family, impale their prey on thorns and barbs. They seem to have an uncanny memory for the location of their food stores, and they have been known to find prey stored for up to eight months. ▪ This bird is called 'Loggerhead' because of its large head.

I.D.: *Sexes similar. Adult:* black tail and wings; gray crown and back; white underparts; barred flanks; black mask extends above the bill; hooked bill. *In flight:* white wing patches; white-edged tail. *Juvenile:* brownish-gray, barred upperparts.
Size: *L* 9 in. (23 cm).
Range: rare migrant and summer resident in the southern U.S. Rockies; very rare north of Yellowstone NP.
Habitat: open areas with shrublands and grasslands.
Nesting: typically on the Great Plains; in a low crotch in a shrub or small tree; bulky cup nest is made with twigs and grass and lined with fine materials; female incubates 5–6 eggs for 15–17 days.
Feeding: swoops down on prey from a perch or attacks in pursuit; regularly eats small birds, rodents and shrews; will commonly take insects if they are available; also eats carrion.
Voice: *Male:* bouncy hiccup, *hugh-ee hugh-ee*, during summer; infrequently a harsh *shack-shack* year-round.
Similar Species: *Northern Shrike* (p. 181): winter resident; adult is larger, and has finely barred underparts; immature has a faint mask and brown-gray, unbarred upperparts. *Northern Mockingbird* (p. 234): lacks the black mask; generally more sleek and slim.

PLUMBEOUS VIREO

Vireo plumbeus

The distinctive 'spectacles' of the Plumbeous Vireo frame the bird's eyes and identify this songbird as it flits about in the trees. The white frames are among the boldest of eye rings belonging to songbirds. ▪ During courtship, male Plumbeous Vireos fluff out their yellow flanks and bob ceremoniously to their prospective mates. The slow, high-pitched song is richer in quality than that of the Red-eyed Vireo, and it is more commonly heard in the Rocky Mountains. ▪ The Plumbeous Vireo was formerly grouped with the Blue-headed Vireo and the Cassin's Vireo as one species, the Solitary Vireo.

I.D.: *Sexes similar:* white 'spectacles'; 2 white wing bars; gray head and upperparts; white underparts; gray flanks; dark tail; stout bill; dark legs.

Size: *L* 5½ in. (14 cm).

Range: uncommon to common migrant and summer visitor throughout the Rockies.

Habitat: coniferous forests mixed with deciduous trees, frequently with dense understorey shrubs, in the montane.

Nesting: in a horizontal fork in a coniferous tree; hanging, basket-like cup nest is made of grass, roots, plant down, spider's silk and cocoons; pair incubates 4 eggs for 14 days.

Feeding: gleans foliage for invertebrates; occasionally hover-gleans to pluck insects from vegetation.

Voice: *Male:* slow, purposeful robin-like notes: *look up ... see me ... here I am.*

Similar Species: *Warbling Vireo* (p. 184), *Red-eyed Vireo* (p. 186) and *Tennessee Warbler* (p. 240): all lack the white 'spectacles.'

183

WARBLING VIREO
Vireo gilvus

The Warbling Vireo may be the most common of the Rocky Mountain vireos, but you must still search a long time before you will spot one. The often-repeated song of this bird, with its oscillating quality, delights anyone listening; the phrases finish on an upbeat as if asking a question of the wilds. In contrast to the bird's velvety voice, however, is its dull plumage. Lacking any splashy field marks, the Warbling Vireo is exceedingly difficult to spot, unless the bird suddenly moves from one leaf-hidden stage to another. ▪ Once the voice of the Warbling Vireo is learned, auditory encounters will soon abound. Searching the treetops for inconspicuous birds may literally be 'a pain in the neck,' but the satisfaction in visually confirming this bird's identity is exceptionally rewarding.

breeding

I.D.: *Sexes similar:* white eyebrow; no wing bars; olive-gray upperparts; greenish flanks, light underparts; gray crown.
Size: L 5¹/₂ in. (14 cm).
Range: common migrant and breeder throughout the Rockies.
Habitat: open deciduous forests and shrubby avalanche slopes in the montane.
Nesting: in a horizontal fork in a deciduous tree or shrub; hanging, basket-like cup nest is made of grass, roots, plant down, spider's silk and a few feathers; pair incubates 4 eggs for 12 days.

Feeding: gleans foliage for invertebrates; occasionally hovers and plucks insects from vegetation.
Voice: *Male:* musical warble: *I love you I love you Ma'am!* or *iggly wiggly iggly piggly iggly eeek! Female:* occasionally sings from the nest.
Similar Species: *Red-eyed Vireo* (p. 186): black eye line extends to the bill; blue-gray crown. *Tennessee Warbler* (p. 240): gray head; olive back. *Orange-crowned Warbler* (p. 241): smaller; darker underparts.

PHILADELPHIA VIREO

Vireo philadelphicus

The few Philadelphia Vireos that range into Banff and Jasper national parks are pioneers stretching the western range of this species, which typically breeds east of the Rocky Mountains. Even in the core of its range, this bird is difficult to observe, because it prefers to perch and sing near the tops of leafy trees. ▪ This vireo's voice resembles that of its Red-eyed cousin so much that few experts can distinguish between them with confidence. ▪ This bird bears the name of the city from which it was first collected. Philadelphia was the center of America's scientific community in the early 1800s, and much of the study of birds and other natural sciences originated in Pennsylvania.

breeding

I.D.: *Sexes similar:* white eyebrow; yellow breast and flanks; grayish head; dark eye line extends to the bill; dark, olive-green upperparts; white belly; thick bill.
Size: *L* 5¼ in. (13 cm).
Range: common spring migrant, common summer resident and uncommon fall migrant in Jasper NP; uncommon fall migrant in Banff NP; vagrant in the U.S. Rockies.
Habitat: willow stands in deciduous forests in the montane.
Nesting: high up in a deciduous tree or shrub; basket-like cup nest hangs from a horizontal fork and is made of grass, roots, plant down and spider's silk; pair incubates 4 eggs for up to 13 days.

Feeding: gleans foliage and other vegetation for invertebrates; frequently hovers to search for food in foliage.
Voice: *Male:* song is a continuous, robin-like run of phrases: *Look-up way-up Tree-top see-me Here-I-am.*
Similar Species: *Red-eyed Vireo* (p. 186): black-bordered, blue-gray cap; lacks the yellow wash on the belly; song is lower pitched. *Warbling Vireo* (p. 184): dusky eye line; lacks the yellow wash on the belly. *Tennessee Warbler* (p. 240): well-defined, gray cap; greenish back.

RED-EYED VIREO
Vireo olivaceus

The Red-eyed Vireo is the undisputed champion of singing endurance. In spring and early summer, male Red-eyes sometimes pause along the Rockies and offer their songs to the mountains. Many other songbirds curtail their courting melodies five or six hours after sunrise, but the Red-eyed Vireo sings continuously through the day. One patient ornithologist estimated that this vigorous vireo sings its memorable phrases up to 21,000 times a day. ▪ For a songbird to have red eyes is quite uncommon; red eyes tend to be more prevalent in non-passerines, such as accipiters, grebes and some herons. ▪ Red-eyed Vireos are frequently parasitized by Brown-headed Cowbirds, which lay their eggs in an unknowing foster home!

breeding

I.D.: *Sexes similar:* white eyebrow; black eye line; black-bordered, blue-gray crown; olive-green upperparts; olive cheek; light underparts; no wing bars; red eyes (seen only at close range).
Size: *L* 6 in. (15 cm).
Range: common spring migrant and summer breeder in the Canadian and northern U.S. Rockies; increasingly uncommon southward through the Rockies.
Habitat: deciduous forests with semi-open canopies and shrublands in the montane.
Nesting: in a horizontal fork in a deciduous tree or shrub; hanging, basket-like cup nest is made of grass, roots, spider's silk and cocoons; female incubates 4 eggs for 11–14 days.

Feeding: gleans foliage for insects, especially caterpillars; also eats berries.
Voice: call is a cat-like *meow. Male:* song is a continuous, robin-like run of phrases: *Look-up way-up tree-top see-me Here-I-am.*
Similar Species: *Philadelphia Vireo* (p. 185): yellow belly; lacks the black border to the blue-gray cap. *Warbling Vireo* (p. 184): dusky eye line does not extend to the bill.

GRAY JAY
Perisoreus canadensis

There is no other Rocky Mountain bird that can equal the Gray Jay for boldness. Small family groups glide slowly and unexpectedly out of spruce forests, attracted by any foreign sound or potential food opportunity. ▪ Gray Jays lay their eggs and begin incubation as early as late February. Their nests are well insulated to conserve heat, and nesting early means the jays will be feeding their quickly growing nestlings when the forests are full of food in spring. ▪ Gray Jays often store food. These jays have specialized salivary glands that they use to coat the food with a sticky mucous, which helps preserve the food. ▪ The Gray Jay is also affectionately known as the Camp Robber, the Canada Jay and the Whisky Jack. This last name is derived from the Algonquin name for this bird, *wiskedjack*.

I.D.: *Sexes similar. Adult:* fluffy, pale gray plumage; long tail; light forehead; darker on the back of the head; dark gray upperparts; light gray underparts; white cheek; dark bill. *Immature:* dark sooty gray overall.
Size: L 11½ in. (29 cm).
Range: common year-round throughout the Rockies.
Habitat: dense and open coniferous and mixed forests, townsites, scenic overlooks and campgrounds from the foothills to the subalpine.
Nesting: in the crotch of a conifer tree; bulky, well-insulated nest is made with plant fibers, roots, moss, twigs, feathers and fur; female incubates 3–4 eggs for 17 days.
Feeding: searches the ground and vegetation for insects, fruit, songbird eggs and nestlings, carrion and berries; stores food items.
Voice: complex vocal repertoire; soft, whistled *quee-oo*; chuckled *cla-cla-cla*; also imitates other birds.
Similar Species: *Clark's Nutcracker* (p. 192): adult has a heavy black bill and black-and-white wings and tail. *Northern Shrike* (p. 181): black mask; black-and-white wings and tail.

STELLER'S JAY
Cyanocitta stelleri

The Steller's Jay is the classic crested jay of areas west of the Continental Divide. With a crest length unequaled by any other North American bird, the Steller's Jay is an unmistakable, raucous resident of the western slopes of the Rockies. It is the provincial bird of British Columbia. ▪ Steller's Jays are frequently encountered in parking areas, viewpoints and day-use areas in most of the national parks in the Rocky Mountains. They are bold, and they will not hesitate to steal food scraps from inattentive picnickers. Steller's Jays also eat acorns and other natural seeds, which they hammer apart with their bill partially open.

▪ George Wilhelm Steller, the first European naturalist to visit Alaska, collected the first specimen—the 'type' specimen—of this species.

Nesting: in the crotch of a conifer tree; bulky stick and twig nest is lined with mud, grass and conifer needles; female incubates 4 eggs for 16 days.

Feeding: searches the ground and vegetation for insects, small vertebrates and various other food items; forages in treetops for nuts, berries and other birds' eggs; visits bird feeders during winter.

I.D.: *Sexes similar:* glossy blue plumage; black head and nape; large, black crest; white streaks on the forehead and chin; wings and tail are accentuated by dark blue.

Size: L 11½ in. (29 cm).

Range: locally uncommon to very common year-round resident throughout the Rockies.

Habitat: coniferous and mixed forests, campgrounds, picnic areas and townsites up to the subalpine.

Voice: harsh, noisy *shack-shack-shack*, along with a variety of other calls.

Similar Species: *Blue Jay* (p. 189): white underparts; black 'necklace'; white wing bar. *Western Scrub-Jay* (p. 190): no crest; pale gray underparts.

BLUE JAY
Cyanocitta cristata

The Blue Jay is typically found in eastern North America, but its steadfast expansion westward has recently led it to the toe of the Rocky Mountains. The Blue Jay has been able to expand its range partly as a result of the spread of human development. Feeders and landfills enable overwintering birds to cope with harsh winters, and forest fragmentation has invited the jays deeper into the once impenetrable forests. ▪ Blue Jays possess one of the most complex vocal repertoires east of the Continental Divide. They readily imitate other birds, barking dogs and even lawnmowers. ▪ Blue Jays cache food for winter; they store acorns, nuts and seeds in a variety of places, such as loose soil, from late summer through fall. ▪ If Blue Jays populate your yard, try identifying individual birds by their characteristic head patterns.

I.D.: *Sexes similar:* blue crest; black 'necklace'; blue upperparts; white underparts; white flecking on the wings; white wing bar; black bill.
Size: *L* 11 in. (28 cm).
Range: rare year-round in the southern U.S. Rockies; very rare summer breeder and uncommon migrant in the Canadian Rockies; typically occurs east of the Continental Divide; population is expanding westward.
Habitat: mixed deciduous forests and townsites with feeders in the eastern foothills.

Nesting: in the crotch of a tree or tall shrub; pair builds a bulky stick nest and incubates 4–5 eggs for 18 days.
Feeding: forages on the ground and among vegetation for nuts, berries, eggs, nestlings and bird seed; also eats insects and carrion.
Voice: noisy, screaming *jay-jay-jay;* nasal *too-wheedle too-wheeled,* like the horn of a Model-T Ford; also imitates other sounds.
Similar Species: *Steller's Jay* (p. 188): dark hood; dark underparts. *Western Scrub-Jay* (p. 190): no crest; light gray underparts. *Pinyon Jay* (p. 191): no crest; blue underparts.

WESTERN SCRUB-JAY
Aphelocoma californica

This aggressive jay of open country is often seen surveying its dry habitat from a perch atop a tall shrub. Western Scrub-Jays do not extend into the high elevations of the Rockies; they prefer lower elevations in the southern Rockies where shrublands prevail. ▪ A scrub-jay, instead of tolerating the presence of a neighboring Steller's Jay, frequently drives it away. ▪ These intelligent birds use 'anvil' sites to pound and break open nuts and seeds. They are also known to rub hairy caterpillars in sand or loose dirt to remove the irritating hairs. ▪ The Western Scrub-Jay was recently given full species status, and it is now separated from the Florida Scrub-Jay and the Island Scrub-Jay.

I.D.: *Sexes similar:* slim body; sky-blue upperparts; long tail; gray and buffy underparts; white throat is slightly streaked and is bordered by a bluish 'necklace'; dark, heavy bill; dark cheek; faint white eyebrow.
Size: *L* 11½ in. (29 cm).
Range: rare to locally common year-round in the southern and central U.S. Rockies.
Habitat: semi-open forests, especially oak and pinyon-juniper forests, up to the lower montane.
Nesting: in a small conifer or small shrub; pair builds the bulky stick nest, usually with an inner cup lined with moss, grass and fur; female incubates 3–6 eggs for 15–17 days.

Feeding: forages on the ground for insects and small vertebrates; also eats other birds' eggs and nestlings, as well as acorns and pinyon nuts.
Voice: harsh, repetitive *ike-ike-ike*; rough, frequently repeated *quick-quick-quick.*
Similar Species: *Pinyon Jay* (p. 191): blue underparts; shorter tail. *Gray Jay* (p. 187): all-gray plumage. *Steller's Jay* (p. 188): large crest; dark hood; dark underparts.

PINYON JAY
Gymnorhinus cyanocephalus

The Pinyon Jay is a highly gregarious and loud species that acts more like a small crow than a jay. During the non-breeding season, this non-crested jay forages in flocks, consisting of family members, that roam over the countryside in search of food. The group members take turns being on the look-out for danger while the rest concentrate on feeding activities. ▪ When the source of pinyon cones fails periodically, these jays disperse widely in search of alternative food sources; they venture far from their typical ranges. ▪ Pinyon Jays do not establish pair bonds until their third year. Once the bond is formed, pairs remain together year-round. ▪ *Gymnorhinus* is Greek for 'naked nose'—an usual trait for a jay—and *cyanocephalus* means 'blue-headed.'

I.D.: *Sexes similar:* all–blue-gray plumage; light streaks on the throat; long, pointed bill; short tail.
Size: *L* 9–11½ in. (23–29 cm).
Range: locally common year-round in the southern U.S. Rockies.
Habitat: pinyon-juniper woodlands up to the montane.
Nesting: in pinyons, junipers and shrubs; large, bulky nest is made of sticks, twigs and fibers; female incubates 4–5 eggs for up to 17 days.
Feeding: searches the ground and vegetation for pinyon nuts, seeds and insects; also eats berries and other birds' eggs and nestlings.
Voice: warning call is a low *krawk-krawk-krawk.*
Similar Species: *Western Scrub-Jay* (p. 190): light gray underparts; long tail.

CLARK'S NUTCRACKER

Nucifraga columbiana

The Clark's Nutcracker is a hardy, raucous and gregarious bird that is a familiar sight in the Rockies. It is often encountered in public day-use areas, surveying from a perch and swooping boldly to take advantage of the generosity or neglect of the human visitors. ■ When Captain William Clark, of the Lewis and Clark expedition, collected the first specimen, the bird's large, straight, black bill misled the famous western explorer into believing it was a woodpecker; it was originally categorized as being of the genus *Picicorvus*, meaning 'woodpecker-crow.' ■ Despite its name, this bird actually cracks more conifer cones than nuts with its crowbar-like bill.

I.D.: *Sexes similar:* light gray head, back and underparts; large, black bill; black wings with flashy white inner wing patches. *In flight:* black central tail feathers; white outer tail feathers.
Size: L 12–13 in. (30–33 cm).
Range: uncommon to common resident throughout the Rockies.
Habitat: open coniferous and mixed forests, scenic overlooks, krummholz forests and townsites from the foothills to the alpine. *Winter:* moves to lower elevations.
Nesting: on a horizontal limb; twig and stick platform nest is lined with grass and strips of

bark; pair incubates 2–4 eggs for 16–22 days, starting in March.
Feeding: forages on the ground and among trees for pinecones and pinyon nuts; hammers the cones and nuts with its bill; also eats insects; stores food for winter.
Voice: loud, harsh, squawking *kra-a-a-a-a.*
Similar Species: *Gray Jay* (p. 187): gray wings and tail. *Pinyon Jay* (p. 191): all–blue-gray plumage. *Northern Mockingbird* (p. 234): smaller overall; smaller bill; body plumage is not uniformly gray.

BLACK-BILLED MAGPIE

Pica pica

The beauty of this bird is too often overlooked because its raucous and aggressive demeanor overshadows its gorgeous, panda-like plumage. The long, shiny tail of the Black-billed Magpie is one of the longest of any North American bird. Most residents are jaded by the omnipresence of magpies, but foreign visitors to our parks are often captivated by their beauty and approachability. ■ The abundance of hoofed mammals in many Rocky Mountain parks provides magpies and other scavengers with a dependable food source during harsh winters. Winter- and predator-killed elk, deer, moose and bison are fundamental building blocks for the Rocky Mountain food web. ■ A well-planned day trip in Colorado can yield as many as 10 members of the corvid family (including the Chihuahuan Raven, which is not found in the Rockies), more than anywhere else in North America. ■ Black-billed Magpies also occur in Europe, North Africa, Arabia and Asia.

I.D.: *Sexes similar:* long, black tail; black head, breast and back; rounded, black-and-white wings; black undertail coverts; black bill; white belly.
Size: L 18–22 in. (46–56 cm).
Range: common to very common year-round throughout the Rockies.
Habitat: open forests, agricultural areas, riparian thickets, townsites and campgrounds up to and the montane.

Nesting: in a tree or tall shrub; domed stick and twig nest is often held together with mud; female incubates 5–8 eggs for up to 24 days.
Feeding: forages on the ground for insects, carrion and garbage; picks insects and ticks off large ungulates.
Voice: loud, nasal, frequently repeated *yeck-yeck-yeck;* also many other vocalizations.
Similar Species: none.

AMERICAN CROW
Corvus brachyrhynchos

Someone once suggested that if humans were given feathers and wings, very few would be as clever as crows. These are wary, intelligent birds capable of solving simple problems, which makes them excel at self-preservation. ▪ In fall, when their reproductive duties are completed, American Crows group together in flocks of thousands. A flock of crows is called a 'murder'—a term that is understandable for those who have seen Alfred Hitchcock's *The Birds*—but the aggregation is merely a get-together in preparation for an evening flight to the roost. ▪ *Corvus brachyrhynchos*, despite sounding cumbersome, is Latin for 'raven with the small nose.'

I.D.: *Sexes similar:* all-black body; fan-shaped tail; black bill and legs; slim, sleek head and throat.
Size: L 17–21 in. (43–53 cm); W 37 in. (94 cm).
Range: uncommon to common migrant and breeder in most of the Rockies; common winter resident in the U.S. Rockies.
Habitat: urban areas, agricultural fields and shrublands in the foothills and the montane.
Nesting: in coniferous or deciduous trees

and on power poles; large stick and branch nest is lined with fur and soft plant materials; female incubates 4–6 eggs for up to 18 days.
Feeding: very opportunistic; feeds on carrion, small vertebrates, other birds' eggs and nestlings, berries, seeds, invertebrates and human garbage.
Voice: distinctive, far-carrying, repetitive *caw-caw-caw.*
Similar Species: *Common Raven* (p. 195): larger; wedge-shaped tail; shaggy throat.

194

COMMON RAVEN
Corvus corax

Glorified in traditional cultures worldwide, the Common Raven does not act by instinct alone. Whether tumbling aimlessly through the air, delivering complex, meaningful vocalizations or sliding playfully down a snowy bank on its back, this raucous bird demonstrates behavior many think of as being exclusively human.
■ Few birds naturally occupy as large a natural range as the raven, but the Rockies remain one of the most reliable places in which to experience their habits. It seems that little goes on in the Rockies without the omnipresent raven surveying the scene.

I.D.: *Sexes similar:* all-black plumage; heavy, black bill; wedge-shaped tail; shaggy throat; rounded wings.
Size: L 24 in. (61 cm); W 50 in. (127 cm).
Range: common year-round throughout the Rockies.
Habitat: grasslands, shrublands, townsites, campgrounds and landfills from the foothills to the alpine.
Nesting: on power poles, steep cliffs and tall conifer trees; large stick and branch nest is lined with fur and soft plant materials; female incubates 4–6 eggs for 18–21 days.
Feeding: very opportunistic; feeds on carrion, small vertebrates, other birds' eggs and nestlings, berries, invertebrates and hoofed mammal afterbirth.
Voice: deep, guttural, far-carrying, repetitive *craww-craww* or *quork quork;* also many other vocalizations.
Similar Species: *American Crow* (p. 194): smaller; rounded tail; slim throat; slimmer bill; call is a higher-pitched *caw.*

195

HORNED LARK
Eremophila alpestris

Horned Larks are birds of open, treeless country. They are found in every type of unforested area—alpine and arctic tundra, sea coasts, native grasslands, agricultural areas and mountain tops. Horned Larks are frequently encountered when you are driving along backroads in open country. These small birds prefer running to flying, but they will desperately take to the air to avoid oncoming cars, revealing their black tail in the process. ■ As a result of this bird's wide range, there are no less than 21 recognized subspecies throughout North America. It is our region, however, that is celebrated in this bird's scientific name, which means 'lark of the mountains.'

I.D.: *Male:* small black 'horns' (often not raised); black line running under the eye from the bill to the cheek; light yellow to white face; dull brown upperparts; black breast band; dark tail with white outer tail feathers; light throat. *Female:* less distinctive head patterning; duller plumage overall.

Size: *L* 7 in. (18 cm).

Range: common breeder and migrant in the Canadian and Colorado Rockies; uncommon to rare breeder elsewhere in the Rockies; uncommon winter resident in the U.S. Rockies.

Habitat: open areas, including alpine tundra, fields and roadways up to the alpine.

Nesting: on the ground; in a shallow scrape lined with grass, plant fibers and roots; female chooses the nest site and incubates 3–4 eggs for up to 12 days.

Feeding: gleans the ground for seeds; occasionally feeds its young on insects during the breeding season.

Voice: tinkling *tsee-titi*, given in flight.

Similar Species: *Open-country sparrows* (pp. 266–75) and *longspurs* (pp. 282–83 & 323): all lack the facial pattern and the black outer tail feathers.

PURPLE MARTIN

Progne subis

In a few scattered localities in the extreme southwestern Rockies, Purple Martins congregate at large apartment-style nest boxes to raise their young. Adults spiral around the nests, coming and going from foraging forays. The young perch clumsily at the opening of their apartment cavity, impatiently waiting for their parents to return with a mouthful of flying insects. Although the aerial maze of flying birds may at first glance appear chaotic, the complex is quite efficiently negotiated by the busy flyers. ▪ House Sparrows and European Starlings frequently invade unkempt martin houses. Human landlords of these complexes should clean the boxes and plug the holes until the earliest of the spring martins arrive and perch beside their locked apartments. ▪ The genus name of our largest swallow, *Progne*, refers to the daughter of Pandion, Prokne, who had changed herself into a swallow in Greek mythology.

I.D.: *General:* dark blue, glossy body; slightly forked tail; pointed wings; small bill. *Male:* dark underparts. *Female:* gray underparts.
Size: *L* 7–8 in. (18–20 cm).
Range: rare to uncommon summer resident at low elevations in the southern U.S. Rockies.
Habitat: *Nesting:* near semi-open aspen or ponderosa pine forests, often near water. *In migration:* over rivers, reservoirs and agricultural areas.
Nesting: communal; nest is usually built in a human-made, apartment-style bird house, rarely in tree cavities or other natural cavities; nest materials include feathers, grass, mud and vegetation; female incubates 4–5 eggs for 15–16 days.
Feeding: mostly while in flight; usually eats flies, ants, bugs, dragonflies and mosquitoes; may also walk on the ground, taking insects and rarely berries.
Voice: rich, fluty, robin-like *pew-pew*, often heard in flight.
Similar Species: *European Starling* (p. 232): longer bill; lacks the forked tail. *Barn Swallow* (p. 202): deeply forked tail; creamy brown underparts.

TREE SWALLOW
Tachycineta bicolor

Tree Swallows are our most common roadside swallows, perching all summer long by their fencepost nest boxes. When conditions are favorable, these busy birds are known to return to their nest site and feed their young 10 to 20 times an hour. When they leave their nests to forage, Tree Swallows frequently cover their eggs with feathers from the nest. These swallows are so enticed by feathers, that nest-building parents might swoop down to get feathers tossed in the breeze. ▪ Unlike other North American swallows, female Tree Swallows do not acquire their full adult plumage until their second or third year. ▪ In the bright spring sunshine, the back of the Tree Swallow appears blue, while prior to fall migration the back appears to be green. ▪ The scientific name *bicolor* is Latin for 'two colors,' in reference to this bird's dark and light plumage.

I.D.: *Sexes similar. Adult:* iridescent blue-green head and upperparts; white underparts; no white on the cheek; dark rump; small bill; long, pointed wings; shallowly forked tail. *Female:* slightly duller. *Immature:* brown above; white below.
Size: L 5¹/₂ in. (14 cm).
Range: common migrant and breeder throughout the Rockies.
Habitat: open areas, such as beaver ponds, marshes, fields, townsites and open woodlands, up to the subalpine.

Nesting: in a tree cavity or nest box; nest is made of weeds, grass and feathers; female incubates 4–6 eggs for up to 19 days.
Feeding: catches flies, beetles and ants on the wing; also takes stoneflies, mayflies and caddisflies over water.
Voice: alarm call is a metallic, buzzy *klweet*.
Similar Species: *Violet-green Swallow* (p. 199): white cheek; white rump patches. *Bank Swallow* (p. 201): brown upperparts. *Northern Rough-winged Swallow* (p. 200): light brown smudge on the upper breast.

VIOLET-GREEN SWALLOW

Tachycineta thalassina

The Violet-green Swallow is possibly the highest foraging of the Rocky Mountain swallows. These western birds can feed more than 100 ft. (30 m) above the ground to catch high-flying insects. ▪ Swallows occasionally eat mineral-rich soil, egg shells and exposed shellfish fragments, possibly to recoup the minerals lost in egg laying. ▪ Swallows are swift and graceful flyers, routinely traveling at speeds of 30 m.p.h. (48 km/h). W.L. Dawson, a noted 20th-century ornithologist, once vividly described these masters of flight as 'the children of Heaven.' ▪ The scientific name *thalassina* is Latin for 'sea green,' a tribute to this bird's body color.

I.D.: *Sexes similar:* iridescent blue-green plumage; white underparts; white on the cheek; white rump patches; small bill; long, pointed wings; shallowly forked tail; small feet. *Female:* duller and more bronze than the male.
Size: L 5¼ in. (13 cm).
Range: locally common migrant and breeder throughout the Rockies.
Habitat: open environments, including beaver ponds, marshes, townsites and mixed woodlands, up to the lower subalpine.
Nesting: in a tree cavity, rock crevice or nest box; nest is made of weeds, grass and feathers; female incubates 4–6 eggs for up to 15 days.
Feeding: catches flying insects, such as leafhoppers, leafbugs, flies, ants and wasps; drinks on the wing.
Voice: buzzy, trilling *tweet tweet;* harsh *chip-chip.*
Similar Species: *Tree Swallow* (p. 198): lacks the white cheek and the white rump patches. *Bank Swallow* (p. 201) and *Northern Rough-winged Swallow* (p. 200): brown upperparts; lack the white cheek.

NORTHERN ROUGH-WINGED SWALLOW
Stelgidopteryx serripennis

The Northern Rough-winged Swallow cruises at low altitudes when foraging. Frequently, Rough-wings catch insects just as they are emerging from the water's surface. ▪ An early 20th-century ornithologist once caught a Northern Rough-winged Swallow and released it 30 mi. (48 km) from its nest. He immediately drove back to the site where he had captured the bird, only to find it feeding its nestlings. ▪ Unlike other Rocky Mountain swallows, male Northern Rough-wings, have curved barbs along the outer edge of their primary wing feathers. The purpose of this saw-toothed edge remains a mystery. The ornithologist who initially named this bird must have been very impressed with its wings: *Stelgidopteryx* (scaper wing) and *serripennis* (saw feather) refer to this unusual characteristic.

I.D.: *Sexes similar:* brown upperparts; light brownish-gray underparts; small bill; dark cheek; dark rump. *In flight:* long, pointed wings; notched tail.

Size: L 5¹/₂ in. (14 cm).

Range: uncommon to locally common breeder throughout the Rockies.

Habitat: open areas, such as rivers, lakes and marshy areas, up to the lower subalpine.

Nesting: occasionally in small colonies; at the end of a burrow lined with leaves and dry grass; sometimes reuses kingfisher burrows, rodent burrows and other land crevices.

Feeding: catches flying insects on the wing; occasionally eats insects from the ground; drinks on the wing.

Voice: generally quiet; occasionally a quick, short, squeaky *brrrtt.*

Similar Species: *Bank Swallow* (p. 201): dark breast band. *Tree Swallow* (p. 198): female has green upperparts and a clean white breast. *Violet-green Swallow* (p. 199): female has green upperparts, white cheek and rump patches and a white breast.

BANK SWALLOW
Riparia riparia

A colony of Bank Swallows is in a constant flurry of activity as the parents bring mouthfuls of insects to their insatiable young. All that activity attracts predators, but few are able to catch these swift-flying birds. Skunks and badgers are known to dig into the colony from above to get to the vulnerable nestlings. ▪ In medieval Europe, it was thought that swallows spent winter in the mud at the bottom of swamps, since they were not seen during that season. ▪ *Riparia* is from the Latin for 'riverbank,' which is a common nesting site for this bird. If you approach a colony by canoe, the birds will burst from their burrows in the hundreds and circle nervously until the river carries you away. ▪ In Europe, the Bank Swallow is known as the Sand Martin.

I.D.: *Sexes similar:* brown upperparts; light underparts; brown breast band; long, pointed wings; shallowly forked tail; white throat; dark cheek; small legs.
Size: L 5¼ in. (13 cm).
Range: locally common migrant and uncommon breeder in most of the Rockies.
Habitat: steep banks, lakeshores and open areas up to the lower subalpine.
Nesting: colonial; in a burrow in a steep earthen bank; pair excavates the cavity and incubates 4–5 white eggs for up to 16 days.

Feeding: catches flying insects; drinks on the wing.
Voice: twittering chatter: *speed-zeet speed-zeet.*
Similar Species: *Northern Rough-winged Swallow* (p. 200): lacks the dark breast band. *Violet-green Swallow* (p. 199): green upperparts; white cheek and rump patches; lacks the dark breast band. *Tree Swallow* (p. 198): lacks the dark breast band; greenish upperparts.

BARN SWALLOW

Hirundo rustica

Because of its close association with human structures, the Barn Swallow is the most familiar of the North American swallows. It builds its cup-shaped mud nest under the eaves of barns, outbuildings and sheds. In these places the reproductive practices of the bird can be carefully studied, especially the parents' dive-bombing nest-defense strategy. ■ 'Swallow tail' is a term used to describe something that is deeply forked; among Rocky Mountain swallows, however, it is only the Barn Swallow that displays this feature. Barn Swallows also occur in Europe. ■ *Hirundo* is Latin for 'swallow'; *rustica* is Latin for 'rural.'

I.D.: *Sexes similar:* long, deeply forked tail; rust-colored throat and forehead; blue-black upperparts; rust- to buff-colored underparts; long, pointed wings.

Size: *L* 7 in. (18 cm).

Range: very common local breeder and locally common migrant throughout the Rockies.

Habitat: rivers, lakes, marshes, bridges, culverts and other structures in open country and cities in the foothills and the montane.

Nesting: on a wall under a roof, on a bridge, in a culvert or in a cave; cup nest is made of mud; pair incubates 4–7 eggs for 12–17 days.

Feeding: catches flying insects on the wing.

Voice: constantly buzzy, electric chatter: *zip-zip-zip*; also *kvick-kvick.*

Similar Species: *Cliff Swallow* (p. 203): squared-off tail; light-colored rump and underparts.

CLIFF SWALLOW
Petrochelidon pyrrhonota

If the Cliff Swallow were to be renamed in the 20th century, it would probably be called the Bridge Swallow or the Building Swallow: there seems to be a colony of Cliff Swallows under just about every low-elevation bridge that spans a large river. Unlike Barn Swallows, however, which have all but abandoned natural structures, Cliff Swallows continue to build their all-mud nests on natural, rocky cliffs as well. The colonial nests are rarely built lower than 8 ft. (2.4 m) from the ground, unless they are over water, where they may be just 3 ft. (91 cm) above the surface. During years of high run off and prolonged rains, floods can wipe out entire nesting colonies of Cliff Swallows.

- The Cliff Swallow is the species that predictably returns each spring to the Capistrano mission in California.

I.D.: *Sexes similar:* square tail; buffy rump; blue-gray head and wings; cream-colored forehead; rusty cheek, nape and throat; buffy breast; white belly; spotted undertail coverts.
Size: L 5¹/₂ in. (14 cm).
Range: locally common migrant and breeder throughout the Rockies.
Habitat: steep banks, cliffs, bridges and buildings near watercourses; forages over water, fields and marshes up to the lower subalpine.

Nesting: colonial; under bridges, on cliffs and on buildings; pair builds a gourd-shaped mud nest with a small opening on the bottom; pair incubates 4–5 eggs for up to 16 days.
Feeding: catches flying insects on the wing; occasionally eats berries; drinks on the wing.
Voice: twittering chatter: *churrr-churrr*; also an alarm call: *nyew*.
Similar Species: *Barn Swallow* (p. 202): deeply forked tail; dark rump; rust-colored underparts.

BLACK-CAPPED CHICKADEE
Poecile atricapillus

Flocks of this exceptionally friendly bird appear to be a welcoming committee for walkers along trails, greeting them into the chickadee's world of shrubs, dry leaves and insect eggs. ▪ Black-capped Chickadees occur at lower elevations throughout central North America. They commonly visit backyard feeders during winter, and they are easily enticed to land on an outstretched hand that offers a sunflower seed. ▪ Most songbirds, including Black-capped Chickadees, have both songs and calls. Bird songs are delivered primarily during courtship, to attract mates and to defend territories. Calls, which can be heard year-round, are used to establish flock cohesion and contact. ▪ The scientific name *atricapillus* is Latin for 'black crown' (or 'black hair').

I.D.: *Sexes similar:* black cap and bib; white cheek; gray back and wings; white underparts; light buff sides; dark legs.
Size: L 5–6 in. (13–15 cm).
Range: uncommon to common year-round throughout the Rockies.
Habitat: aspen forests, riparian woodlands, urban areas, backyard feeders, willow groves and mixed forests up to the montane.
Nesting: in a natural cavity or an abandoned woodpecker nest; can excavate a cavity in soft, rotting wood; lines the nest with fur, feathers, moss, grass and cocoons; female incubates 6–8 eggs for up to 13 days.
Feeding: gleans vegetation, branches and the ground for small insects and spiders; visits backyard feeders; also eats conifer seeds and invertebrate eggs.
Voice: call is a chipper, whistled *chick-a-dee-dee-dee*; song is a simple, whistled *swee-tee*.
Similar Species: *Mountain Chickadee* (p. 205): white eyebrow; black eye line. *Boreal Chickadee* (p. 207): gray-brown cap and flanks. *Chestnut-backed Chickadee* (p. 206): rusty back and flanks; dark brown cap.

MOUNTAIN CHICKADEE

Poecile gambeli

The Mountain Chickadee breeds at higher elevations than all other chickadees. Largely restricted to the Rocky Mountain region, where it is the most common chickadee, the Mountain Chickadee routinely nests at 8000–10,000 ft. (2400– 3000 m). ▪ In winter, these residents band together with other birds to forage in mixed flocks, at times close to timberline. It is more common, however, for them to move down to the plains for winter. ▪ The scientific name *gambeli* honors William Gambel, a 19th-century ornithologist who died of typhoid fever in the Sierra Nevada Mountains at the age of 28. 'Chickadee' is an onomatopoeic derivation from these birds' calls.

I.D.: *Sexes similar:* black cap and bib; white eyebrow; black eye line; white cheek; gray upperparts and tail; light gray underparts.
Size: L 5¹/₄ in. (13 cm).
Range: very common to common resident throughout the Rockies.
Habitat: coniferous forests, especially old-growth spruce-fir forests, and occasionally shrubby areas, aspen forests and urban areas in the montane and the subalpine.
Nesting: in a natural cavity or abandoned woodpecker nest; can excavate a cavity in soft, rotting wood; lines the nest with fur, feathers, moss and grass; incubates 5–9 eggs for up to 14 days.

Feeding: gleans vegetation, branches and the ground for small insects and spiders; visits backyard feeders; also eats conifer seeds and invertebrate eggs.
Voice: song is a sweet, clear, whistled *fee-bee-bay*; call is *chick a-dee a-dee a-dee*.
Similar Species: *Black-capped Chickadee* (p. 204): lacks the white eyebrow and the black eye line. *Boreal Chickadee* (p. 207): gray-brown cap and flanks. *Chestnut-backed Chickadee* (p. 206): rusty back and flanks; dark brown cap.

CHESTNUT-BACKED CHICKADEE
Poecile rufescens

This West Coast chickadee extends its range into a narrow region of the Rocky Mountains. Following the cool, moist cedar and fir forests eastward, Chestnut-backed Chickadees reach their eastern limit in western Alberta and northwestern Montana. ▪ When intruders approach the nest of a chickadee, both parents flutter their wings and hiss loudly at the perceived threat. ▪ Chickadee nests are not only attractive to the small birds but also to insects. Bumblebees have been known to invade a chickadee's cavity and chase the small bird from its nest. ▪ The scientific name *rufescens* is from the Latin *rufescene*, meaning 'to become reddish.'

I.D.: *Sexes similar:* dark brown cap; black bib; rusty back and flanks; white cheek; light underparts; gray wings and tail.
Size: L 4³/₄ in. (12 cm).
Range: uncommon but regular winter resident in Glacier and Waterton Lakes NPs and northern Idaho; rare elsewhere in the Canadian Rockies; typically west of the Continental Divide.
Habitat: moist coniferous forests in the foothills and the montane.
Nesting: typically west of the Rockies; excavates a cavity in soft, rotting wood or uses a natural cavity or an abandoned woodpecker nest; lines the nest with fur, feathers, moss and grass; incubates 6–7 eggs for up to 15 days.
Feeding: gleans vegetation, branches and the ground for small insects and spiders; also eats conifer seeds.
Voice: rapid, whistled *tsick-a-dee-dee*.
Similar Species: *Mountain Chickadee* (p. 205): white eyebrow; black eye line. *Boreal Chickadee* (p. 207): gray-brown cap and flanks. *Black-capped Chickadee* (p. 204): black cap; gray back; buffy flanks.

BOREAL CHICKADEE
Poecile hudsonicus

These small birds burn so much energy that they must replenish their stores almost daily to survive winter. Chickadees do not have sufficient fat reserves to survive prolonged stretches of cold weather, which inhibits their foraging, but Boreal Chickadees are likely more cold hardy than their Black-capped cousins. Like jays, many chickadees store food for winter—they often hide seeds or dead insects in holes and bark crevices—and they have a remarkable ability to remember and find their stores. All chickadees enter into a state known as torpor during cold winter nights. While in torpor, the bird's metabolism slows slightly, so that the bird uses less energy during the night. ▪ The scientific name *hudsonicus* refers to the northern, Hudsonian region of Canada.

I.D.: *Sexes similar:* gray-brown cap; black bib; gray-brown flanks; light gray underparts; light brownish back; white cheek patch.
Size: L 5–5¹/₂ in. (13–14 cm).
Range: common year-round in the Canadian and northern U.S. Rockies.
Habitat: mature and young coniferous forests, especially spruce and fir, and occasionally pine forests up to the subalpine.
Nesting: excavates a cavity in soft, rotting wood or uses a natural cavity or abandoned woodpecker nest in a conifer tree; female lines the nest with fur, feathers, moss and grass; female incubates 5–8 eggs for around 15 days.
Feeding: gleans vegetation, branches and infrequently the ground for small tree-infesting insects, including their pupae and eggs, and spiders; also eats conifer seeds.
Voice: soft, nasal, whistled *scick-a day day day.*
Similar Species: *Mountain Chickadee* (p. 205): white eyebrow; black eye line. *Black-capped Chickadee* (p. 204): black cap; buffy flanks. *Chestnut-backed Chickadee* (p. 206): rusty back and flanks; dark brown cap.

JUNIPER TITMOUSE
Baeolophus ridgwayi

Despite the Juniper Titmouse's somber plumage, its behavior is bright and cheerful. This active little bird pecks and pries every crack with an enthusiasm plainly expressed by its raised crest. ■ Juniper Titmice are very inquisitive—if a pair are in the woods, they will be attracted to the presence of all who enter. ■ Until very recently, the Juniper Titmouse and the Oak Titmouse were considered one species: the Plain Titmouse. (The Oak Titmouse is found in western California.) ■ 'Titmouse' is a term that reflects these birds' high-pitched calls and their mouse-like, scurrying habits.

I.D.: *Sexes similar:* uniform gray plumage; small visible crest; no wing bars or eye ring; dark eye.

Size: L 5³/₄ in. (15 cm).

Range: locally rare breeder in the southern U.S. Rockies.

Habitat: mature pinyon-juniper woodlands, ponderosa pine forests and riparian forests in the foothills.

Nesting: excavates a cavity in soft, rotting wood or uses a natural cavity or an abandoned woodpecker nest (chosen by the female); lines the nest with fur, feathers, moss and grass; female incubates 6–8 eggs for 14–16 days.

Feeding: gleans vegetation, branches and the ground for small insects and spiders; also eats seeds.

Voice: song is a clearly whistled *witt-y witt-y witt-y*; call is a chickadee-like *tsick-a-dee-dee*.

Similar Species: *Bushtit* (p. 209): no crest; dark legs; brown cheek. *Boreal Chickadee* (p. 207): black bib; gray-brown cap. *Mountain Chickadee* (p. 205): black cap; white eyebrow; black bib.

BUSHTIT
Psaltriparus minimus

The character of the home reflects the quality of the occupant, and the Bushtit sets a fine example. The architecture of its intricately woven nest is worthy of close inspection. ▪ The Bushtit is best described as a tiny, gray cottonball with a long, narrow tail. It is constantly on the move, bouncing from one shrubby perch to another. Bushtits travel in bands of up to 40 birds, filling the shrublands with their bell-like tinkles. ▪ Bushtits are typically found west of our region, but they extend into the Rockies in Utah and Colorado. ▪ *Psaltriparus* is derived from the Greek word *psaltris*, 'player of the lute' (or zither), and *parus*, the Latin name for a titmouse.

I.D.: *Sexes similar:* uniform, gray plumage; light brown cheek; long tail; no crest. *Male:* dark eyes. *Female:* light-colored eyes.
Size: L 4½ in. (11 cm).
Range: rare resident on the western slopes of the southern U.S. Rockies.
Habitat: shrubland, pinyon-juniper forests and riparian woodlands in the foothills.
Nesting: pair builds a sock-like, hanging nest, woven with moss, lichens, cocoons, spiders silk, fur and feathers, that can take up to 50 days to complete; pair incubates 5–7 eggs for 12 days.

Feeding: gleans vegetation for insects; also eats small seeds.
Voice: *Male:* simple, thin, high-pitched whistle: *tsit tsit tsit tsit.*
Similar Species: *Juniper Titmouse* (p. 208): small crest; relatively shorter tail; light-colored legs; lacks the brown cheek patch. *Boreal Chickadee* (p. 207): brown cap; black bib. *Ruby-crowned Kinglet* (p. 222): distinct wing bars and eye ring; proportionately shorter tail.

RED-BREASTED NUTHATCH
Sitta canadensis

Red-breasted Nuthatches frequently join in on bird waves—groups of warblers, chickadees and kinglets moving through the woods. The nuthatches' unusual body form and nasal cries easily set them apart from the other songbirds. ▪ The Red-breasted Nuthatch smears the entrance of its nesting cavity with sap. This sticky doormat might inhibit ants and other animals from entering the nest chamber—invertebrates can be the most serious threat to nesting success, because they frequently transmit diseases and parasitize nestlings. ▪ The Red-breasted Nuthatch's distinctive, nasal calls are heard more and more often as spring arrives. ▪ The scientific name *canadensis* means 'of Canada'—a reference to its northerly nesting habits.

I.D.: *General:* rusty underparts; gray-blue upperparts; white eyebrow; black eye line; black cap; straight bill; short tail; white cheek. *Male:* deeper rust on the breast; black crown. *Female:* light red wash on the breast; gray crown.

Size: L 4¹/₂ in. (11 cm).

Range: uncommon to common resident throughout the Rockies.

Habitat: spruce-fir, lodgepole pine and other coniferous forests up to the subalpine.

Nesting: excavates a cavity or uses an abandoned woodpecker nest; usually smears the entrance with sap; nest is made of bark shreds, grass and fur; female incubates 5–6 eggs for 12 days.

Feeding: forages down trees while probing under loose bark for larval and adult invertebrates; eats many pine and spruce seeds during winter; visits feeders.

Voice: slow, continually repeated, nasal *yank-yank-yank.*

Similar Species: *White-breasted Nuthatch* (p. 211): lacks the black eye line and the red underparts. *Pygmy Nuthatch* (p. 212): brown cap; lacks the black eye line. *Mountain Chickadee* (p. 205): black bib; lacks the red breast.

WHITE-BREASTED NUTHATCH

Sitta carolinensis

Nuthatches make their gravity-defying, headfirst struts seem routine. While foraging on a tree trunk, a White-breasted Nuthatch will frequently pause in mid-descent, arch its head at right angles to the trunk and call noisily. ▪ Unlike a woodpecker or the Brown Creeper, a nuthatch does not use its tail as a brace against a tree trunk. In fact, its tail is so short that it couldn't possibly serve that purpose. Nuthatches clasp the trunk through foot power alone. ▪ The White-breasted Nuthatch is known to jam tufts of fur into crevices near the nesting hole, but the purpose of this behavior remains a mystery. ▪ The scientific name *carolinensis* means 'of the Carolinas'—an indication of this bird's more southern breeding distribution than its red-breasted cousin.

♂

I.D.: *Sexes similar:* white underparts; white face; gray-blue back; rusty undertail coverts; short tail; straight bill; short legs. *Male:* black cap. *Female:* dark gray cap.

Size: L 5³/4 in. (15 cm).

Range: common year-round in Rocky Mountain NP; uncommon in the central and northern U.S. Rockies; rare and local resident in the Canadian Rockies.

Habitat: aspen, ponderosa pine and pinyon-juniper forests in the foothills and the lower montane.

Nesting: in a natural cavity or an abandoned woodpecker nest in a large deciduous tree; lines the cavity with bark, grass, fur and feathers; female incubates 5–8 eggs for up to 14 days.

Feeding: forages down trees headfirst in search of larval and adult invertebrates; also eats many nuts and seeds; regularly visits feeders.

Voice: frequently repeated *yarnk-yarnk-yarnk*.

Similar Species: *Pygmy Nuthatch* (p. 212): brown cap; buff-colored underparts; light nape patch. *Red-breasted Nuthatch* (p. 210): black eye line; rusty underparts. *Chickadees* (pp. 204–7): all have a black bib.

211

PYGMY NUTHATCH
Sitta pygmaea

The Pygmy Nuthatch is one of the most energetic residents of the U.S. Rockies. It hops continuously up and down trunks and treetops, probing and calling incessantly. Its voice is quite unlike the nasal, rhythmic calls of the other nuthatches.
▪ Pygmy Nuthatches are quietly gregarious, always appearing in small flocks that increase in size during fall and winter. At night, Pygmy Nuthatches retreat to communal roosts in tree and building cavities. Up to 100 birds have been recorded snuggling together in a single roosting site. Pygmy Nuthatches are even sociable during the nesting season: a pair might have up to three 'helpers' looking after their nestlings.

I.D.: *Sexes similar:* brown cap bordered by a black eye line; white cheek and throat; gray-blue back; short tail; pale underparts; straight bill.
Size: L 4¹/₄ in. (11 cm).
Range: very common year-round in Rocky Mountain NP; locally common in Montana; rare year-round in the Canadian Rockies.
Habitat: ponderosa pine and aspen forests in the montane.
Nesting: often in an abandoned woodpecker cavity; occasionally excavates its own nest site; lines the nest with soft plant material, wood

chips, fur and feathers; female incubates 6–8 eggs for 15–16 days.
Feeding: forages up and down trunks and outer limbs for adult and larval invertebrates; also eats pine seeds.
Voice: high-pitched *te-dee te-dee*, unlike the other nuthatches.
Similar Species: *White-breasted Nuthatch* (p. 211): larger; black crown; red undertail coverts. *Red-breasted Nuthatch* (p. 210): black eye line; reddish underparts. *Boreal Chickadee* (p. 207): black bib.

BROWN CREEPER
Certhia americana

Creepers are among the most inconspicuous birds in North America. Embracing old coniferous forests, the Brown Creeper often goes unnoticed until a flake of bark appears to come alive. ▪ The Brown Creeper forages by spiraling up trunks. Once it reaches the upper branches, the creeper floats down to the base of a neighboring tree to begin another ascent. ▪ The thin whistle of a Brown Creeper is so high-pitched that it is frequently not heard by birders. ▪ There are many species of creepers in Europe and Asia, but the Brown Creeper is the only one found in North America.

I.D.: *Sexes similar:* brown back is heavily streaked with grayish white; white eyebrow; white underparts; downcurved bill; long, pointed tail feathers; rusty rump.
Size: L 5¹/₄ in. (13 cm).
Range: common resident in the southern and central U.S. Rockies; uncommon but regular in the northern U.S. Rockies; uncommon year-round in the Canadian Rockies.
Habitat: mainly coniferous forests, such as spruce, fir, limber pine, lodgepole pine and Douglas-fir, up to the lower subalpine.
Nesting: under loose bark; nest is made with grass and conifer needles woven together with spider silk; female incubates 5–6 eggs for 15–17 days.
Feeding: hops up trunks and large limbs, probing loose bark for adult and larval invertebrates.
Voice: faint, high-pitched *trees-trees-trees see the trees.*

Similar Species: *Nuthatches* (pp. 210–12): all have a gray-blue back. *Black-and-white Warbler* (p. 252): black-and-white plumage; shorter tail. *Woodpeckers* (pp. 161–70): all lack the brown back streaking and have a straight bill.

ROCK WREN
Salpinctes obsoletus

Rock Wrens have the most unusual habit of 'paving' a walkway to their nests. They occasionally make this gravel welcome mat by carefully placing up to 1500 stones and pebbles, although, typically, only a few stones are used. The exact purpose of this paving is not clear: it might protect the nest from moisture, or it might make the nest easier to find in the monotonous terrain. ■ Rock Wrens are found in rocky areas throughout the West. Coastal cliffs, desert outcrops and mountain cliffs are some of the varied breeding habitats preferred by these birds. ■ *Salpinctes* is from the Greek word for 'trumpeter,' in reference to this bird's loud call.

I.D.: *Sexes similar:* gray-brown upperparts; light underparts; white throat; finely streaked, white breast; rusty brown rump and tail; downcurved bill; tail is trimmed with buff-colored tips.
Size: *L* 6 in. (15 cm).
Range: common resident in the southern and central U.S. Rockies; increasingly rare in spring and summer north into Montana and southern Canada.
Habitat: rocks, cliffs and open, rocky slopes in the montane.
Nesting: in a small crevice or hole in a cliff; places small stones at the opening; nest is

made of grass and rootlets and lined with a variety of items; incubates 5–6 eggs for up to 14 days.
Feeding: forages on the ground and picks up insects and spiders from around and under rocks.
Voice: harsh *tra-lee tra-lee tra-lee*; long, drawn out, melodious *keree keree keree*, *chair chair chair*, *deedle deedle deedle*, *tur tur tur*, *keree keree trrrrrr*.
Similar Species: *Canyon Wren* (p. 215): clean white throat; brown underparts; no eyebrow. *House Wren* (p. 217): brown upperparts; shorter bill.

CANYON WREN
Catherpes mexicanus

The lively song of the Canyon Wren is heard far more often than this bird is seen. The song, which echoes hauntingly through canyons, cascades and ripples down melodic scales, finishing on an unexpected upbeat. ■ Because of its somewhat flattened body shape, the Canyon Wren is able to easily pass through narrow crevices. These small birds forage tirelessly during the hottest parts of the day, searching nooks and crevices with great vigilance for hidden insects and spiders. Their smooth strides are quite similar to those of a small rodent. ■ While foraging and moving about its territory, a Canyon Wren will quickly raise and lower its hind quarters every few seconds, which is a useful identifying behavior. ■ *Catherpes* is the Latinized form of the Greek word *katherpein*, meaning 'to creep.'

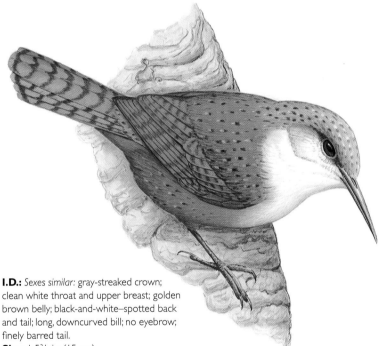

I.D.: *Sexes similar:* gray-streaked crown; clean white throat and upper breast; golden brown belly; black-and-white–spotted back and tail; long, downcurved bill; no eyebrow; finely barred tail.
Size: L 5¾ in. (15 cm).
Range: uncommon local breeder in the central and southern U.S. Rockies, typically west of the Continental Divide.
Habitat: open cliffs, canyons, boulder piles and rocky slopes in the montane.
Nesting: in a crevice under rocks, on a ledge or on a shelf in a cave; cup nest of moss, twigs and spiders silk is lined with fur and feathers; female incubates 5–6 eggs for up to 18 days; both parents feed the young.

Feeding: gleans rocks, exposed ground and vegetation for insects and spiders.
Voice: descending, whistled *dee-ah dee-ah dee-ah dah-dah-dah*.
Similar Species: *Rock Wren* (p. 214): lightly streaked throat; faint eye line; gray back; light belly. *Other wrens* (pp. 216–19): all have an eyebrow.

BEWICK'S WREN
Thryomanes bewickii

The long, narrow tail of the Bewick's Wren waves gently from side to side as this small bird roams about. Almost mouse-like in its traveling, this wren curiously investigates all the nooks and crevices of its territory. ▪ The Bewick's Wren is one of the hardiest of its family; it routinely overwinters through much of its range. ▪ John James Audubon chose to honor Thomas Bewick in the name of this spirited bird. Bewick was an exceptionally talented wood engraver whom Audubon visited during one of his trips to England.

I.D.: *Sexes similar:* long white eyebrow; long tail; gray-brown upperparts; light gray underparts; tail is trimmed with white spots; slender, downcurved bill.
Size: *L* 5¹/₄ in. (13 cm).
Range: rare breeder in the southern U.S. Rockies.
Habitat: shrublands, especially pinyon-juniper and sagebrush, in the foothills.
Nesting: typically along the Pacific Coast and east of the Rockies to the Appalachians; often in a natural cavity or an abandoned wood-

pecker nest; also in bird boxes; nest is made with sticks and grass and lined with feathers; female incubates 5–7 eggs for up to 14 days.
Feeding: gleans the ground and vegetation for insects, especially beetles, caterpillars, grasshoppers and spiders.
Voice: bold and clear *chick-click, for me-eh, for you.*
Similar Species: *Marsh Wren* (p. 219): heavily streaked back; shorter tail. *House Wren* (p. 217): shorter tail; faint eyebrow. *Rock Wren* (p. 214): gray crown and upper back; lacks the long white eyebrow.

HOUSE WREN

Troglodytes aedon

The loud, bubbly song of the House Wren spills out from dense tangles and shrubs. This small bird sings as though its lungs were bottomless, a characteristic shared by many wrens. This strong voice was recognized by the Chippewa, whose name for the House Wren, *O-du-ná-mis-sug-ud-da-we'-shi*, means 'big noise for its size.' ■ Most wrens carry their tails cocked up at a right angle to the rest of the body. This trait alone should help identify these often drably dressed birds. ■ In Greek mythology, Aedon was the queen of Thebes, whom Zeus transformed into a nightingale. The wonderfully bubbling call of the House Wren is somewhat similar to a nightingale's.

I.D.: *Sexes similar:* unstreaked, brown upperparts; faint eyebrow; short 'cocked up' tail is finely barred with black; faint eye ring; throat is lighter than the underparts.

Size: *L* 4³/₄ in. (12 cm).

Range: locally common breeder in the U.S. Rockies; uncommon to rare in the Canadian Rockies.

Habitat: aspen forests, shrublands and dense understorey vegetation up to the montane.

Nesting: typically at low elevations; often in a natural cavity or abandoned woodpecker nest; also in bird boxes; nest is made with sticks and grass and lined with feathers, fur and other soft materials; incubates 6–8 eggs for up to 19 days.

Feeding: gleans the ground and vegetation for insects, especially beetles, caterpillars, grasshoppers and spiders.

Voice: smooth, running, bubbly warble— *tsi-tsi-tsi-tsi oodle-oodle-oodle-oodle*—that lasts about 2–3 seconds.

Similar Species: *Winter Wren* (p. 218): shorter tail; darker overall; dark barring on the flanks. *Bewick's Wren* (p. 216): long tail; long, white eyebrow.

WINTER WREN
Troglodytes troglodytes

The sweet, warbling voice of the Winter Wren serenades forests of spruce and fir. The song of the Winter Wren is distinguished by its melodious, bubbly tone and its uninterrupted length. The length of the song alone facilitates identification, because it eliminates all other forest songsters. When not singing, the Winter Wren can be observed in woodlands, skulking beneath the dense understorey.
■ *Troglodytes* is Greek for 'creeping in holes' or 'cave dweller.' This bird's common name may refer to the fact that a few winter in the northern U.S. ■ The Winter Wren also breeds across Europe and Asia.

I.D.: *Sexes similar:* very short, 'cocked up' tail; dark brown upperparts; light brown underparts; fine, light eyebrow; dark barring on the flanks.
Size: L 4 in. (10 cm).
Range: locally common breeder and migrant in the Canadian and northern U.S. Rockies; rare migrant in the Rockies south of Montana.
Habitat: subalpine fir and Engelmann spruce forests with dense understoreys, often near water, in the subalpine.
Nesting: in an abandoned woodpecker cavity, in a natural hole, under bark or under upturned tree roots; bulky nest is made with twigs, moss, grass and fur; male frequently builds up to 4 'dummy' nests prior to egg-laying; female incubates 6–7 eggs for up to 16 days.

Feeding: forages on the ground and on trees for beetles, wood borers and other invertebrates.
Voice: *Male:* song is a tumbling warble of quick notes, often more than 8 seconds long.
Similar Species: *House Wren* (p. 217): tail is longer than the leg; less barring on the flanks. *Bewick's Wren* (p. 216): long tail; long, white eyebrow.

MARSH WREN
Cistothorus palustris

The energetic and reclusive Marsh Wren is usually associated with cattail marshes and dense, wet meadows. Although it prefers to keep a low profile by staying hidden in the deep vegetation, its distinctive song is one of the characteristic voices of our freshwater wetlands. Patient observers might be rewarded with a brief glimpse of a Marsh Wren perching atop a cattail reed as it quickly evaluates its territory.
▪ Marsh Wrens occasionally destroy the nests and eggs of other Marsh Wrens and blackbirds. Red-winged Blackbirds, in turn, occasionally destroy the nest and eggs of Marsh Wrens. ▪ The scientific name *palustris* is Latin for 'marsh.'

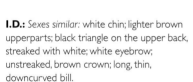

I.D.: *Sexes similar:* white chin; lighter brown upperparts; black triangle on the upper back, streaked with white; white eyebrow; unstreaked, brown crown; long, thin, downcurved bill.
Size: L 5 in. (13 cm).
Range: locally common to rare migrant and breeder throughout the Rockies.
Habitat: cattail and bulrush marshes up to the lower subalpine.
Nesting: typically across central North America; in cattail marshes; globe-like nest is woven with cattails, bulrushes, weeds and grass and lined with cattail down; female incubates 4–6 eggs for 12–16 days.
Feeding: gleans vegetation and flycatches for adult aquatic invertebrates, especially dragonflies and damselflies; occasionally eats other birds' eggs.

Voice: *Male:* rapid series of *zig-zig-zig-zig*, like an old sewing machine.
Similar Species: *Bewick's Wren* (p. 216): longer tail; lacks the streaked back. *House Wren* (p. 217): faint eyebrow; lacks the white streaking on the back.

AMERICAN DIPPER
Cinclus mexicanus

The American Dipper is among the world's most unusual songbirds. Along fast-flowing mountain waters, it stands bobbing up and down on a stream-side rock. In its search for food, the dipper dives into the water, disappearing momentarily below the stream's surface. Its stout body form, strong claws and thick feathers enable the dipper to survive in cold, fast-flowing water. ■ John Muir wrote: "Find a fall, or cascade, or rushing rapid ... and there you will find the complementary Ouzel, flitting about in the spray, diving in foaming eddies, whirling like a leaf among beaten foam-bells; ever vigorous and enthusiastic, yet self-contained, and neither seeking nor shunning your company." ('Water Ouzel' is an old name for the American Dipper.)

I.D.: *Sexes similar. Adult:* slate gray plumage; head and neck are darker than the body; short tail; short neck; flesh-colored legs; straight, black bill; stout body. *Immature:* lighter bill; light underparts.
Size: L 7¹/₂ in. (19 cm).
Range: locally common year-round in the Rockies.
Habitat: *Summer:* fast-flowing creek, stream and river edges from the foothills to the upper subalpine. *Winter:* also visits the open shores of lakes, large rivers and marshes.

Nesting: under a rock ledge, overhang, uprooted tree or bridge; bulky globe nest is made of moss and grass; nest entrance faces the water; female incubates 4–5 eggs for up to 17 days.
Feeding: wades or flies through the water or plunges below the surface for aquatic larval insects, fish fry and eggs.
Voice: vocal throughout the year; song is clear and melodious; alarm call is a harsh *tzeet.*
Similar Species: none.

GOLDEN-CROWNED KINGLET

Regulus satrapa

Golden-crowned Kinglets are hyperactive foragers that keep busy on outer branches in the Rockies' conifer forests. These small birds move in flocks, often ornamenting spruces, firs and pines like Christmas tree decorations. ▪ Kinglets are surprisingly hardy birds that are able to withstand winters throughout much of the Rockies. ▪ The Golden-crowned Kinglet is the smallest songbird in North America. These tiny birds are remarkably fearless of people and have been known to allow themselves to be petted and even, on occasion, to be picked up. ▪ *Regulus* is derived from the Latin word for 'king.'

I.D.: *General:* olive back; darker wings and tail; light underparts; dark cheek; 2 white wing bars; black eye line; white eyebrow; black border to the crown. *Male:* reddish-orange crown. *Female:* yellow crown.
Size: *L* 4 in. (10 cm).
Range: uncommon to common spring migrant and breeder throughout the Rockies; uncommon winter resident in the U.S. Rockies.
Habitat: mixed and pure forests of Engelmann spruce, white spruce, lodgepole pine, subalpine fir, Douglas-fir and ponderosa pine up to the subalpine.

Nesting: usually in a spruce tree; hanging nest is made of moss, lichens, twigs and leaves; female incubates 8–9 eggs for about 15 days.
Feeding: gleans and hovers for insects, berries and occasionally sap.
Voice: faint, high-pitched, accelerating *tsee-tsee-tsee-tsee, why do you shilly-shally?*
Similar Species: *Ruby-crowned Kinglet* (p. 222): eye ring; lacks the black border to the crown. *Golden-crowned Sparrow* (p. 280): chunkier body; much larger; brown-mottled back.

RUBY-CROWNED KINGLET
Regulus calendula

Each summer, Ruby-crowned Kinglets are one of the most persistent voices in mountain coniferous forests. Their distinctive songs echo through the mountains from spring to August. ■ The male's small ruby crown is held erect during court-ship to impress prospective mates. Throughout most of the year, however, the crown remains hidden among the green feathers on top of the bird's head. ■ Mass movements of kinglets have been known to frustrate birders. At times, these small birds dominate the birding scene; birdwatchers would dearly like something to filter out all the Ruby-crowned Kinglets from the similar wood warblers.

I.D.: *General:* olive-green upperparts; dark wings and tail; 2 strong, white wing bars; incomplete eye ring; light underparts; short tail; flicks its wings. *Male:* small red crown (usually not seen). *Female:* no crown.
Size: *L* 4 in. (10 cm).
Range: common to very common migrant and breeder throughout the Rockies.
Habitat: spruce-fir forests, especially lodge-pole pine, Douglas-fir and black spruce, from the foothills to the subalpine.

Nesting: usually in a spruce tree; hanging nest is made of moss, lichens, twigs and leaves; female incubates 7–9 eggs for up to 16 days.
Feeding: gleans and hovers for insects and spiders; infrequently eats seeds and berries.
Voice: song is an accelerating and rising *tea-tea-tea-tew-tew chewy chewy chewy cheweee!*
Similar Species: *Golden-crowned Kinglet* (p. 221): dark cheek; black border to the crown; male has an orange crown; female has a yellow crown. *Orange-crowned Warbler* (p. 241): no eye ring or wing bars.

BLUE-GRAY GNATCATCHER
Polioptila caerulea

The Blue-gray Gnatcatcher constantly waves its long tail during its treetop foraging trips. When the wind blows, the gnatcatcher's long tail catches the wind and often appears to nearly topple the small bird. Nevertheless, Blue-gray Gnatcatchers are energetic birds, and they constantly flit about in deciduous treetops.
■ During courtship, a male gnatcatcher accompanies his prospective mate around his territory. Once the bond is established, the pair remains close during nest building and egg laying. ■ Although these bird undoubtedly eat gnats, these insects do not represent a substantial portion of their diet. ■ The scientific name *caerulea* is from the Latin word for 'blue.'

breeding

I.D.: *General:* blue-gray upperparts; long tail; white eye ring; pale gray underparts; no wing bars; black uppertail with white outer tail feathers. *Breeding male:* darker upperparts; black border on the side of the forecrown.
Size: L 4^1/$_2$ in. (11 cm).
Range: rare migrant and summer resident in the southern and central U.S. Rockies.
Habitat: pinyon-juniper forests and riparian woodlands in the foothills and the montane.
Nesting: typically across the eastern U.S. and in the southwest; on a limb or in a crotch in a deciduous tree; lichen-covered cup nest is made with plant fibers and grass and bound by spider silk; female incubates 3–4 eggs for up to 15 days.

Feeding: gleans vegetation and flycatches for insects, spiders and other invertebrates.
Voice: call is a banjo-like, high-pitched twang: *chee. Male:* song is a low warble, often beginning with *zee-u zee-u.*
Similar Species: *Ruby-crowned Kinglet* (p. 222) and *Golden-crowned Kinglet* (p. 221): olive-green overall; short tail; wing bars. *Gray Catbird* (p. 233): much larger; red undertail coverts.

223

WESTERN BLUEBIRD
Sialia mexicana

The Western Bluebird is dressed with the colors of the cool sky on its back and the warm, setting sun on its breast. ▪ These open-country specialists nest in cavities, and they have responded well to nest boxes erected throughout much of their range. Western Bluebirds are the preferred tenants of nesting boxes, but they can be usurped from nesting sites by aggressive House Sparrows and European Starlings. ▪ Throughout most of their range, Western Bluebirds manage to raise two broods each year. The second clutch of eggs is laid just as the first brood has left the nest, but the first brood continues to depend on their parents for food. During the fall migration, both broods often join the parents on their southern voyage.

I.D.: *General:* chestnut red breast; light gray belly and undertail coverts; dark bill and legs. *Male:* deep blue head, back and wings; chestnut red flanks. *Female:* light eye ring; gray-brown head and back; blue wings and tail.

Size: *L* 7 in. (18 cm).

Range: uncommon migrant and summer resident and in the southern and central U.S. Rockies; rare in the Canadian Rockies.

Habitat: open forests, low-elevation grasslands in the montane.

Nesting: typically west of the Rockies; in an abandoned woodpecker cavity, natural cavity or nest box; nest is built of stems, conifer needles and twigs; female incubates 4–6 eggs for up to 17 days.

Feeding: swoops from a perch and pursues flying insects; also forages on the ground for invertebrates.

Voice: song is a harsh *cheer cheerful charmer*; call is a soft *few* or a harsh *chuck*.

Similar Species: *Mountain Bluebird* (p. 225): lacks the red underparts. *Lazuli Bunting* (p. 287): white belly; conical bill; darker upperparts; white wing bars. *Townsend's Solitaire* (p. 226): never has a reddish breast; buffy patches in the wings and tail.

MOUNTAIN BLUEBIRD
Sialia currucoides

The plumage of the male Mountain Bluebird is like a piece of mountain sky come to life. Just as the last spring snows are retreating from the mountain landscape, Mountain Bluebirds arrive from the south. These spring migrations routinely consist of small groups of birds, but, on occasion, Mountain Bluebirds migrate in flocks numbering over 100 birds. ▪ Because of their early spring arrival, late spring snowstorms occasionally prove fatal for many Mountain Bluebirds. ▪ The Mountain Bluebird is the state bird of Idaho and Nevada. ▪ Mountain Bluebirds breed in Alaska, farther north than any other North American bluebird.

I.D.: *General:* black eye, bill and legs. *Male:* sky blue body; upperparts are darker than the underparts. *Female:* sky blue wings, tail and rump; blue-gray back and head; gray underparts.
Size: *L* 7 in. (18 cm).
Range: uncommon to common migrant and breeder throughout the Rockies.
Habitat: open forests, forests edges, burned forests and mountain grasslands from the upper foothills to the subalpine; alpine meadows in late summer and early fall.
Nesting: in an abandoned woodpecker cavity, natural cavity or nest box; nest is built of plant stems, grass, conifer needles and twigs and frequently lined with a few feathers; female incubates 5–6 pale blue eggs for 13 days.

Feeding: swoops from a perch for flying and terrestrial insects; also forages on the ground for a variety of invertebrates, such as beetles, ants and bugs.
Voice: call is a low *turr turr. Male:* song is a short warble of *chur*s.
Similar Species: *Western Bluebird* (p. 224): male has a chestnut red breast. *Steller's Jay* (p. 188) and *Blue Jay* (p. 189): prominent crest. *Western Scrub-Jay* (p. 190): longer tail; blue is less intense. *Pinyon Jay* (p. 191): larger; larger bill. *Townsend's Solitaire* (p. 226): peach-colored patches in the wings and tail; white outer tail feathers.

225

TOWNSEND'S SOLITAIRE
Myadestes townsendi

The Townsend's Solitaire is a relatively plain bird that is mainly restricted to the western mountain ranges. This slim thrush is frequently observed in the mountains, perched on an exposed limb, surveying the area for insects. ▪ During the summer months, solitaires are rarely seen in groups, and this solitary tendency is represented in the name 'solitaire.' Only during winter do Townsend's Solitaires group together, with flocks descending on berry trees. ▪ These mountain thrushes overwinter south of Montana. ▪ John Kirk Townsend may be one of the most unsung of the early American ornithologists. He made great contributions to our region, including the Rocky Mountain region's first checklist in 1839.

I.D.: *Sexes similar. Adult:* gray body; darker wings and tail; peach-colored wing patches (very evident in flight); white eye ring; white outer tail feathers; long tail. *Immature:* brown body is heavily spotted with buff; pale eye ring.

Size: *L* 8¹/₂ in. (22 cm).

Range: common resident in the southern and central U.S. Rockies; common migrant and breeder in the Canadian Rockies; uncommon migrant and breeder in the northern U.S. Rockies.

Habitat: Engelmann spruce, subalpine fir and lodgepole pine forests, avalanche slopes and abandoned mine shafts in the montane and the lower subalpine.

Nesting: on the ground, in a bank or in a hollow snag; cup nest is built with twigs, grass and conifer needles; incubates 4 eggs for up to 13 days; eggs are light blue, patterned with brown.

Feeding: flycatches and gleans vegetation and the ground for invertebrates and berries.

Voice: call is a harsh *piink. Male:* song is a long, bubbly warble.

Similar Species: *Northern Mockingbird* (p. 234): lighter underparts; lacks the peach-colored wing patches. *Gray Catbird* (p. 233): black cap; red undertail coverts. *Bluebirds* (pp. 224–225): females lack the peach-colored wing and tail patches and the white outer tail feathers; female Mountain Bluebird has a faint rusty breast.

VEERY
Catharus fuscescens

The Veery's voice, like a tumbling waterfall, descends with a liquid ripple. It is heard far more often than this shy forest bird is seen. ▪ Perhaps the most terrestrial of the North American thrushes, the Veery nests and forages on the ground. Unlike the robin, the Veery does not walk or run; rather, it travels in springy hops. ▪ When startled by an intruder, the Veery either flushes or faces the threat, exposing its whitish underparts. ▪ 'Veery' is a feeble onomatopoeic version of this bird's airy song; *fuscescens* is from the Latin word for 'dusky,' in reference to the bird's color.

I.D.: *Sexes similar:* brownish back; thin, gray eye ring; moderately spotted throat; light underparts; gray flanks; flesh-colored legs.
Size: *L* 7 in. (18 cm).
Range: uncommon spring migrant and breeder in Waterton Lakes NP; locally common to uncommon in the U.S. Rockies.
Habitat: deciduous forests, with a dense, shrubby understorey, in the lower montane.
Nesting: on the ground; bulky nest is made with leaves and moss; female incubates 3–4 eggs for up to 15 days.

Feeding: gleans the ground and lower vegetation for invertebrates and berries.
Voice: *Male:* song is a musical, tumbling, spiraling *da-vee-ur, vee-ur, vee-ur, veer, veer, ver.*
Similar Species: *Swainson's Thrush* (p. 228): bold eye ring; golden face; olive-brown upperparts. *Gray-cheeked Thrush* (p. 321): olive-brown upperparts with bold breast spots; typically a migrant. *Hermit Thrush* (p. 229): reddish rump and tail; brownish back; bold eye ring.

227

SWAINSON'S THRUSH

Catharus ustulatus

The upward spiral of the Swainson's Thrush's song lifts the soul with each note and leaves the listener breathless at its conclusion. This inspiring song can be heard late on spring evenings—the Swainson's Thrush is routinely the last of the daytime singers to be silenced by the night. ▪ Swainson's Thrushes are most frequently observed perched high in treetops. ▪ At higher elevations, the Swainson's Thrush is replaced by the Hermit Thrush. ▪ William Swainson was an English zoologist and illustrator; his name also graces the Swainson's Hawk. ▪ This bird was formerly known as the Olive-backed Thrush.

I.D.: *Sexes similar:* olive-brown upperparts; bold, white eye ring; golden cheeks; moderately spotted throat and breast; white belly and undertail coverts; brownish-gray flanks.
Size: *L* 7 in. (18 cm).
Range: common migrant and breeder in the Canadian Rockies; uncommon to common migrant and breeder elsewhere in the Rockies.
Habitat: coniferous and mixedwood forests and steep ravines up to the montane.
Nesting: usually in a shrub or small tree;

small cup nest is built with grass, moss, leaves, roots and lichens; female incubates 3–4 eggs for 12–13 days.
Feeding: gleans vegetation and forages on the ground for invertebrates; also eats berries.
Voice: song is a slow, rolling, rising spiral: *whip-poor-will-a-will-e-zee-zee-tee*; call is a sharp *wick.*
Similar Species: *Hermit Thrush* (p. 229): grayish head and back; gray face; heavily spotted breast; lacks the bold eye ring. *Veery* (p. 227): lacks the bold eye ring, the golden face and the olive-brown back.

HERMIT THRUSH

Catharus guttatus

Beauty in forest birds is often gauged by sound and not appearance. Given this criterion, the Hermit Thrush is certainly one of the most beautiful birds to inhabit Rocky Mountains forests. ▪ Many features of the Hermit Thrush can be remembered by association with its name: its memorable song always begins with a single, lone (hermit-like) note; and its rump and tail are red, which reminds one of a lonely old hermit wearing nothing but a pair of red long underwear. ▪ The scientific name *guttatus* is Latin for 'spotted' or 'speckled,' in reference to the breast.

I.D.: *Sexes similar:* reddish-brown tail and rump; gray-brown head and back; brown wings; black-spotted breast; light undertail coverts; gray flanks; pale eye ring.
Size: *L* 7 in. (18 cm).
Range: common migrant and breeder throughout the Rockies.
Habitat: spruce-fir forests, avalanche slopes and lodgepole pine forests in the upper montane and the subalpine.
Nesting: occasionally on the ground, but usually in a small tree or shrub; cup nest is built with grass, twigs and mud; female incubates 4 eggs for up to 13 days.

Feeding: forages on the ground and gleans vegetation for insects and other invertebrates; also eats berries.
Voice: call is *chuck. Male:* song is a warbling, upward spiral, always preceded by a lone, thin note.
Similar Species: *Swainson's Thrush* (p. 228): golden cheek; olive-brown back and tail. *Veery* (p. 227): lightly streaked upper breast. *Fox Sparrow* (p. 275): stockier build; conical bill; brown breast spots.

229

AMERICAN ROBIN
Turdus migratorius

The ubiquitous American Robin is a familiar bird to most North Americans, because it favors the pleasant surroundings of suburbia. Despite its intimate association with backyards and city parks, the robin is also widespread and common throughout the Rocky Mountains. Its *tut-tut-tut* alarm notes are frequently heard along trails as the bird retreats ahead of an intrusion. The familiarity that the American Robin offers could bring some reassurance to wary visitors, uncomfortable in the wilds of the Rockies. ▪ American Robins sometimes attempt to overwinter around hot springs and open water in the southern Rockies. ▪ The American Robin was named by English colonists after the Robin Redbreast of their native land. Both birds look and behave in a similar fashion, even though they're only distantly related.

I.D.: *Sexes similar:* gray-brown back; darker head; white throat streaked with black; white undertail coverts; incomplete, white eye ring; yellow, black-tipped bill. *Female:* dark gray head; light red-orange breast. *Male:* deeper, brick red breast; black head. *Juvenile:* heavily spotted breast.
Size: *L* 10 in. (25 cm).
Range: common to very common breeder and migrant throughout the Rockies; common winter resident in the Rockies south of Montana.
Habitat: townsites, forests, ranchlands, forest edges and roadsides up to the subalpine.

Nesting: in a coniferous or deciduous tree or shrub; cup nest is well built of grass, moss and loose bark and cemented with mud; female incubates 4 baby blue eggs for 11–16 days.
Feeding: forages on the ground and among vegetation for larval insects, adult insects, other invertebrates and berries.
Voice: song is an evenly spaced warble: *cheerily cheer-up cheerio;* call is a rapid *tut-tut-tut.*
Similar Species: *Varied Thrush* (p. 231): adult has a black breast band and 2 orange wing bars; juvenile has wing bars and a white belly.

VARIED THRUSH

Ixoreus naevius

The haunting courtship song of the Varied Thrush is unlike any other sound in nature. The long, drawn-out whistles carve through the spring air in the Rockies. The low tones of the Varied Thrush's song ensure that the sound can pass through the dense western coniferous forests typical of its breeding habitat. ▪ During harsh spring storms, many Varied Thrushes (as well as other songbirds) perish. Early spring is one of the harshest times of year, because food supplies are at a minimum. ▪ Varied Thrushes are typically found in the temperate rain forests of the West Coast, but they extend east across Washington and B.C. into the Rocky Mountains.

I.D.: *General:* dark upperparts; orange eyebrow; 2 orange wing bars; orange throat and belly. *Male:* black breast band; black-blue upperparts. *Female:* brown upperparts; faint breast band.
Size: *L* 9¹/₂ in. (24 cm).
Range: common migrant and breeder in the Canadian and northern U.S. Rockies, especially west of the Continental Divide.
Habitat: spruce-fir forests, especially Engelmann spruce and lodgepole pine, up to the subalpine.

Nesting: typically west of the Rockies; often against the trunk of a conifer; bulky cup nest is made of twigs, leaves, moss and grass; female incubates 3–4 eggs for 14 days.
Feeding: forages on the ground and among vegetation for insects, seeds and berries.
Voice: *Male:* long steam-whistle–like notes, always delivered at different pitches.
Similar Species: *American Robin* (p. 230): adult lacks the black breast and the orange wing bars.

231

EUROPEAN STARLING
Sturnus vulgaris

European Starlings have not yet invaded the Rockies to the same extent as they have the rest of North America. Throughout much of the continent, the starling is one of the most abundant urban birds. About 100 European Starlings were released in New York's Central Park in 1890 and 1891, as part of the local Shakespearean society's plan to introduce to the city all the birds mentioned in their favorite author's play. The starlings spread quickly across the continent, often at the expense of many native cavity-nesting birds that are unable to withstand the aggression of the introduced invaders. As the Rocky Mountains are continuously developed and urbanized, European Starlings will expand their range into these areas as well.

breeding

Habitat: forest edges, townsites, agricultural areas, landfills and roadsides up to the lower montane.
Nesting: in an abandoned woodpecker cavity, natural cavity, nest box or almost any other cavity; nest is made of grass, twigs and straw; female incubates 4–6 bluish eggs for 12–14 days.

I.D.: *Sexes similar:* short, squared tail; pointed, triangular wings in flight. *Breeding adult:* blackish, iridescent plumage; yellow bill. *Fall adult:* brown plumage overall; white spotting on the underparts; dark bill. *Juvenile:* gray-brown plumage; brown bill.
Size: L 8¹/₂ in. (22 cm).
Range: locally common migrant and summer breeder throughout the Rockies; common winter resident only in the southern U.S. Rockies.

Feeding: very diverse diet, including many invertebrates, berries, seeds and garbage, taken from the ground and vegetation.
Voice: rambling whistles, squeaks and gurgles; imitates other birds throughout the year.
Similar Species: *Brewer's Blackbird* (p. 293): longer tail; black bill. *Brown-headed Cowbird* (p. 295): adult male has a longer tail and a shorter bill; juvenile has streaked underparts, a stout bill and a longer tail.

GRAY CATBIRD

Dumetella carolinensis

The Gray Catbird's courtship activities involve an unusual 'mooning' display: the male raises his long, slender tail to show off his red undertail coverts. ▪ Gray Catbirds vigorously defend their nesting territories. These birds are so thorough in chasing away intruders that the nesting success of neighboring warblers and sparrows increases as a result of the catbird's vigilance. ▪ This bird's vocal repertoire contains a wide array of musical and harsh sounds, including the cat-like call that leads many people to mistake this bird for a friendly feline. ▪ *Dumetella* is Latin for 'small thicket,' which is quite an appropriate genus name for a bird that inhabits dense tangles.

I.D.: *Sexes similar:* dark gray overall; black cap and tail; red undertail coverts; black eyes, bill and legs; long tail.

Size: L 8¹/₂ in. (22 cm).

Range: uncommon migrant and common breeder in Waterton Lakes NP, western Montana and Idaho; uncommon to rare elsewhere in the Rockies.

Habitat: dense thickets and shrublands, often near water, in the foothills.

Nesting: in a dense shrub or thicket; bulky cup nest is loosely built with twigs, leaves and grass and lined with fine materials; female incubates 4 eggs for up to 15 days.

Feeding: forages on the ground and in vegetation for a wide variety of ants, beetles, grasshoppers, caterpillars, moths and spiders; also eats berries and visits feeders.

Voice: call is a cat-like *meoow. Male:* song is of variable warbles, usually in pairs.

Similar Species: *Gray Jay* (p. 187), *Pinyon Jay* (p. 191) and *Western Scrub-Jay* (p. 190): all lack the black cap and the red undertail coverts.

233

NORTHERN MOCKINGBIRD
Mimus polyglottos

The amazing vocal repertoire of birds reaches its pinnacle in the Northern Mockingbird, which has been known to sing over 400 different song types. Northern Mockingbirds can imitate other sounds so perfectly that computerized auditory analysis is often unable to detect differences between the original source and the mockingbird. ▪ During winter, mockingbirds establish and defend territories in berry-rich areas. ▪ To flush insects and to scare off predators, mockingbirds frequently raise their wings and tails. ▪ The scientific name *polyglottos* is Greek for 'many tongues,' in reference to the bird's varied vocal repertoire.

I.D.: *Sexes similar. Adult:* gray upperparts; dark wings and tail; 2 white wing bars; white outer tail feathers; light gray underparts; long black tail. *In flight:* large white patch at the base of the black primaries. *Juvenile:* paler overall; spotted breast.

Size: *L* 10 in. (25 cm).

Range: rare migrant in the southern U.S. Rockies; rare to uncommon elsewhere in the Rockies.

Habitat: dense tangles, shrublands, thickets, agricultural areas and riparian forests up to the lower montane.

Nesting: typically across the southern U.S.; often in a small shrub or small tree; cup nest is built with twigs, grass, fur and leaves; female incubates 3–5 eggs for 12–13 days.

Feeding: gleans vegetation and forages on the ground for beetles, ants, wasps and grasshoppers; also eats berries; visits feeders for suet and raisins.

Voice: song is a variable musical medley, with the phrases often repeated 3 times or more; call is a harsh *chair*; habitually imitates other songs and noises.

Similar Species: *Northern Shrike* (p. 181) and *Loggerhead Shrike* (p. 182): hooked bill; adults have a black mask; juveniles are stockier, and less vocal. *Townsend's Solitaire* (p. 226): prominent eye ring; lacks the white in the wings.

SAGE THRASHER
Oreoscoptes montanus

The Sage Thrasher is well named: this bird is intricately linked to open sagebrush country. These thrashers can be regularly seen in our area, but only in the flats of sagebrush that penetrate the Rocky Mountain foothills. ■ This bird was formerly known as the Mountain Mockingbird or Sage Mockingbird, because of its mannerisms, which are similar to a mockingbird's: while perched, the Sage Thrasher slowly raises and lowers its tail; while running along the ground, it holds its tail high. ■ 'Thrasher' is derived from 'thrush'—these birds unfortunately do not 'thrash' with their long tails. ■ *Oreoscoptes* is Greek for 'mimic of the mountains'—really a misconception because most of their range lies outside of the Rockies.

I.D.: *Sexes similar:* gray-brown upperparts; heavily streaked underparts; yellow eyes. *In flight:* 2 white wing bars; white-tipped tail; short, straight bill.
Size: *L* 8¹/₂ in. (22 cm).
Range: uncommon migrant and breeder in the central and southern U.S. Rockies.
Habitat: sagebrush flats and shrublands in the lower foothills and the lower montane.
Nesting: usually in sagebrush; bulky cup nest is made of grass, twigs and leaves and lined with fine vegetation; pair incubates 3–5 eggs for up to 17 days

Feeding: forages on the ground and among vegetation for invertebrates and their larvae; also eats berries.
Voice: *Male:* song is sustained, lasting up to 2 minutes, with the phrases usually repeated without a pause.
Similar Species: *Brown Thrasher* (p. 236): long, reddish tail; reddish back; heavily streaked underparts. *Northern Mockingbird* (p. 234): juvenile has less heavily streaked underparts and large, white wing patches.

BROWN THRASHER
Toxostoma rufum

Male Brown Thrashers have the largest vocal repertoire of any Rocky Mountain bird: more than 3000 song variations. Thrashers will frequently repeat phrases twice, often combining them into complex choruses. ■ Because the Brown Thrasher nests on or close to the ground, the eggs and nestlings are vulnerable to predation by weasels, skunks, raccoons and foxes. ■ Brown Thrashers are among the most aggressive and vigilant defenders of their nests: pairs have been known to attack curious onlookers to the point of drawing blood. ■ Most of the eight species of North American thrashers live in the Southwest.

I.D.: *Sexes similar:* reddish-brown upperparts; white underparts with heavy, brown streaking; long, downcurved bill; orange-yellow eyes; long, rufous tail; white wing bars.
Size: L 11½ in. (29 cm).
Range: rare migrant and summer resident in the southern U.S. Rockies; very rare in the Rockies north of Colorado.
Habitat: dense shrubs and thickets in the foothills.
Nesting: usually in a low shrub; cup nest is made of grass, twigs and leaves and lined with fine vegetation; pair incubates 4–5 eggs for up to 14 days

Feeding: gleans the ground and vegetation for larval and adult invertebrates; occasionally tosses leaves aside; also eats seeds and berries.
Voice: repeats a variety of phrases, typically resembling *dig-it dig-it*, *hoe-it hoe-it*, *pull-it-up*, *pull-it-up*; pauses between phrases.
Similar Species: *Sage Thrasher* (p. 235): gray back; shorter bill and tail. *Hermit Thrush* (p. 229): shorter tail; gray-brown back and crown; dark brown eyes.

AMERICAN PIPIT
Anthus rubescens

In summer and fall, the American Pipit is linked to harsh, treeless environments: it only breeds in the alpine and arctic tundra. The alpine meadows it inhabits run along the spine of the Rocky Mountains, extending as far south as Colorado. Although this region is covered by snow and ice for most of the year, several species of birds have adapted to this habitat alone. ▪ Many American Pipits arrive on their breeding territories already paired up—courtship and pair formation often occur at lower elevations—which is thought to save valuable time in a place with a very brief summer. ▪ The pipit bobs its short tail continuously as it forages.

breeding

I.D.: *Sexes similar:* faintly streaked, gray-brown upperparts; lightly streaked 'necklace' on the upper breast; streaked breast and flanks; black legs; black tail with white outer tail feathers; buff-colored underparts; slim body.
Size: *L* 6–7 in. (15–18 cm).
Range: common migrant and breeder throughout the Rockies.
Habitat: alpine tundra and wet alpine meadows.
Nesting: in a shallow depression; small cup nest is made with coarse grass and sedges,

and is sometimes lined with fur; frequently has an overhanging canopy; female incubates 4–5 eggs for 13–15 days.
Feeding: gleans the ground and vegetation for terrestrial and freshwater invertebrates and seeds.
Voice: familiar flight call is *pip-it pip-it.* Male: harsh, sharp *tsip-tsip* or *chiwee.*
Similar Species: *Horned Lark* (p. 196): black horns and facial markings. *Brewer's Sparrow* (p. 266): unstreaked breast; conical bill; stout body.

BOHEMIAN WAXWING
Bombycilla garrulus

Bohemian Waxwings are highly social birds that have been known to pass berries down a line to a hungry bird. Tight flocks of Bohemians appear irregularly in the Rockies during winter. They have quite a variable winter distribution: they might be entirely absent for several winters and then suddenly be numerous one year. ▪ Waxwings get their common name from the colorful spots on their wing tips. The 'waxy spots' are colorful enlargements of the feathers' shafts. The body feathers of waxwings are also noteworthy: they blend together wondrously to form a cohesive coat. ▪ Bohemia is allegedly the ancestral home of the gypsies—an appropriate name for this northern wanderer.

I.D.: *Sexes similar. Adult:* cinnamon crest; black mask; black throat; soft gray-brown body; yellow, terminal tail band; red undertail coverts; white, red and yellow spots on the wings. *Juvenile:* brown-gray above; streaked underparts; light throat; no mask; white wing patches.

Size: *L* 8 in. (20 cm).

Range: common, but irregular; year-round in the Canadian Rockies; uncommon migrant and irregular winter resident in the U.S. Rockies.

Habitat: open coniferous forests, frequently near water, and townsites up to the subalpine.

Nesting: in a conifer; cup nest is made with twigs, grass, moss and lichens and sometimes lined with fur; female incubates 4–6 eggs for 12–16 days.

Feeding: gleans vegetation or catches flying insects on the wing; depends on berries and fruit in winter.

Voice: faint, high-pitched whistle: *zirr-r-r zirr-r-r.*

Similar Species: *Cedar Waxwing* (p. 239): smaller; slight yellow wash on the belly; lacks the red undertail coverts.

CEDAR WAXWING
Bombycilla cedrorum

The Cedar Waxwing's courtship display involves the passing of a berry to a potential mate. If the other bird is receptive, the berry is passed back and forth between the birds until the fruit is eventually eaten by the female. ▪ Cedar Waxwings are among of the last birds to nest in the Rocky Mountains. The delay in nesting is to ensure that the berry crop is well developed when the nestlings are growing quickly and in need of food. ▪ Waxwings frequently are the most numerous birds at fruit trees, but they are easily 'bullied' by robins and starlings, forcing the beautiful waxwings to whistle patiently from nearby trees. In fall, flocks of waxwings gorging themselves on fermented fruit are occasionally rendered flightless from intoxication.

I.D.: *Sexes similar. Adult:* cinnamon crest; brown upperparts; black mask; yellow wash on the belly; gray rump; yellow, terminal tail band; white undertail coverts; red spots on the wings. *Juvenile:* no mask; streaked underparts; gray-brown body.
Size: *L* 7 in. (18 cm).
Range: common breeder and uncommon to rare winter resident throughout the Rockies.
Habitat: forest edges, deciduous forests, shrublands and riparian woodlands in the foothills and the montane.

Nesting: in a coniferous or deciduous tree or shrub; cup nest is made with twigs, grass, moss and lichens and often lined with fine grass; female incubates 3–5 eggs for 12–16 days.
Feeding: gleans vegetation or catches flying insects on the wing; also eats berries and fruit, especially during fall and winter.
Voice: faint, high-pitched whistle: *tseee-tseee-tseee.*
Similar Species: *Bohemian Waxwing* (p. 238): adult is larger, has red undertail coverts and has yellow and white wing spots; juvenile has red undertail coverts and white wing patches.

239

TENNESSEE WARBLER
Vermivora peregrina

Migrating Tennessee Warblers are not easily overlooked: their loud, three-part calls pierce mature forests. ▪ On their breeding grounds, Tennessee Warblers usually inhabit the upper half of trees. During migration, however, these long-distance migrants can be observed on the forest floor. ▪ Alexander Wilson discovered this species along the Cumberland River in Tennessee, and he named it after that state. Although a migrant through Tennessee, this warbler breeds almost exclusively in Canada. ▪ The scientific name *peregrina* is Latin for 'wandering.'

breeding

I.D.: *Breeding male:* gray crown; olive-green back, wings and tail; white eyebrow; black eye line; white underparts; thin bill. *Breeding female:* yellow breast; olive-gray head; yellowish eyebrow. *Non-breeding:* yellow underparts; dark green head; yellow eyebrow; white underparts.

Size: L 4³/₄ in. (12 cm).

Range: uncommon migrant and breeder in the Canadian and northern U.S. Rockies; rare to very rare elsewhere in the Rockies.

Habitat: coniferous or mixed mature forests and occasionally spruce bogs in the montane and the lower subalpine.

Nesting: on the ground or on a raised hummock; female builds a small cup nest of grass, moss and roots and lines it with fur; female incubates 5–6 eggs for 12 days.

Feeding: gleans foliage and buds for small insects, caterpillars and other invertebrates; also eats berries; visits suet feeders.

Voice: *Male:* accelerating, loud, sharp *ticka-ticka-ticka swit-swit-swit-swit chew-chew-chew-chew-chew.*

Similar Species: *Warbling Vireo* (p. 184): stouter bill; lacks the blue-gray cap. *Orange-crowned Warbler* (p. 241): lacks the eye line and the blue-gray head.

ORANGE-CROWNED WARBLER

Vermivora celata

Don't bother looking for the Orange-crowned Warbler's telltale orange crown—its most distinguishing characteristic is the lack of distinctive field marks. Conspicuously absent are wing bars, an eye ring and a colorful breast, rump or flank. Orange-crowned Warblers are the plainest of the warbler clan; even this bird's golden-orange crown is concealed by its olive head feathers. ▪ Wood warblers are strictly confined to the New World. The 109 species (56 occurring in North America) originated in South America, where they have the highest diversity. ▪ *Vermivora* is Latin for 'worm eating'; *celata* is from the Latin for 'hidden,' a reference to this bird's inconspicuous crown.

I.D.: *Sexes similar:* olive-gray body; lighter undertail coverts; dark eye line; yellowish eyebrow; faintly streaked underparts; thin bill; faint orange crown patch.

Size: *L* 5 in. (13 cm).

Range: common spring migrant and summer breeder in the Canadian Rockies; less common in the northern U.S. Rockies; uncommon to locally common in Idaho and Colorado.

Habitat: deciduous or mixed forests, shrubby avalanche slopes, pinyon-juniper woodlands and riparian forests from the upper foothills to the lower subalpine.

Nesting: on the ground or occasionally in a low shrub; well-hidden, small cup nest is made of coarse grass; incubates 4–5 eggs for 12–14 days.

Feeding: gleans foliage for invertebrates, berries, nectar and sap.

Voice: *Male:* faint trill that breaks downward halfway through.

Similar Species: *Tennessee Warbler* (p. 240): blue-gray head; olive back; dark eye line. *Ruby-crowned Kinglet* (p. 222): broken eye ring; wing bars. *Wilson's Warbler* (p. 258): female has no eyebrow, yellower underparts and light-colored legs.

NASHVILLE WARBLER
Vermivora ruficapilla

The Nashville Warbler makes rare appearances in the Rockies during its spring and fall migrations, when it sings continuously from deciduous forests. ▪ These warblers have a most unusual distribution. There are two distinct populations: one in the East and one in the West. The Nashville Warblers that filter through our area arrive from the West. ▪ Nashville Warblers were first described as being from Tennessee, although they do not breed in that state. This misnomer is not an isolated incident: the Tennessee, Palm, Magnolia, Cape May, Connecticut and Prairie warblers all bear names that falsely reflect their breeding grounds.

♂

I.D.: *Male:* blue-gray head; white eye ring; yellow-green upperparts; yellow underparts; small red crown. *Female* and *Immature:* light eye ring; olive-gray head; yellow underparts; yellow-green upperparts.
Size: *L* 4³/₄ in. (12 cm).
Range: locally common breeder in western Montana and northern Idaho; very rare spring migrant throughout the Rockies.
Habitat: open deciduous forests and second-growth woodlands, especially aspen and birch forests with low shrubs, in the montane.

Nesting: typically east or west of the Rockies; on the ground; female constructs a cup nest of grass, bark strips, moss, conifer needles and fur; female incubates 4–5 eggs for 11–12 days.
Feeding: gleans foliage for insects, such as caterpillars, flies and aphids.
Voice: *Male:* first part of the song is high-pitched, then *see-it see-it see-it see-it, ti-ti-ti-ti-ti.*
Similar Species: *Virginia's Warbler* (p. 243): whiter underparts; grayer upperparts. *MacGillivray's Warbler* (p. 256): male has a slate gray hood and lacks the yellow throat. *Common Yellowthroat* (p. 257): female lacks the gray head.

VIRGINIA'S WARBLER
Vermivora virginiae

No-one has ever met a warbler they didn't like, and the Virginia's Warbler is no exception. In fine warbler fashion, it moves about continuously in its shrubby Southwest neighborhoods, dancing between half-hidden perches. ■ The Virginia's Warbler is the most abundant species of warbler, in the appropriate habitat. In our region it breeds in the foothills of Colorado and Utah, at 7500–8000 ft. (2300–2400 m). ■ This southwestern warbler is very active. It is often observed flying in low shrubs and thickets, twitching its tail while feeding. ■ Army surgeon William Wallace Anderson collected the first specimen of the Virginia's Warbler in New Mexico. When he sent it to the Smithsonian, he asked Spencer Fullerton Baird to name the unknown bird after his wife, Virginia.

I.D.: *Male:* gray head and back; yellow breast; white throat; white belly; yellow undertail coverts; white eye ring; yellow-green rump; faint reddish crown patch. *Female:* duller overall.
Size: L 4³/₄ in. (12 cm).
Range: uncommon spring migrant and summer breeder in the southern U.S. Rockies.
Habitat: dense thickets of mountain mahogany and open pinyon-juniper, ponderosa pine and shrub oak habitats in the foothills and the lower montane.

Nesting: typically in the Southwest; on the ground, often hidden by vegetation; loose cup nest is made of leaves, moss, grass and rootlets; female (probably) incubates the 4 eggs.
Feeding: gleans and flycatches from the ground and among foliage for a variety of invertebrates, including insects.
Voice: song is *che-we-che-we-che-we-che-we—wit-a-wit-wit-wit-wit.*
Similar Species: *Nashville Warbler* (p. 242): more yellow on the underparts, especially the throat; lacks the yellow rump.

243

YELLOW WARBLER
Dendroica petechia

The Yellow Warbler is active and inquisitive, flitting from branch to branch in search of juicy caterpillars, aphids and beetles. From May through June, its lively courtship song and golden plumage refresh aspen forests. ■ Yellow Warblers are among the most frequent victims of cowbird parasitism. Unlike many bird species of the forest interior, however, Yellow Warblers recognize the foreign eggs and will either abandon the nest or simply build another nest over top of the eggs. ■ Often mistakenly called wild canaries, Yellow Warblers often leave their nesting grounds before the end of July, just after their young have fledged. ■ The scientific name *petechia* is Latin for 'red spots on the skin.'

breeding

I.D.: *Sexes similar:* canary yellow body; black bill and eyes; dark green wings and tail. *Breeding male:* red breast streaks. *Breeding female:* faint red breast streaks.

Size: *L* 5 in. (13 cm).

Range: common migrant and breeder in the Canadian and northern U.S. Rockies; common to uncommon summer breeder in the central and southern U.S. Rockies.

Habitat: wet shrubby meadows, willow tangles and shrubby avalanche slopes, usually near water, in the montane.

Nesting: in a fork in a deciduous tree or small shrub; female builds a compact cup nest

of grass, plant down, lichens and spider silk; female incubates 4–5 eggs for 11–12 days.

Feeding: gleans foliage and vegetation for invertebrates, especially caterpillars, inch worms, beetles, aphids and cankerworms.

Voice: *Male:* song is a fast, frequently repeated *sweet-sweet-sweet I'm so-so sweet.*

Similar Species: *Orange-crowned Warbler* (p. 241): lacks the beady, black eyes; male has red streaks and yellower plumage. *American Goldfinch* (p. 311): black wings and tail; male often has a black forehead. *Wilson's Warbler* (p. 258): female has a shorter, darker tail and yellower underparts.

MAGNOLIA WARBLER
Dendroica magnolia

The Magnolia Warbler is widely regarded as the most beautiful wood warbler in North America. Like a customized Cadillac, the Magnolia has all the luxury options—eyebrows, wing bars, a 'necklace,' a yellow rump and breast, tail patches and a dark cheek. As if aware of their beauty, Magnolia Warblers frequently seem to flaunt their colors at close range. These beautiful warblers forage on lower branches, and they often closely approach patient birdwatchers. ■ Magnolia Warblers tend to migrate at night. If they are blown off course into the Rockies, they might move during the following day to correct their misdirection. ■ There is a debate over the origin of this bird's name: some sources claim it bears the name of French botanist Pierre Magnol, while others claim it was named after being collected from a magnolia tree.

breeding

I.D.: *Male:* yellow underparts with black streaks; black mask; white eyebrow; blue-gray crown; dark upperparts; white wing bars. *Female:* lacks the black mask; duller overall. *In flight:* yellow rump; white tail patches.
Size: *L* 5 in. (13 cm).
Range: rare migrant and summer breeder in the Canadian Rockies; very rare migrant in the U.S. Rockies.
Habitat: open coniferous and mixed forests, often near water, in the montane and the lower subalpine.

Nesting: typically in the boreal and eastern deciduous forests; on a horizontal limb in a conifer; pair constructs a loose cup nest with grass, twigs and rootlets; female incubates 4 eggs for 11–13 days.
Feeding: gleans vegetation and buds, and occasionally flycatches, for beetles, flies, wasps and caterpillars; sometimes eats berries.
Voice: *Male:* song is a quick, rising *pretty pretty lady!* or *wheata wheata wheet-zu*.
Similar Species: *'Audubon's' Yellow-rumped Warbler* (p. 246): male has a yellow crown and lacks the yellow belly and the white eyebrow.

YELLOW-RUMPED WARBLER
Dendroica coronata

The Yellow-rumped Warbler is the most abundant and widespread North American wood warbler. Although this bird is common to most experienced bird-watchers, it is still often sought out in the Rockies. Yellow-rumped Warblers come in two forms: the 'Audubon's Warbler,' which has a yellow throat, and the 'Myrtle Warbler,' which has a white throat. 'Myrtles' are more prevalent in the northeastern Rockies and 'Audubons' in the southern and western Rockies, but both forms occur throughout our range. ▪ The two forms of the Yellow-rumped Warbler were once considered separate species, but because of their overlapping ranges in the Rockies, and because they interbreed, they are now considered a single species. ▪ The scientific name *coronata* is Latin for 'crowned,' referring to this bird's yellow crown.

breeding 'Audubon's Warbler'

I.D.: *General:* dark upperparts; yellow rump; white tail patches; yellow 'shoulder' patch, white belly; white undertail coverts; dark cheek. *'Audubon's Warbler':* yellow throat; large, white wing patches; yellow crown extending to the back of the head; male has a blue-black back; female has gray-brown upperparts. *'Myrtle Warbler':* white throat; thin, white wing bars; male has blue-black upperparts; female has gray-brown upperparts.
Size: *L* 5¹/₂ in. (14 cm).
Range: very common migrant and summer breeder throughout the Rockies; common winter resident in the southern U.S. Rockies.
Habitat: *Breeding:* all forested areas, especially conifer forests, throughout the

foothills and the montane. *Fall migration:* commonly in subalpine regions.
Nesting: in the crotch or horizontal limb of a conifer; female constructs a compact cup nest with grass, bark strips, moss, lichens and spider silk; female incubates 4–5 eggs for up to 13 days.
Feeding: hawks, hovers or gleans vegetation and buds for beetles, flies, wasps, plant lice, and caterpillars; sometimes eats berries.
Voice: call is a sharp *chip*. *Male:* song is a tinkling trill that rises or falls at the end; much variation between races and individuals.
Similar Species: *Magnolia Warbler* (p. 245): male has a yellow belly and a white eyebrow, but lacks the yellow crown.

BLACK-THROATED GRAY WARBLER
Dendroica nigrescens

The Black-throated Gray Warbler's spunky *weezy-weezy-weezy-wee-zee* song is very similar to the songs of the Townsend's and Hermit warblers, its close relatives. Both those warblers, however, have considerably more yellow in their plumage. ■ Male and female Black-throated Grays have very similar plumages, except that the male has more black markings where the female is gray and white. ■ This insect eater is highly migratory, and it spends most of the fall through winter in Mexico and South America. The Black-throated Gray Warbler is rarely found at higher mountain elevations. It is closely associated with pinyon-juniper woodlands during the breeding season.

I.D.: *General:* blue-gray back; black head; white eyebrow and 'mustache' stripe; yellow lore; lightly streaked breast and flanks; white belly and undertail; black legs; 2 white wing bars. *Male:* black bib and crown. *Female:* paler overall.
Size: *L* 5 in. (13 cm).
Range: common migrant and summer breeder in Utah, western Colorado, southern Idaho and southwestern Wyoming; accidental elsewhere in the Rockies.

Habitat: tall, dense pinyon-juniper woodlands; occasionally in other coniferous woodlands.
Nesting: usually in a conifer, well out on a horizontal branch; small cup nest is made of grass, moss, lichens, feathers and fur; female (primarily) incubates the eggs.
Voice: lazy, oscillating *weezy-weezy-weezy-wee-zee*, often rising or falling at the end.
Similar Species: *Townsend's Warbler* (p. 248): yellow face and underparts; green upperparts.

247

TOWNSEND'S WARBLER

Dendroica townsendi

The Townsend's Warbler lives high in tree spires. Conifer crowns are penthouses for many neotropical warblers; many species choose to nest and feed exclusively at these great heights. The Townsend's Warbler would often escape detection if not for its constant flitting about and its characteristic song. ■ While most wood warblers spend the winter months in the New World tropics, the Townsend's Warbler commonly overwinters in western California. ■ This western warbler bears the name of one of the West's most pioneering ornithologists, John Kirk Townsend.

breeding

I.D.: *General:* yellow underparts streaked with black; black cheek; olive-green upperparts; 2 wing bars; white undertail coverts. *Male:* black throat, crown and cheek patch. *Female:* yellow throat; white belly; dusky cheek.
Size: *L* 5 in. (13 cm).
Range: uncommon to common spring migrant and summer resident in the Canadian and northern U.S. Rockies; rare to uncommon in the central and southern U.S. Rockies.
Habitat: mature coniferous forests, usually not far from water, in the montane and the subalpine.

Nesting: in the crotch or horizontal limb of a conifer; compact cup nest is built with grass, moss, lichens and spider silk; female incubates 4–5 eggs for 12 days.
Feeding: gleans vegetation and buds and flycatches for beetles, flies, wasps and caterpillars.
Voice: *Male:* 2 songs: *dzeer dzeer dzeer dzeer, tseetsee* and *weazy weazy seesee.*
Similar Species: *Black-throated Green Warbler* (p. 321): yellow cheek; lacks the yellow breast. *Black-throated Gray Warbler* (p. 247): lacks the yellow breast; very little yellow in the face.

PALM WARBLER
Dendroica palmarum

For a few days each spring, Palm Warblers pass through the Rockies on their way to their muskeg breeding grounds. Migrating Palm Warblers are lively transients; they can generally be found low in shrubs or hopping along trails and forest clearings. The Palm Warbler's yellow throat gleams surprisingly in sunlight, while the dull red cap strikes a dark contrast. ■ The Palm Warbler's most distinctive trait is perhaps its incessant habit of wagging its tail, whether it is perched or hopping along on the ground. ■ This warbler is misnamed: it is rarely seen among palms, even on its tropical wintering grounds. 'Bog Warbler' would have been a more appropiate, though less charismatic, name.

I.D.: *Sexes similar:* chestnut cap; light yellow throat and undertail coverts; white under-parts streaked with brown; yellow eyebrow; olive-brown upperparts.

Size: L 5¹/₂ in. (14 cm).

Range: vagrant along the eastern slopes of the Rockies.

Habitat: semi-open habitats, including bogs, fields and wetlands bordered by woodlands, in the lower montane.

Nesting: typically in northern bogs in the boreal forest; on the ground or on a short shrub; small cup nest is made with grass,

weeds and feathers; incubates 4–5 eggs for 12 days.

Feeding: gleans the ground and short vegetation for grasshoppers, beetles, moths and flies.

Voice: *Male:* song is a weak trill with a quick finish.

Similar Species: *Yellow-rumped Warbler* (p. 246): yellow rump; darker upperparts; white wing bars. *Orange-crowned Warbler* (p. 241): lacks the rufous crown and the streaked underparts. *Chipping Sparrow* (p. 264): stouter body; unstreaked underparts; no yellow in the plumage.

BAY-BREASTED WARBLER
Dendroica castanea

Bay-breasted Warblers, which weigh just slightly more than $^1/_2$ oz. (14 g), visit mature coniferous mountain forests during their spring and fall migrations between the northern boreal forest and the South American tropics. ■ Like most wood warblers, the Bay-breasted Warbler is a neotropical migrant that winters in the New World tropics. Deforestation in both their summer and winter habitats, environmental contaminants and migration hazards have all contributed to their decline over the past decades. These birds are truly international residents, so their conservation requires the efforts of several nations.

breeding

I.D.: *Breeding male:* chestnut crown, throat and flanks; black mask; creamy belly and undertail coverts; cream patch behind the ear; 2 white wing bars. *Female:* pale face, throat and flanks; cream-colored underparts; faint chestnut cap; 2 white wing bars.
Size: *L* 5 $^1/_2$ in. (14 cm).
Range: very rare spring migrant throughout the Rockies; very rare summer resident in the Canadian Rockies.
Habitat: riparian and coniferous forests in the montane.

Nesting: typically in the boreal forest; usually on a horizontal conifer branch; cup nest is loosely built of grass, twigs, moss and bark; female incubates 4–5 eggs for 13 days.
Feeding: gleans vegetation and terminal branches for caterpillars and adult invertebrates; usually forages at the mid-level of trees.
Voice: extremely high-pitched *seee-seese-seese-seee.*
Similar Species: *Cape May Warbler:* very rare through the Rockies; red cheek; lacks the reddish flanks and crown.

BLACKPOLL WARBLER

Dendroica striata

The Blackpoll Warbler is best known in our region as a migrant; it owes its breeding status in the Rockies to a few records in Jasper and Banff national parks. Never numerous, the spring migrants follow the eastern slopes of the Rockies north to their northern summer homes. ■ Blackpolls are the greatest migrants among the warblers. Weighing less than two 25-cent coins, these birds are known to fly south over the Atlantic Ocean, leaving land at Cape Cod and not landing again until they reach the coast of Venezuela. ■ A persistent springtime birder in the Rockies could be rewarded by a glimpse of a Blackpoll Warbler. The presence of such a natural wonder injects awe into a perceptive soul. ■ The scientific name *striata* is from the Latin word for 'striped.'

breeding

I.D.: *General:* 2 white wing bars; orange legs. *Breeding male:* black cap and upperparts; white cheek; black-streaked underparts. *Breeding female:* streaked, greenish upperparts; black-streaked or white underparts; dirty cheek.
Size: L 5¹/₂ in. (14 cm).
Range: uncommon migrant throughout the Rockies; common summer resident in the northern Canadian Rockies.
Habitat: black spruce forests, muskeg bogs, burns and occasionally mixed forests in the montane and the lower subalpine.

Nesting: in a stunted spruce tree; well-concealed nest is made of twigs, bark shreds, grass, lichens and fur; female incubates 4–5 eggs for about 12 days.
Feeding: gleans buds, leaves and branches for larval insects, aphids and scale insects; also flycatches for insects.
Voice: high-pitched, uniform *tsit tsit tsit.*
Similar Species: *Black-throated Gray Warbler* (p. 247): dark legs; lacks the pure white cheek. *Black-and-white Warbler* (p. 252): dark legs; striped, black-and-white crown.

BLACK-AND-WHITE WARBLER
Mniotilta varia

In general appearance this warbler seems quite normal, but the foraging behavior of the Black-and-white Warbler lies in sharp contrast to most of its kin. Rather than dancing quickly between twig perches like most warblers, Black-and-white Warblers have a foraging strategy similar to an entirely unrelated group of birds—the nuthatches. As if possessed by nuthatch envy, Black-and-white Warblers hop gingerly up and down tree trunks in search of food. Even a novice birdwatcher can easily identify this two-toned and oddly behaved warbler. A keen ear also helps: the gentle oscillating song—like a wheel in need of greasing—is easily identified and remembered.

breeding

I.D.: *General:* black-and-white–streaked crown; black upperparts; 2 white wing bars; black legs; streaked flanks. *Breeding male:* black cheek and throat. *Breeding female:* gray cheek; white throat.

Size: L 5¼ in. (13 cm).

Range: rare migrant along the eastern slopes of the Rockies; very rare elsewhere in the Rockies.

Nesting: typically in the boreal and eastern deciduous forests; often on the ground; in a shallow scrape lined with grass, leaves and fine plant materials; female incubates 5 eggs for 10 days.

Feeding: forages on tree trunks for insect eggs, larval insects, beetles, spiders and other invertebrates.

Voice: oscillates between 2 high notes: *wee-see wee-see wee-see* (like the wheel of a squeaky wheelbarrow).

Similar Species: *Black-throated Gray Warbler* (p. 247): small yellow lore; lacks the striped crown. *Blackpoll Warbler* (p. 251): orange legs; solid black cap.

AMERICAN REDSTART
Setophaga ruticilla

Through the continuous butterfly-like quivering of its wings and tail, the male American Redstart's hot orange patches spark life into any dark forest. These birds behave like over-energized wind-up toys, flitting from branch to branch in continual pursuit of prey. Always in motion, redstarts rhythmically sway their tails even while perched. ■ American Redstarts behave in much the same way in their Central American wintering grounds, where they are locally known as *candelita* (little candle). ■ The genus name *Setophaga* is Greek for 'insect-eater.'

I.D.: *Adult male:* black overall; salmon-red shoulder, wing and tail patches; white belly and undertail coverts. *Female:* olive-green upperparts; gray-green head; yellow shoulder, wing and tail patches; white belly and undertail coverts. *Immature male:* resembles a female, but with breast streaks.
Size: L 5¼ in. (13 cm).
Range: uncommon to common migrant and breeder in the Rockies north of Colorado; uncommon migrant and rare breeder in the southern U.S. Rockies.
Habitat: mature deciduous forests, shrubbery, avalanche slopes, willow patches and lowland forests, usually near water, in the foothills.

Nesting: in the fork of a shrub or short tree; tight cup nest is made of plant down, grass, roots and bark shreds, and lined with feathers and soft materials; female incubates 4 eggs for 12 days.
Feeding: actively gleans foliage and hawks for insects and spiders on leaves, buds and branches.
Voice: *Male:* wonderfully variable (but confusing) series of *tseets*, often given at different pitches.
Similar Species: male is distinctive; female and immature can resemble other warblers, but they have yellow patches on their wings and tails.

OVENBIRD
Seiurus aurocapillus

A visual identification of an Ovenbird in the Rockies is an experience shared by a fortunate few. It is this bird's distinctive song that is most often experienced during its brief mountain passage. The loud, pulsing song has a strange quality to it that makes it difficult to locate the source. ■ Ovenbirds almost stubbornly refuse to become airborne, preferring to escape through dense tangles and shrubs.
■ The scientific name *aurocapillus* is from the Latin for 'golden hair,' an allusion to the Ovenbird's infrequently seen crown. 'Oven' refers to the shape of its ground nest.

I.D.: *Sexes similar:* olive-brown upperparts; white eye ring; heavily streaked breast and flanks; rufous crown bordered by black; pink legs; white undertail coverts; no wing bars.
Size: *L* 6 in. (15 cm).
Range: rare to uncommon migrant on the eastern slopes of the Rockies; accidental elsewhere in the Rockies.
Habitat: riparian and deciduous forests and shrubbery; occasionally in mixed woods with semi-open undergrowth.
Nesting: typically across the boreal and deciduous forests; on the ground; oven-shaped, domed nest is made of grass and weeds and lined with fine materials; female incubates 4–5 eggs for 11–13 days.
Feeding: gleans the ground for worms, snails, insects and occasionally seeds.
Voice: loud, distinctive *teacher Teacher TEACHER TEACHER!!*, increasing in speed and volume; the emphasis is on the *cher*.
Similar Species: *Swainson's Thrush* (p. 228) and *Hermit Thrush* (p. 229): larger; lack the rufous-and-black crown. *Northern Waterthrush* (p. 255): light eyebrow; lacks the rufous crown; darker upperparts.

NORTHERN WATERTHRUSH

Seiurus noveboracensis

The Northern Waterthrush is not much of a visual bird—a gratifying sight of it arises all too infrequently in the lives of birdwatchers. Instead, Northern Waterthrushes are well recognized and admired through their song, whose quality seems perfectly suited to their inhospitable haunts. Waterthrushes, perhaps better than any other birds of the Rockies, raise the need for aspiring birders to learn the calls and songs of these creatures. ■ The scientific name *noveboracensis* is the Latin for 'of New York'—this bird was originally known as the New York Warbler.

I.D.: *Sexes similar:* pale yellow eyebrow; streaked breast; spotted throat; olive-brown upperparts; pinkish legs; often teeters.
Size: L 5–6 in. (13–15 cm).
Range: uncommon migrant and summer resident north of Wyoming; rare to uncommon migrant in the southern U.S. Rockies.
Habitat: deciduous riparian thickets, forests and streams in the montane.
Nesting: often on the ground, on a mossy mound or low on a broken stump or branch;

usually near water; small, well-hidden cup nest is made of moss, leaves and fine bark shreds; female incubates 4–5 eggs for 13 days.
Feeding: gleans foliage and the ground for invertebrates, frequently tossing aside vegetation with its bill; also dips into shallow water for aquatic invertebrates and very occasionally for small fish.
Voice: loud, penetrating *chew chew chew chew where-where-where-where-where.*
Similar Species: *Ovenbird* (p. 254): russet crown; lacks the pale eyebrow.

255

MACGILLIVRAY'S WARBLER

Oporornis tolmiei

Keeping to the densest and most impenetrable shrubs in the Rockies, the MacGillivray's Warbler is a very difficult bird to observe. To get a clear view you must often crouch down, peer deep into dark bushes and strain your neck in rapid response to the bird's faintly perceptible actions. A hard-earned glimpse of this bird is often satisfying, however, because the male MacGillivray's Warbler is certainly one of the most beautiful warblers in the Rockies. ■ Audubon named this warbler in honor of William MacGillivray, who edited and reworked the manuscript of Audubon's classic work but never set foot in North America. Another Scotsman, William Tolmie, is remembered in this bird's scientific name. Tolmie spent his adult life on the Pacific coast of North America, where he undoubt-edly had several encounters with this endearing warbler.

I.D.: *General:* yellow underparts; olive-green upperparts; broken, white eye ring; pinkish legs. *Male:* dark slate gray hood; black bib. *Female* and *Immature:* light gray-brown hood.

Size: L 5–5³/₄ in. (13–15 cm).

Range: common spring migrant and summer resident in the greater Yellowstone area, western Montana, eastern Idaho, western Alberta and eastern B.C.; uncommon migrant and summer breeder elsewhere in the Rockies.

Habitat: dense, deciduous riparian thickets and forests, shrubby understoreys and wooded urban areas from the foothills to the lower subalpine.

Nesting: in low trees or shrubs, between vertical stems; small cup nest is made with weeds and grasses; female incubates 4 eggs for up to 13 days.

Feeding: gleans low vegetation and the ground for beetles, bees, leafhoppers, insect larvae and other invertebrates.

Voice: clear, high-pitched, rolling *sweeter sweeter sweeter sugar sugar.*

Similar Species: *Nashville Warbler* (p. 242): yellow chin; complete eye ring. *Common Yellowthroat* (p. 257): female lacks the incomplete eye ring and the grayish throat.

COMMON YELLOWTHROAT
Geothlypis trichas

There is a great diversity of wood warblers in North American, so it isn't surprising that one has taken to inhabiting wetlands. The Common Yellowthroat shuns the forests so loved by most of its kin; instead it chooses to bound around in a world of cattails, bulrushes and willows. ▪ Although yellowthroats might stubbornly refuse to reveal themselves to a waiting pair of binoculars, their oscillating song is heard with very little effort. ▪ Common Yellowthroat nests are often parasitized by Brown-headed Cowbirds, which are primarily birds of open country and commonly target nests in less forested habitats.

I.D.: *General:* yellow throat; green upperparts; orange legs. *Breeding male:* black mask with a pale border. *Female:* no mask.

Size: L 4¹/₂–5¹/₂ in. (11–14 cm).

Range: common to fairly common migrant and summer resident throughout the Rockies.

Habitat: cattail marshes, riparian willow and alder clumps, sedge wetlands and beaver ponds from the foothills to the lower subalpine.

Nesting: low to the ground, usually in a small shrub or among reeds, cattails, bulrushes or other emergent vegetation; large, compact nest is made of weeds, grass and dead leaves; female incubates 3–5 eggs for 12 days.

Feeding: gleans vegetation and hovers for adult and larval insects, including dragonflies, spiders and beetles; occasionally eats seeds.

Voice: oscillating, clear *witchety witchety witchety-witch.*

Similar Species: male is distinctive. *Nashville Warbler* (p. 242): similar to a female yellowthroat, but with a complete eye ring and darker upperparts.

257

WILSON'S WARBLER
Wilsonia pusilla

Even a lazy-eyed glance into willow shrubs is sure to catch the energetic activity of a Wilson's Warbler busily hopping around at eye level. The yellow sparkle flickers quickly through the leaves and branches, as if a moment of motionlessness would seize its muscles and glue it in place. Because of this continuous dazzle, the Wilson's Warbler is one of the most pleasant songbirds to meet in the Rockies. Its lively movements do not seem to tire the small birds, but birdwatchers frequently feel exhausted: to view a Wilson's Warbler, for extended periods, one must often echo the birds actions and dart quickly from place to place in pursuit of this golden gem.
■ This bird is most deserving of its rich name. Named after Alexander Wilson, this bird epitomizes the energetic devotion that that pioneering ornithologist exhibited in the study of North American birds.

I.D.: *General:* yellow underparts; yellow-green upperparts; beady, black eyes; black bill; orange legs. *Breeding male:* black cap. *Female:* cap is very faint or absent.

Size: L 4¹/₂–5 in. (11–13 cm).

Range: fairly common summer resident throughout the Rockies; very common migrant in the southern U.S. Rockies; uncommon migrant in the central U.S. Rockies; common migrant in the Canadian and northern U.S. Rockies.

Habitat: shoreline willow and alder thickets, wet meadows, avalanche slopes, re-vegetated burns and krummholz areas from the foothills to the upper subalpine.

Nesting: on the ground, sunken into soft substrate, or in a low shrub or thicket; neat cup nest is made of moss, grass and leaves and occasionally lined with fine grass; female incubates 4–6 eggs for 10–13 days.

Feeding: gleans vegetation, hovers and catches insects on the wing; eats mostly adult and larval invertebrates.

Voice: during spring and summer, a chatty series that falls off at the end: *chi chi chi chi chet chet.*

Similar Species: male is distinctive. *Yellow Warbler* (p. 244): male is similar to a female Wilson's, but with red breast streaks, lighter upperparts and a shorter tail.

YELLOW-BREASTED CHAT
Icteria virens

At nearly 8 in. long, the Yellow-breasted Chat is quite literally a warbler and a half. In some ways it behaves like a typical warbler, with a curiosity and flitting habits that seem misplaced in so large a bird, but it is highly territorial, more like a catbird than a warbler. ■ Chats are bizarre birds, and they often attract attention to themselves through strange vocalizations and noisy thrashing in dense undergrowth. ■ 'Chat' is a wonderfully descriptive and imaginative name; anyone who encounters this bird will certainly leave with a 'chatty' impression of it.

I.D.: *Sexes similar:* white 'spectacles'; white 'jaw' line; heavy, black bill; yellow breast; white undertail coverts; olive-green upperparts; long tail; gray-black legs.

Size: *L* 7¹/₂ in. (19 cm).

Range: uncommon to fairly common migrant and summer breeder along the mesas and foothills of Colorado and Utah; very rare along the Rockies north of central Wyoming.

Habitat: riparian shrublands, shrubby coulees and oak, mahogany and skunkbrush woodlands in the foothills.

Nesting: low in a shrub or small tree; well-concealed, bulky nest is made of leaves, straw and weeds, with a tight inner cup woven with bark and plant fibers; female incubates 3–4 eggs for about 11 days.

Feeding: gleans low vegetation for insects.

Voice: whistles, *kuks* and 'laughs,' linked together or alone in no obvious arrangement.

Similar Species: *Nashville Warbler* (p. 242): much smaller; white eye ring; thinner bill.

259

WESTERN TANAGER
Piranga ludoviciana

No other bird found routinely in the Rockies can match the tropical splendor of a male Western Tanager. The golden body of the male, accentuated by black wings and a black tail, is often highlighted by a red crown. Indeed, the exotic appearance of the tanager is well deserved, because its family roots extend deeply into the rainforests of the New World. ■ The song of the male tanager can be difficult to learn, because it closely parallels the phrases of the robin's song. The tanager's hiccup-like *pit-a-tik* call, however, which drips frequently from its treetop perches, is distinctive. ■ 'Tanager' is derived from *tangara*, the Tupi name for this group of birds in the Amazon basin.

♂ ♀

breeding

I.D.: *Breeding male:* yellow underparts, wing bars and rump; black back, wings and tail; often red on the forehead or the entire head (variable); light-colored bill. *Breeding female:* olive-green overall; lighter underparts; darker upperparts; faint wing bars.
Size: *L* 7 in. (18 cm).
Range: common migrant and summer resident in the U.S. Rockies; uncommon migrant and summer resident in the Canadian Rockies.
Habitat: mature coniferous or mixedwood forests, especially Douglas-fir and ponderosa pine, and oak, pinyon-juniper and aspen woodlands from the foothills to the lower subalpine.

Nesting: on a horizontal branch or in fork in a conifer, well out from the trunk; cup nest is loosely built of twigs, grass and other plant materials and lined with fine vegetation; female incubates 4 eggs for 13–14 days.
Feeding: gleans vegetation and catches flying insects on the wing; eats wasps, beetles, flies and other insects, including caterpillars; also eats fruit.
Voice: call is a hiccup-like *pit-a-tik. Male:* song is hoarse and robin-like: *hurry, scurry, scurry, hurry.*
Similar Species: male is distinctive. *Bullock's Oriole* (p. 297) and *Baltimore Oriole* (p. 296): females have thinner bills and darker olive plumage.

GREEN-TAILED TOWHEE

Pipilo chlorurus

Sneaking into the southwestern backdoor of the Rockies, the Green-tailed Towhee follows the sagebrush and scrub flats into the mountains. In this dry community, its springtime courtship chorus carries above the sounds of most other birds. ▪ A classic double-scratcher at loose debris (quickly jumping forward and jumping back), the Green-tailed Towhee goes through life under the shade of small shrubs. If it cannot skulk away from threats, it will unwillingly flush, producing an annoyed mewing call. ▪ Echoing the common name, the scientific name *chlorurus* means 'green-tailed.'

I.D.: *Sexes similar. Adult:* rufous crown; metallic green upperparts; white throat outlined in black; sooty gray face and breast; gray legs; conical, gray bill. *Immature:* streaked upperparts; streaked underparts; pale throat outlined in black.

Size: L 6¹/₂–7 in. (17–18 cm).

Range: fairly common migrant and summer breeder and very rare winter resident in the southern U.S. Rockies; increasingly scarce with increasing elevation and latitude; uncommon migrant and breeder in the central U.S. Rockies.

Habitat: dry shrublands, primarily scrub oak, mountain mahogany, sagebrush, saltbrush, serviceberry and pinyon-juniper, in the lowlands and the foothills.

Nesting: on the ground or very low in a bush; deep, bulky, thick-walled cup nest is made of twigs, grass and bark shreds and lined with fine materials; female incubates 3–4 eggs for 11 days.

Feeding: scratches the ground for insects, seeds and berries; drinks morning dew from leaves; occasionally visits feeding stations.

Voice: 'squeally' and raspy trills: *swee-too weet chur cheee-churr.*

Similar Species: *Chipping Sparrow* (p. 264): clear white eyebrow; black eye line; lacks the green back. *American Tree Sparrow* (p. 263): clear-white throat; black breast spot; lacks the green upperparts. *Canyon Towhee:* lacks the white throat and the green back.

SPOTTED TOWHEE

Pipilo maculatus

Where dried leaves have accumulated on the ground under shrubs, one might easily hear a Spotted Towhee. This large sparrow, its side stained with orange or rufous, is a noisy forager, scratching at loose leaves with both feet. ▪ Spotted Towhees rarely leave their sub-arboreal world, except to proclaim their courtship song and to evaluate a threat in their territory. These cocky, spirited birds can often be enticed into view by 'squeaking' or 'pishing,' noises that alert curious birds to an intrusion. ▪ Until recently, the Spotted Towhee was grouped together with the Eastern Towhee, a spotless, eastern bird, as a single species known as the Rufous-sided Towhee.

I.D.: *Male:* black hood, back, wings and tail; rufous flanks; dark, conical bill; white spotting on the wings; white outer tail coverts; white belly and undertail. *Female:* somewhat paler overall.

Size: L 7–8¹/₂ in. (18–22 cm).

Range: common migrant and summer resident in the southern U.S. Rockies; rare migrant and summer visitor in the central U.S. Rockies; locally common breeder in the northern U.S. Rockies; very rare in the Canadian Rockies; rare winter resident in southern Colorado.

Habitat: shrubby fields, riparian shrublands, especially scrub oak, and dry woodlands, especially pinyon-juniper, in the lowlands and the foothills.

Nesting: low in a bush, on the ground under cover or in a brushy pile; cup nest is made with leaves, grass and bark shreds and lined with fine material; female (primarily) incubates 3–4 eggs for 12–13 days.

Feeding: scratches the ground vigorously for insects and seeds, including caterpillars, moths, beetles, ants and other common invertebrates; visits feeding stations periodically.

Voice: song is *here here here PLEASE*; call is a raspy or whining *chee*.

Similar Species: *Black-headed Grosbeak* (p. 285): red eyes; much heavier bill; lacks the rufous on the sides. *'Oregon' Dark-eyed Junco* (p. 282): smaller; pale rufous on the back as well as the sides.

AMERICAN TREE SPARROW
Spizella arborea

If you wanted to let the activities of birds guide your yearly calendar, there might be no better subject to follow than the American Tree Sparrow. With its unassuming but doggedly regular migratory habits, this species quietly announces the arrivals of spring and fall. The gentle flow of the American Tree Sparrow through the Rockies usually frames the emergence of willow leaves, and it is rarely seen perched atop anything but bare branches. ▪ While both its common and scientific names (*arborea* means 'tree') might imply that this is a forest-dwelling bird, tree sparrows are most often found in semi-open areas. As an Arctic-nesting bird that prefers bushes to trees, perhaps a more appropriate name would be 'Arctic Shrub Sparrow.'

I.D.: *Sexes similar:* pale rufous cap; unstreaked breast; dark, central breast spot; gray face; soft gray underparts; mottled brown upperparts; dark legs; dark upper mandible; light lower mandible.
Size: L 5½–6½ in. (14–17 cm).
Range: uncommon migrant and winter visitor in the Colorado, Utah, Wyoming and Montana Rockies; rare migrant elsewhere in the Rockies.
Habitat: brushy thickets, roadside shrubs, semi-open fields and agricultural areas in the lowlands.
Nesting: typically along the arctic tundra-taiga transition zone; usually on the ground; often on a raised tussock or other dry area; small cup nest is woven with grass, moss and bark shreds and lined with feathers and fur; female incubates 3–5 eggs for 12–13 days.
Feeding: scratches exposed soil or snow for native plant seeds and occasionally insects; occasionally visits feeding stations during migration and winter.
Voice: sometimes practices its breeding song before departing for the Arctic: *tseet* notes followed by a warble or trill.
Similar Species: *Chipping Sparrow* (p. 264): clear black eye line; white eyebrow; lacks the central breast spot. *Swamp Sparrow* (p. 322): lacks the central breast spot and white wing bars.

CHIPPING SPARROW

Spizella passerina

If you hear a rapid trill in a Rocky Mountain forest, you will probably have to track down the singer to be sure of its species: both the Chipping Sparrow and the Dark-eyed Junco sing similar tunes. ▪ Chipping Sparrows are bright, cheery summer inhabitants of many types of forests. They are found from the forest floor to the spires of conifers, nodding their white eyebrows toward attentive naturalists. ▪ This sparrow commonly nests at eye level, so you could have the fortune of watching the breeding and nest building rituals close-up. ▪ 'Chipping' refers to this bird's call, while *passerina* is Latin for 'little sparrow.'

I.D.: *Sexes similar:* prominent rufous cap; white eyebrow; black eye line; light gray, unstreaked underparts; mottled brown upperparts; all-dark bill; 2 faint wing bars; light-colored legs.

Size: L 5–6 in. (13–15 cm).

Range: common to abundant migrant and summer breeder throughout the Rockies.

Habitat: dry coniferous forests, mixed forests, pure deciduous forests and forest edges from the lowlands to the upper subalpine.

Nesting: usually low to mid-level in a coniferous tree; compact cup nest is woven with grass, rootlets and fine weeds and lined with fur (often using black horsehair if available); female incubates 3–4 eggs for 11–14 days.

Feeding: hops along the ground and outer branches gleaning seeds, especially from grasses, dandelions and clovers; also eats adult and larval invertebrates; occasionally visits feeding stations.

Voice: simple, long, frequently heard trill; call is a high-pitched *chip*.

Similar Species: *American Tree Sparrow* (p. 263): central breast spot; lacks the bold white eyebrow and the black eye line. *Swamp Sparrow* (p. 322): lacks the white eyebrow, the black eye line and the wing bars.

CLAY-COLORED SPARROW

Spizella pallida

Short, plaintive buzzes, despite their insect-like qualities, are produced by this small, subdued sparrow as it darts from aspen edges and shrubby fields. Clay-colored Sparrows are often overlooked because of their plumage, habit and voice—all expertly contribute to an introverted lifestyle. ■ Despite its subdued nature, a Clay-colored Sparrow can be spotted if a little time and patience are used to find the source of its odd song. This sparrow often perches motionlessly on an exposed branch, as if it knows that its drab characteristics provide adequate concealment and protection. ■ The subtlety of the Clay-colored Sparrow contributes to its unassuming beauty. By having to study the bird closely to assure its identification, the observer unknowingly gains an appreciation of the delicate shading, texture and form so often over-looked in birds with more colorful plumage.

breeding

I.D.: *Sexes similar:* light brown cheek edged with darker brown; light brown, unstreaked breast; white eyebrow; light 'jaw' stripe; dark crown with a pale stripe through the center; pale bill; light-colored legs.
Size: L 5–5¹/₂ in. (13–14 cm).
Range: common summer breeder and uncommon migrant in the Canadian and northern U.S. Rockies; uncommon to rare breeder and migrant in the central U.S. Rockies; rare elsewhere in the Rockies.
Habitat: forest edges, birch and willow shrubs, patches of rose bushes, semi-open areas and open deciduous forests in the lower montane.
Nesting: very low in a grassy tuft or small bush; cup nest is woven with grass and small roots and lined with fine materials, including fur; pair incubates 3–4 bluish-green, speckled eggs for 10–12 days.
Feeding: forages on the ground and gleans low vegetation for seeds; also eats grass-hoppers and other insects.
Voice: call is a soft *chip*; song is an insect-like, repeated, flat buzz that usually skips between 2–3 pitches.
Similar Species: *Brewer's Sparrow* (p. 266): less contrast in the face markings; faint eye ring; faint (if present) crown stripe.

265

BREWER'S SPARROW
Spizella breweri

Strip away all the breast streaks, caps, crown stripes and facial markings that adorn most other sparrows and you're left with the Brewer's Sparrow. ■ This drab sparrow has a very interesting distribution in the Rockies: as a bird of open country, it lives in hot, dry sagebrush flats and chilly alpine areas, but nowhere in-between. ■ Thomas Mayo Brewer, M.D., made significant contributions to the understanding of the breeding behavior of North American birds. Unfortunately, he is best remembered as leading the 'winning side' of the House Sparrow war, which resulted in the introduction of that species to North America.

breeding

I.D.: *Sexes similar:* light brown, unstreaked underparts; brown cheek patch; faint eye ring; finely streaked, brown upperparts; pale bill; light throat; pale eyebrow and 'jaw' stripes; light-colored legs.

Size: L 5–5¹/₂ in. (13–14 cm).

Range: common summer breeder throughout the Rockies; common migrant in the southern Rockies; uncommon migrant in the northern Rockies.

Habitat: willow and birch shrubbery, krummholz and avalanche slopes in the subalpine, and (in the southern Rockies) in grasslands, prairies and sagebrush shrublands in the lowlands.

Nesting: in a low, dense shrub; small, compact cup nest is woven with grass and roots and lined with fine materials and fur; pair incubates 3–5 eggs for 11–13 days.

Feeding: forages on the ground and gleans low vegetation for adult and larval invertebrates and seeds.

Voice: extremely variable, canary-like song with buzzes and trills, up to 10 seconds long; often includes trills of different speeds and pitches in the same song.

Similar Species: *Clay-colored Sparrow* (p. 265): more pronounced facial markings and crown stripe; no eye ring.

VESPER SPARROW
Pooecetes gramineus

Living on the flat plains that swarm with multitudes of confusing sparrows, the Vesper Sparrow offers birdwatchers a welcome relief: a chestnut patch tucked neatly on the bird's shoulder announces its identity in flight. While perched, its dress is off-the-rack sparrow drab, but its song is simple and customized. This grass-loving bird is one of the lead singers of the prairie chorus, backed up by a multitude of prairie bells. ■ 'Vesper' is from the Latin for 'evening,' a time when this bird sings. The scientific name refers to this species's preferred habitat: *Pooecetes* is Greek for 'grass dweller,' and *gramineus* is Latin for 'grass-loving.'

I.D.: *Sexes similar:* chestnut shoulder patch; white outer tail feathers; pale yellow lore; weak flank streaking; white eye ring; dark upper mandible; lighter lower mandible; light-colored legs.

Size: L 5¹/₂–6¹/₂ in. (14–17 cm).

Range: common summer resident in the U.S. Rockies; uncommon summer resident in the Canadian Rockies.

Habitat: grasslands, semi-open shrublands, agricultural areas and railway rights-of-way from the lowlands to the montane.

Nesting: in a scrape on the ground, often under a canopy of grass; small cup nest is woven with grass and lined with finer materials; female (primarily) incubates 4–5 eggs for 11–13 days.

Feeding: walks and runs along the ground, picking up grasshoppers, beetles, cutworms and seeds.

Voice: 4 characteristic, preliminary notes followed by an aimless melody: *here-here there-there, everybody-down-the-hill.*

Similar Species: *Savannah Sparrow* (p. 271): lacks the white outer tail feathers and the chestnut shoulder patch. *Baird's Sparrow* (p. 322): well-defined 'necklace'; lacks the white outer tail feathers. *Lincoln's Sparrow* (p. 277): buffy wash on the breast; lacks the white outer tail feathers.

LARK SPARROW
Chondestes grammacus

Good habitat for the Lark Sparrow is easy to spot: the air is dry, the landscape is baked by blazing summer days and the sweet smell of sage soaks the arid flats. There, the Lark Sparrow can be observed singing atop short bushes or on rocky ledges, proclaiming itself to its distinct habitat. ■ Arid sagebrush flats and grasslands are limited in the Rockies, so the Lark Sparrow is not typically thought of as a bird of these mountains. Attentive naturalists could have the fortune of spotting one of these handsome sparrows, however, should the appropriate habitat be encountered. The sight of a typical Great Plains bird in the Rocky Mountains reinforces to the visitor the multitude of ecoregions and the great diversity of life that occurs within this region.

I.D.: *Sexes similar:* distinctive 'helmet' made up of a white throat, eyebrow and crown stripe and a few black lines breaking up an otherwise chestnut-red head; pale, unstreaked breast; central breast spot; black tail with white outer tail feathers; soft brown, mottled back and wings; light-colored legs.
Size: *L* 6 in. (15 cm).
Range: common summer resident and uncommon migrant in the extreme southern Rockies; vagrant in the central U.S. Rockies; locally uncommon in the northern U.S. Rockies; vagrant in the Canadian Rockies.
Habitat: grasslands, semi-open shrublands, agricultural areas, sagebrush and pinyon-juniper woodlands in the lowlands and the foothills.

Nesting: on the ground or in a low bush; bulky cup nest is made of grass and twigs and lined with finer material; occasionally reuses abandoned thrasher or mockingbird nests; female incubates 4–5 eggs for 11–12 days.
Feeding: walks or hops on the ground, gleaning seeds; also eats grasshoppers and other invertebrates.
Voice: melodious and variable song that consists of short trills, buzzes, pauses and clear notes.
Similar Species: no other sparrow has the distinctive head pattern.

SAGE SPARROW
Amphispiza belli

The harsh, arid areas of the southwestern Rockies are home to a select few special-ized birds. As its name suggests, the Sage Sparrow thrives in this region of sage-brush and hard, packed soil. Almost like a mouse, this sparrow runs swiftly among the short shrubs with its head lowered and its tail held high. ▪ The Sage Sparrow is rarely seen in the Rockies, and a quick glimpse of one scurrying on the ground or diving from its sagebrush perch is all you can reasonably expect. ▪ The scientific name honors John Graham Bell, New York's finest taxidermist—he taught that skill to a young Theodore Roosevelt. Bell traveled with Audubon to the Yellowstone River, and together they documented many of the species described in this book.

I.D.: *Sexes similar:* white underparts; central breast spot; finely streaked flanks; gray-brown, mottled upperparts; faint, light eyebrow and 'jaw' line; dark tail; light legs; faint eye ring; faint wing bars.
Size: *L* 5–6 in. (13–15 cm).
Range: locally uncommon migrant and sum-mer resident in the southern U.S. Rockies.
Habitat: dry sagebrush flats and semi-desert shrublands in the lowlands.
Nesting: typically in the Great Basin; usually in a fork in a sagebrush; occasionally on the ground or under a bush; cup nest is woven with twigs, grass and bark shreds and lined with fine materials; female incubates 3–4 bluish-white eggs, speckled with brown, for 13–16 days.
Voice: high-pitched tinkles: *tsit-tsoo-tsee-tsay.*
Similar Species: *Black-throated Sparrow* (p. 322): black throat. *Lark Sparrow* (p. 268): red facial markings. *Brewer's Sparrow* (p. 266): brown plumage; lacks the central breast spot.

LARK BUNTING
Calamospiza melanocorys

Where the grasslands collide with the eastern slopes of the Rockies, you might be lucky to witness the annual courtship of the Lark Bunting. Like a large butterfly, the male flutters, beating his wings slowly and deeply, and rises high above the flat prairie. His bell-like, tinkling song spreads over the flat landscape, until he folds in his wings and floats to the ground like a falling leaf. ▪ The Lark Bunting's courtship behavior might be influenced by times before fenceposts and power poles. Because there were no high points on which to perch, Lark Buntings learned to deliver their songs on the wing. ▪ The scientific name *melanocorys* is Greek for 'black lark'; although the Lark Bunting, the state bird of Colorado, is not related to the Sky Lark, its manner of singing in flight reminded pioneering naturalists of that European bird.

♂

breeding

I.D.: *General:* dark, conical bill. *Breeding male:* all-black plumage; large, white wing and tail-tip patches. *Female:* large, white wing patch; mottled brown upperparts; lightly streaked underparts; pale eyebrow.
Size: *L* 7 in. (18 cm).
Range: rare migrant and uncommon summer resident in the Colorado Rockies; rare northward to Yellowstone; uncommon summer resident all along the eastern edge of the U.S. Rockies.
Habitat: shortgrass prairie, sagebrush flats and open areas in the southeastern lowlands.

Nesting: typically on the Great Plains; on the ground, sheltered by a canopy of grasses or a small bush; cup nest is loosely built with grass, roots and other plant materials and lined with plant down and fur; female (primarily) incubates 4–5 pale blue eggs for 11–12 days.
Feeding: walks or hops along the ground gleaning insects, including grasshoppers, beetles and ants, seeds and waste grain.
Voice: rich and warbling, with clear notes.
Similar Species: all other sparrows lack the white wing patch. *Bobolink* (p. 288): male has a creamy nape, a white rump and white back patches.

SAVANNAH SPARROW
Passerculus sandwichensis

The Savannah Sparrow is a common bird of the open country. Its dull brown plumage and streaked breast conceal it perfectly in the long grass of its preferred habitat. It's most often seen darting across roads, highways and open fields. Savannah Sparrows resort to flight only as a last alternative; they prefer to run swiftly and inconspicuously through the long grass, like feathered voles. ▪ The common and scientific names of this bird reflect its broad distribution: 'Savannah' refers to the city in Georgia, while *sandwichensis* is derived from Sandwich Bay in the Aleutians off Alaska.

I.D.: *Sexes similar:* finely streaked breast; light, streaked underparts; mottled, brown upperparts; yellow lore; light 'jaw' line; light legs; light bill.

Size: L 5–6¹/₂ in. (13–17 cm).

Range: common to very common summer breeder throughout the Rockies.

Habitat: *Breeding:* moist meadows, marshy edges and weedy fields in the lowlands. *Fall migration:* forages in the subalpine and the alpine.

Nesting: on the ground, in a scrape sheltered by a canopy of grass or a small bush; cup nest is woven with grass and lined with finer materials; pair incubates 3–4 eggs for 12–13 days.

Feeding: walks or runs on the ground, occasionally scratching for seeds and insects.

Voice: clear, distinct *tea tea tea teeeeea Today!*

Similar Species: *Vesper Sparrow* (p. 267): white outer tail feathers; chestnut shoulder patches. *Lincoln's Sparrow* (p. 277): buffy 'jaw' line; buffy wash across the breast; grayer face. *Baird's Sparrow* (p. 322): buffy head and nape. *Grasshopper Sparrow* (p. 272): unstreaked breast.

271

GRASSHOPPER SPARROW
Ammodramus savannarum

This open-country bird is named not for its diet but rather for one of its buzzy, insect-like songs. Males sing two completely different, squeaky courtship songs, one short and the other sustained. ▪ The courtship flight is brutish: the males chase the females through the air, buzzing at a frequency that is inaudible to our ears. ▪ If a nesting female Grasshopper Sparrow is flushed from her nest, she will run quietly away, swiftly separating herself from the danger. ▪ *Ammodramus* is Greek for 'sand runner,' and *savannarum* is Latin for 'savanna,' its typical habitat.

I.D.: *Sexes similar:* unstreaked breast; unmarked face; buffy cheek; flat head; pale legs; mottled, brown upperparts; beady, black eyes; sharp tail; pale crown stripe.
Size: L 4¹/₂–5¹/₄ in. (11–13 cm).
Range: uncommon migrant and summer resident in northwestern Montana; rare to very rare migrant elsewhere in the Rockies.
Habitat: grasslands, weedy fields and native prairies up to the montane.
Nesting: on the Great Plains; occasionally semi-colonial; in a shallow depression on the ground, usually under a dome of bent grass; small cup nest is woven with grass and lined with plant fibers, fur and small roots; female incubates 4–5 eggs for 12–13 days.
Feeding: gleans the ground and low plants, pecking and scurrying through the grass; eats mainly grasshoppers; also eats other invertebrates and seeds.
Voice: song is an insect-like buzz: *pit-tuck zee-ee-e-e-e-e-e-e.*
Similar Species: *LeConte's Sparrow* (p. 273): buffy-orange face markings. *Nelson's Sharp-tailed Sparrow* (p. 274): orangish face; gray cheeks and shoulders. *Baird's Sparrow* (p. 322): faint 'necklace'; 2 stripes bordering a white chin.

LECONTE'S SPARROW
Ammodramus leconteii

With sputtering wing beats, flushed LeConte's Sparrows fly weakly over their marshy habitats before they unexpectedly seem to crash into the mass of grasses. LeConte's Sparrows are secretive birds that are usually difficult to observe; even singing males choose low perches from which to offer their love ballads. ▪ The LeConte's Sparrow's song is very similar to that of a Grasshopper Sparrow, but it is even weaker, briefer and more buzzy. ▪ Dr. John LeConte is best remembered as being one of the pre-eminent American entomologists of the 19th century, but he was interested in all areas of natural history.

I.D.: *Sexes similar:* buffy-orange face markings; gray cheek; orange breast; lightly streaked breast; light crown stripe; mottled brown upperparts; light legs.
Size: L 4¹/₂–5 in. (11–13 cm).
Range: uncommon summer resident in Jasper NP; rare in the northern U.S. Rockies and elsewhere in the Canadian Rockies.
Habitat: flooded sedge and grass meadows and willow flats in the lower montane.
Nesting: typically in the prairies and grass-lands of southern Canada and the north-central U.S.; on the ground or very low in a shrub; well-concealed cup is placed in dry areas of marshland and woven with grass; female incubates 3–5 eggs for 12–13 days.

Feeding: forages on the ground and gleans low vegetation for insects, spiders and seeds.
Voice: *Male:* quick, insect-like buzz: *take-it ea-zy!*
Similar Species: *Nelson's Sharp-tailed Sparrow* (p. 274): gray nape with white streaks on the back. *Grasshopper Sparrow* (p. 272): lacks the dark streaking on the breast. *Baird's Sparrow* (p. 322): lacks the buffy-orange in the face.

273

NELSON'S SHARP-TAILED SPARROW
Ammodramus nelsoni

Its hard to find a Nelson's Sharp-tailed Sparrow without getting your feet wet. As a species of marshy areas, these colorful sparrows unexpectedly pop out of their soggy hiding places, occasionally perching completely exposed at close distances.

▪ These birds have a very unusual breeding strategy: males rove around the marsh mating with all available females. Both sexes are promiscuous, and this sparrow does not establish pair bonds or territories.

▪ Edward William Nelson was the chief of the U.S. Biological Survey and president of the American Ornithologists' Union. When he was 17, he traveled to the Rockies, but his greatest contribution was the creation of the Migratory Bird Treaty, still in effect today.

I.D.: *Sexes similar:* orangish face; gray cheek; gray nape; lightly streaked breast; white stripes on the back; light bill.

Size: L 5–5³/₄ in. (13–15 cm).

Range: very rare migrant along the eastern slopes of the Canadian Rockies.

Habitat: marshlands with tall emergent and shoreline vegetation.

Nesting: typically across the Canadian prairies; on the ground or low in upright grass or sedge stems; bulky cup nest is woven with dry grass and sedges and lined with fine materials; female incubates 3–5 eggs for 11 days.

Feeding: runs or walks along the ground gleaning ants, beetles, grasshoppers and often invertebrates; also eats seeds.

Voice: raspy *ts tse-sheeeee*.

Similar Species: *LeConte's Sparrow* (p. 273): lacks the gray nape and the white stripes on the back. *Grasshopper Sparrow* (p. 272): lacks the streaking on the breast. *Savannah Sparrow* (p. 271): yellow is restricted to the lores.

FOX SPARROW
Passerella iliaca

Despite this large sparrow's shrub-loving tendencies, it is commonly met along paths through Rocky Mountain forests. ■ It is not so much the bird's handsome plumage but its noisy habits that strike the observer's attention. The Fox Sparrow is a ruthless and noisy forager. By scratching vigorously on the forest floor, this large sparrow shifts dry leaf litter, often betraying its own presence in the understorey. The voice of the Fox Sparrow is one of the most distinctive in the Rockies. It is as inspiring to the attentive listener as the bugles of elk or the howls of wolves. ■ It is the Fox Sparrow's rufous-red lower back and tail that give it its name.

I.D.: *Sexes similar:* heavily streaked underparts; grayish upperparts; reddish tail and flight feathers; streaking on the breast often merges to a central spot; light gray bill; light legs.
Size: L 6¹/₂–7¹/₂ in. (17–19 cm).
Range: rare migrant and fairly common summer breeder in most of the Rockies; rare in Yellowstone and Rocky Mountain NPs.
Habitat: riparian willow flats, dense woodland thickets, avalanche slopes, open forests, forest edges and willow meadows up to the subalpine.
Nesting: on the ground or low in a shrub or small tree; cup nest is woven with twigs, grass,

moss and bark shreds and often lined with the hair of large mammals; female incubates 3–4 eggs for 12–14 days.
Feeding: scratches the ground to uncover seeds, berries and invertebrates. *In migration:* visits backyard feeding stations, foraging on seeds that have dropped to the ground.
Voice: variable; long, warbling *All I have is what's here dear, won't you won't you take it?*
Similar Species: *Song Sparrow* (p. 276): generally has an eye line and an eyebrow; lighter breast streaking. *Hermit Thrush* (p. 229): lighter breast streaking; thin bill. *Swainson's Thrush* (p. 228): olive tail; light breast streaks; prominent eye ring.

SONG SPARROW
Melospiza melodia

What surprises are produced by this bird! The Song Sparrow's drab, heavily streaked plumage doesn't prepare you for its symphonic song. This common sparrow usually begins with three sharp *hip-hip-hip* notes, and then ends its tune with a prolonged melody. Many beginner birdwatchers hesitate at the song of the Song Sparrow, because the tune conjures up ideas of a far more exotic species. The Song Sparrow stands among the great Rocky Mountain songsters for its song's complexity, rhythm and emotion.

■ Song Sparrows (and many other songbirds) learn to sing by eaves-dropping on their fathers or on rival males. This influence is so great that by the time the male is a few months old, he will have the basis for his song.

■ The scientific name *melodia* means 'melody' in Greek.

I.D.: *Sexes similar:* heavy breast streaking that often converges into a central spot; gray face with a dark eye line; white 'jaw' line (as if milk has dribbled from its bill); red-brown crown (often erect) with a gray stripe; mottled back; white throat; plumage is variable throughout its range.

Size: L 5¹/₂–7 in. (14–18 cm).

Range: uncommon migrant and common summer breeder throughout the Rockies; uncommon winter resident in the U.S. Rockies.

Habitat: willow shrublands and shrubby riparian areas in the foothills and the lower montane.

Nesting: usually on the ground; occasionally in a shrub or small tree; cup nest is woven with grass, leaves and bark shreds and lined with fine materials; female incubates 3–5 eggs for 12–14 days.

Feeding: gleans the ground, shrubs and trees for cutworms, beetles, grasshoppers, ants, various bugs and seeds; also eats wild fruit and visits feeding stations.

Voice: 1–3 distinctive introductory notes, followed by a pleasant melody: *Hip Hip Hip Hurray Boys, the spring is here again* or *Maids Maids Maids, hang up your tea kettle kettle kettle.*

Similar Species: *Fox Sparrow* (p. 275): heavier breast streaking; generally a plain face. *Lincoln's Sparrow* (p. 277): lightly streaked breast with a buffy wash; buffy 'jaw' line. *Savannah Sparrow* (p. 271): lightly streaked breast; yellow lore; lacks the gray face.

LINCOLN'S SPARROW
Melospiza lincolnii

There is a certain beauty in the Lincoln's Sparrow that is greater than the sum of its feather patterns. The sights, sounds and smells of this bird's natural habitat seem to magnify the bird's appearance. ▪ The Lincoln's Sparrow appears to be more fearful than many other sparrows in the Rockies. It only sits openly on exposed vegetation and look-out perches when it is defending its nest or singing its bubbly courtship song. ▪ The nesting territories of Lincoln's Sparrows are frequently flooded by snow melt and swollen streams through the spring and early summer. ▪ This sparrow bears the name of Thomas Lincoln, a young companion to Audubon on his voyage to Labrador.

I.D.: *Sexes similar:* lightly streaked breast with a buffy wash; buffy 'jaw' line; gray eyebrow; brown cheek; dark cap; white belly; gray collar; brown-gray, mottled upperparts; very faint, white eye ring.
Size: L 5³/₄ in. (15 cm).
Range: common migrant and summer resident throughout the Rockies.
Habitat: shrubby meadows, shoreline forests, bog edges, wetlands with emergent sedges and tall shoreline vegetation and roadsides from the foothills to the lower subalpine.
Nesting: on the ground, often sunk into soft moss or concealed beneath shrubs; well-hidden cup nest is woven with dry grass and lined with fine materials; female incubates 4–5 eggs for 11–14 days.
Feeding: scratches at the ground, exposing invertebrates and seeds; occasionally visits feeding stations.
Voice: very wren-like warble, *kee kee kee, see see seedle seedle seedle see-see-see-see*, with a trill in the middle.
Similar Species: *Song Sparrow* (p. 276): heavier breast streaking; white 'jaw' line. *Savannah Sparrow* (p. 271): yellow lore; white eyebrow and 'jaw' line.

WHITE-THROATED SPARROW
Zonotrichia albicollis

While the White-throated Sparrow might lack the physical stature of many of the Rockies' most renowned vocalists, its song rings memorably in the ears of all those who have visited northern woods during summer. This handsome sparrow's simple song is freely offered throughout most spring months. The song's purposeful phrases are occasionally delivered late into the night; these midnight trills break late evening chills for attentive campers. ▪ *Zonotrichia* means 'hair-like,' in reference to the striped head of birds of this genus; *albicollis* is Latin for 'white neck.'

I.D.: *Sexes similar:* black-and-white (or brown-and-tan), striped head; white throat; gray cheek; yellow lore; black eye line; gray, unstreaked underparts; mottled, brown upperparts.
Size: L 6¹/₂–7¹/₄ in. (17–18 cm).
Range: uncommon summer resident in the Canadian Rockies; rare migrant and winter visitor elsewhere in the Rockies.
Habitat: willow shrublands, mixed forest edges, mixed deciduous forests, river floodplains and brushy areas in the montane.
Nesting: typically in the boreal forest; usually on the ground, concealed under a fallen log; occasionally in a low shrub; cup nest is woven with grass, twigs and conifer needles and lined with fur and fine materials; female incubates 4–6 eggs for 11–14 days.
Feeding: scratches the ground to expose invertebrates, seeds and fruit; gleans vegetation and catches invertebrates in flight. *Winter:* visits feeding stations.
Voice: clear and distinct *dear sweet Canada Canada Canada*; variable but always recognizable.
Similar Species: *White-crowned Sparrow* (p. 279): lacks the white throat and the yellow lore. *Swamp Sparrow* (p. 322): rusty cap; slightly streaked breast.

WHITE-CROWNED SPARROW

Zonotrichia leucophrys

Among Rocky Mountain sparrows, the White-crown takes center stage, stealing the spotlight from its peers. A large, bold, colorful and vocal bird, the White-crowned Sparrow can be seen by everyone who visits the mountains in summer. ▪ The White-crowned Sparrows found in the Canadian Rockies tend to have white lores, while those in the U.S. Rockies have black lores. ▪ This bird is the most studied sparrow in North America. It has given science tremendous insight on physiology and geographic variation in song dialects. ▪ The scientific name *leucophrys* is Greek for 'white eyebrow.'

I.D.: *Sexes similar:* large, white crown bordered by black; white eyebrow; black eye line; orange-pink bill; gray face; gray, unstreaked underparts; brown, streaked back.
Size: *L* 5¹/₂–7 in. (14–18 cm).
Range: common to very common migrant and summer breeder throughout the Rockies; common winter resident in the Rockies south of Montana.
Habitat: open environments with shrubby meadows, krummholz, alpine and riparian willow shrubs from the montane to the alpine.

Nesting: usually in a shrub or small coniferous tree or on the ground; neat cup nest is woven with twigs, grass, leaves and bark shreds and lined with fine materials; female incubates 3–5 eggs for 11–14 days.
Feeding: scratches the ground to expose insects and seeds; also eats berries, buds and moss caps; visits feeding stations.
Voice: variable; frequently *I-I-I gotta go wee-wee now!*
Similar Species: *White-throated Sparrow* (p. 278): clearly defined, white throat; darker bill; yellow lore. *Golden-crowned Sparrow* (p. 280): golden-yellow fore crown; dark bill.

GOLDEN-CROWNED SPARROW
Zonotrichia atricapilla

Aside from the spectacular views, one of the rewards of climbing peaks in the Canadian Rocky Mountains is walking through the world of the Golden-crowned Sparrow. Breeding in the open, scrubby areas near treeline, Golden-crowned Sparrows offer their sad, flat song to the challenging landscape. ▪ Exhausted people crossing the Northern Rockies during the Gold Rush were further disheartened by the dreary *Oh dear me* call from the surrounding shrubs. Ironically, the only gold most men were to encounter on their trip was on the crowns of these mountaineering songbirds. ▪ The scientific name *atricapilla* is Latin for 'black hair,' in reference to the broad outline of the gold crown.

I.D.: *Sexes similar:* heavy black eyebrows that converge on the nape; golden-yellow fore crown; gray hind crown; gray face; dark bill; long tail; gray-brown, unstreaked underparts; streaked upperparts; faint, white wing bars.
Size: L 6–7 in. (15–18 cm).
Range: uncommon migrant and common summer resident in the Canadian Rockies; rare in Waterton Lakes and Glacier NPs; vagrant elsewhere in the U.S. Rockies.
Habitat: high-elevation meadows, mountain tundra and stunted fir and spruce forests in the upper subalpine and the alpine.

Nesting: usually in a scrape or depression on the ground, near the base of a shrub or small tree; bulky cup nest is woven with grass, twigs, leaves and bark shreds and lined with fine materials; 4–5 eggs.
Feeding: gleans the ground for invertebrates, buds, seeds and occasionally fruit.
Voice: 3–5 notes: *Oh dear me* or *three blind mice.*
Similar Species: *White-crowned Sparrow* (p. 279): lacks the golden-yellow crown. *Harris's Sparrow* (p. 322): black bib; orange-pink bill.

LAPLAND LONGSPUR
Calcarius lapponicus

Lapland Longspurs wheel about in uncountable masses over frozen fields that farmers vacate for the winter. In early fall, Lapland Longspurs can be seen in the lower mountains, but as winter sets in, they move to the foothills and plains. They might have left their beautiful spring plumage behind in the Arctic, but they now show communal grace in their flocking synchrony. ▪ These winter residents of farmlands feed themselves by scraping away the ice and snow to reach the grains the combines could not catch. ▪ This species breeds across northern polar regions, including the area of northern Europe known as Lapland.

non-breeding

I.D.: *Non-breeding:* white outer tail feathers; often has rufous in the wings; light underparts; mottled upperparts; lightly streaked flanks; dark bill; male has pale chestnut on the nape; female lacks the chestnut nape.
Size: L 6¼ in. (16 cm).
Range: uncommon fall migrant along the eastern slopes of the Rockies; rare winter resident in the U.S. Rockies.
Habitat: grasslands, stubble fields. *In migration:* alpine meadows.

Nesting: on the tundra; in a shallow depression on a hummock; cup nest is woven with moss, grass and fur; female incubates 4–6 eggs for 12–13 days.
Feeding: *Winter:* gleans the ground and snow for seeds and waste grain. *Summer:* eats insects and seeds.
Voice: flight song is a rapid warbling; musical calls, plus a dry rattle in flight.
Similar Species: *Snow Bunting* (p. 284): shows white and black patterning in flight; lacks the brown mottling on the back.

281

DARK-EYED JUNCO
Junco hyemalis

Frequently encountered by hikers from Colorado to the Yukon, the Dark-eyed Juncos living in various regions have taken on decidedly different plumages. If one were to travel the length of the mountains, it would prove to be a gratifying personal study to map the ranges of the various subspecies. ■ Juncos are ground dwellers that are frequently observed flushing along wooded trails. The distinctive, white outer tail feathers will flash in alarm as the otherwise dark junco flies down the narrow path before diving into a thicket. ■ The scientific name *hyemalis* is New Latin for 'wintry,' an allusion to this junco's annual arrival in the southern U.S., which usually foretells the coming of the winter.

'Oregon Junco'

'Gray-headed Junco'

I.D.: *General:* all forms have white outer tail feathers and a pink bill. *'Oregon Junco':* reddish-brown back and flanks; white belly; male has a black hood and a gray rump; female has a dark brown hood and a brown rump. *'Pink-sided Junco':* gray head; pink flanks; white belly; light brown back. *'Gray-headed Junco':* chestnut-red back; otherwise gray; black lore. *'Slate-colored Junco':* white belly; male is otherwise all gray; female is otherwise brown-gray. *'White-winged Junco':* 2 white wing bars; male is slate-gray overall; female is brown-gray.
Size: *L* 5–6³/₄ in. (13–17 cm).

'Slate-colored Junco'

'Pink-sided Junco' ♂

'White-winged Junco' ♂

Range: *'Oregon Junco':* very common migrant and summer breeder in the Canadian and northern U.S. Rockies; very common winter resident in the southern U.S. Rockies; uncommon migrant in the Yellowstone area; rare winter resident north of Colorado. *'Pink-sided Junco':* very common migrant and summer breeder and uncommon winter resident in Yellowstone NP; common winter resident in the southern U.S. Rockies. *'Gray-headed Junco':* common year-round resident in the southern U.S. Rockies. *'Slate-colored Junco':* common in the lower valleys of Banff and Jasper NPs and in the Canadian foothills; uncommon migrant and rare winter resident in the central U.S. Rockies. *'White-winged Junco':* rare winter resident in the Colorado Rockies.

Habitat: coniferous and mixed forests, shrublands, roadsides, wooded urban areas, forest edges and avalanche slopes from the foothills to the upper subalpine.

Nesting: usually on the ground, often with an overhanging canopy, or low in a shrub or tree; deep cup nest is woven with grass, bark strips and roots and lined with fine materials and fur; female incubates 3–5 eggs for 12–13 days.

Feeding: scratches the ground for invertebrates, especially spiders, beetles, caterpillars, true bugs, ants and wasps; also eats berries and seeds; commonly visits feeding stations.

Voice: long, dry trill; call is a 'smacking' note.

Similar Species: none.

SNOW BUNTING
Plectrophenax nivalis

When autumn snows dust the eastern slopes of the Rockies, Snow Buntings are surely close behind. Unlike most migrant songbirds found in the Rockies, Snow Buntings arrive in the Rockies in fall and endure winter in small, tight flocks. Although wintering Snow Buntings prefer the endless and expansive open areas of the Great Plains, each winter a few of these hardy songbirds arrive to scratch and peck at exposed seeds and grains in open areas of the Rockies. ▪ As flocks of Snow Buntings lift in unison, the startling black-and-white contrast of their plumage flashes characteristically against the clean white backdrop. ▪ The northern wanderings of summer Snow Buntings are not exceeded by any other songbird. A single individual (likely misguided and lost) has been recorded not far from the North Pole.

♂

♀

non-breeding

Nesting: in the northern Arctic; in a rocky crevice, among boulders or on the ground; bulky cup nest is loosely built of grass, lichens and roots and lined with feathers and fur; female incubates 4–7 eggs for 10–16 days.

I.D.: *Non-breeding:* white underparts; light golden-brown crown and back (male has a paler back); pale bill. *In flight:* black wing tips and tail contrast with the light body plumage.
Size: L 6–7½ in. (15–19 cm).
Range: rare migrant and variably abundant winter visitor throughout the Rockies.
Habitat: grasslands, frozen marshes, roadsides and railways from the lowlands to the montane.

Feeding: *Winter:* gleans the ground and snow for seeds and waste grain. *Summer:* eats insects and seeds.
Voice: spring song is a musical, high-pitched *chi-chi-churee*; call is a whistled *tew*.
Similar Species: *Lapland Longspur* (p. 281): brown, mottled back; doesn't show the white-and-black contrast in flight.

BLACK-HEADED GROSBEAK
Pheucticus melanocephalus

Regardless of whether the nest is tended by the male or the female, young Black-headed Grosbeaks are continually enveloped by a world of song. Black-headed Grosbeaks are brilliant singers that flaunt their voices in performances from tree-tops and from atop their nests. ▪ Although this grosbeak's bill looks like it can crush any seed imaginable, during their stay in the Rockies, Black-headed Grosbeaks also eat many insects. Strangely, these birds regularly dine on monarch butterflies, which are distasteful and even toxic to most birds, owing to their larval diet of milkweed. ▪ The scientific name *melanocephalus* is Greek for 'black-headed.'

I.D.: *General:* large, dark, conical bill. *Male:* orange-brown underparts and rump; black head, back, wings and tail; white wing bars and undertail coverts. *Female:* dark brown upperparts; buffy underparts; lightly streaked flanks; pale eyebrow and crown stripe.
Size: *L* 7–8¹/₂ in. (18–22 cm).
Range: fairly common migrant and summer resident in the southern and central U.S. Rockies; locally common in the northern U.S. Rockies; vagrant in the Canadian Rockies.
Habitat: lowland and foothills forests, primarily pinyon-juniper, oak, ponderosa pine and aspen woodlands in the foothills.

Nesting: in a tall shrub or deciduous tree, often near water; cup nest is loosely woven of twigs and lined with fine grass; female builds the nest in 3–4 days; pair incubates 3–5 eggs for 12–14 days.
Feeding: forages the upper canopy for invertebrates and plant foods; occasionally visits feeding stations.
Voice: long series of robin-like phrases, without any breaks.
Similar Species: male is distinctive. *Rose-breasted Grosbeak* (p. 323): female has a pale bill and a streaked breast. *Purple Finch* (p. 302): female is much smaller and has heavily streaked underparts.

BLUE GROSBEAK
Guiraca caerulea

Male Blue Grosbeaks owe their spectacular spring plumage not to a fresh molt but, oddly enough, to feather wear. While Blue Grosbeaks are wintering in Mexico and Central America, the brown feather tips slowly wear away, leaving the crystal blue plumage that is seen on birds arriving on their breeding grounds. ▪ Blue Grosbeaks occur in fairly low densities throughout their range. ▪ These birds are very expressive: watch for tail spreading, tail flicking and crown raising behaviors on their summer territories. ▪ *Guiraca* is a Native Mexican and South American name for this bird; *caerulea* is from the Latin for 'blue'—a description that just doesn't grasp this bird's true beauty.

I.D.: *Male:* royal blue plumage overall; rusty wing bars; stout, dark bill, black at the base; *Female:* soft brown plumage overall; rusty wing bars; rump can have blue hints.
Size: L 6–7¹/₂ in. (15–19 cm).
Range: uncommon migrant and summer visitor to the southern U.S. Rockies; very rare elsewhere in the Rockies.
Habitat: brushy, weedy fields, pastures, riparian forest edges, hedgerows and tamarisk shrubs in the lowlands.
Nesting: typically in the southern U.S.; in a shrub or low tree; cup nest is woven with twigs, roots and grass and lined with finer

materials, including paper and occasionally shed reptile skins; female incubates 2–5 eggs for 11–12 days.
Feeding: gleans the ground by hopping around, taking insects and occasionally seeds; periodically gleans vegetation; occasionally visits feeding stations.
Voice: sweet, melodious, warbling song with phrases that rise and fall; call note: *chink*.
Similar Species: *Lazuli Bunting* (p. 287): smaller body and bill; male has a bold, chestnut breast band; female lacks the rusty wing bars. *Indigo Bunting* (p. 323): smaller body and bill; no wing bars.

LAZULI BUNTING
Passerina amoena

While hiking through the shrubby habitat of Lazuli Buntings, one might soon notice the complexities of the males' songs. Neighboring males copy and learn from one another, producing 'song territories.' Each male within a song territory has slight differences in the song syllables, producing his own acoustic fingerprint. ▪ Before leaving in the fall, Lazuli Buntings undergo an incomplete molt; they fly to the southwest to complete the change of wardrobe. ▪ This bird is named after the colorful gemstone lapis lazuli. The generally accepted pronunciation of the name is 'LAZZ-you-lie,' but personal variations are acceptable. ▪ The scientific name *amoena* is from the Latin for 'charming, delightful or dressy,' which this bird certainly is.

♂

I.D.: *General:* stout, conical bill. *Male:* turquoise blue hood and rump; chestnut breast; white belly; dark wings and tail; 2 white wing bars. *Female:* soft brown overall; hints of blue on the rump.
Size: *L* 5–6 in. (13–15 cm).
Range: common migrant and summer breeder in the southern U.S. Rockies; increasingly uncommon northward; very rare migrant in the Canadian Rockies.
Habitat: brushy areas, forest edges, willow and alder thickets, sage and oak shrublands and pinyon-juniper woodlands in the lowlands and the foothills.

Nesting: in an upright crotch low in a shrubby tangle; small cup nest is woven with grass and lined with finer grass and hair; female incubates 3–5 eggs for 12 days.
Feeding: gleans the ground and low shrubs for grasshoppers, beetles, other insects and native seeds; visits feeding stations.
Voice: *Male:* song is a fast *swip-swip-swip zu zu ee, see see sip see see.*
Similar Species: *Indigo Bunting* (p. 323): no wing bars; male lacks the chestnut breast. *Western Bluebird* (p. 224): male is larger, has a slimmer bill and has no wing bars.

287

BOBOLINK
Dolichonyx oryzivorus

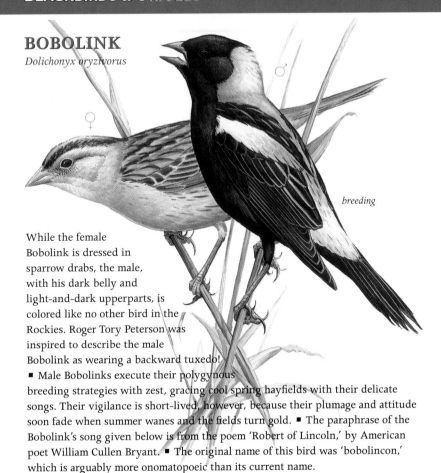

♂

♀

breeding

While the female
Bobolink is dressed in
sparrow drabs, the male,
with his dark belly and
light-and-dark upperparts, is
colored like no other bird in the
Rockies. Roger Tory Peterson was
inspired to describe the male
Bobolink as wearing a backward tuxedo!
▪ Male Bobolinks execute their polygynous
breeding strategies with zest, gracing cool spring hayfields with their delicate
songs. Their vigilance is short-lived, however, because their plumage and attitude
soon fade when summer wanes and the fields turn gold. ▪ The paraphrase of the
Bobolink's song given below is from the poem 'Robert of Lincoln,' by American
poet William Cullen Bryant. ▪ The original name of this bird was 'bobolincon,'
which is arguably more onomatopoeic than its current name.

I.D.: *Breeding male:* black bill, head, wings, tail
and underparts; buff nape; white rump and
wing patch. *Breeding female:* mottled brown
overall; streaked back, flank and rump; pale
eyebrow; dark eye line; light central crown
stripe bordered by brown stripes. *Fall male:*
similar to breeding female, but darker above
and golden-buff below.
Size: *L* 6–8 in. (15–20 cm).
Range: locally common breeder in the
northern and southern U.S. Rockies; possible
breeder in Yellowstone NP; rare to
uncommon migrant in most of the Rockies.
Habitat: tall, grassy meadows, prairies,
hayfields and croplands up to the montane.

Nesting: typically east of the Rockies; on the
ground, well concealed by tall grass; cup nest
is loosely woven with coarse grass, plant
stems and fine materials; female incubates
5–6 eggs for 10–13 days.
Feeding: gleans the ground and low vegetation for adult and larval invertebrates; also
eats many seeds.
Voice: banjo-like twangs: *bobolink bobolink
spink spank spink.*
Similar Species: breeding male is distinctive. *Savannah Sparrow* (p. 271): faint breast
streaks; yellow lore. *Vesper Sparrow* (p. 267):
faint breast streaks; white outer tail feathers.
Grasshopper Sparrow (p. 272): white belly;
golden orange in face.

RED-WINGED BLACKBIRD
Agelaius phoeniceus

No cattail marsh is free from the loud calls and bossy, aggressive nature of the Red-winged Blackbird. The male's bright red shoulders and short, raspy song are his most important tools in the often strategic and intricate displays he uses to defend his territory from rivals.

■ Male Red-winged Blackbirds arrive at the marshes and wetlands of the Rockies a week or so before the females. In the ladies' absence, the males stake out territories through song and visual displays. A flashy and richly voiced male who has managed to establish a large and productive territory can attract several mates to his cattail mansion. ■ In experiments, males whose red shoulders were painted black soon lost their territories to rivals that they had previously defeated.

I.D.: *Male:* all-black, except for the large, red shoulder patch edged in yellow. *Female:* heavily streaked underparts; mottled brown upperparts; faint red shoulder patch; light eyebrow.

Size: L 7¹/₂–9¹/₂ in. (19–24 cm).

Range: common migrant and breeder throughout the Rockies; fairly common winter resident in the southern U.S. Rockies; uncommon winter resident in the northern U.S. Rockies.

Habitat: cattail marshes, wet meadows, croplands and shoreline shrubs up to the lower subalpine.

Nesting: colonial and polygynous; in cattails or shoreline bushes; nest is woven with dried cattail leaves and grass and lined with grass and soft materials; female incubates 3–4 eggs for 10–12 days.

Feeding: gleans the ground for seeds, waste grain and invertebrates; also gleans vegetation, catches insects in flight and eats berries; occasionally visits feeding stations during migration.

Voice: loud, raspy *konk-a-ree* or *eat my CHEEzies.*

Similar Species: male is distinctive (when shoulder patch shows). *Brewer's Blackbird* (p. 293) and *Rusty Blackbird* (p. 292): females lack the streaked underparts.

WESTERN MEADOWLARK
Sturnella neglecta

The Western Meadowlark's trademark song is the voice of the prairies; it rings all too infrequently through low-elevation grasslands in the Rockies. ▪ The yellow breast, with its black V, and the white outer tail feathers serve to attract mates. Potential meadowlark mates face one another, raise their bills high and perform a grassland ballet. ▪ Oddly, the colorful breast and white tail feathers are also used to attract the attention of potential predators. Foxes, hawks and falcons focus on these bold features in pursuit, so the meadowlark can mysteriously disappear into the grass whenever it chooses to turn its back or fold away its white tail flags. ▪ This species, the state bird of Montana, Oregon and Wyoming, was overlooked by the famed Lewis and Clark expedition, which mistakenly thought it was an Eastern Meadowlark. This omission is represented in its scientific name, *neglecta*.

I.D.: *Sexes similar:* yellow underparts; broad, black bib; mottled brown upperparts; short tail; long, pinkish legs; yellow lore; brown crown stripes and eye line; white outer tail feathers; black spotting on the white flanks; slender bill.
Size: L 8–10 in. (20–25 cm).
Range: common migrant and summer breeder and uncommon winter resident north to Waterton Lakes NP; rare migrant elsewhere in the Canadian Rockies.
Habitat: croplands, agricultural areas, grasslands, roadsides and mountain meadows up to the subalpine.

Nesting: in a dry depression or scrape on the ground; domed nest, with a side entrance, is woven into the surrounding vegetation with grass and plant stems; female incubates 3–7 eggs for 13–15 days.
Feeding: walks or runs along the ground, gleaning grasshoppers, crickets and spiders off grass and the ground; also eats seeds.
Voice: rich series of flute-like warbles.
Similar Species: none.

YELLOW-HEADED BLACKBIRD
Xanthocephalus xanthocephalus

In a perfect world, male Yellow-headed Blackbirds would have a song to match their splendid plumage. A spring trip to a wetland, however, often reveals the unfortunate truth: when the male arches his golden head backward, he struggles to produce a painful, pathetic, metallic grind. Although the song of the Yellow-headed Blackbird could be the worst in North America, its quality soon becomes an appreciated aspect of its marshy home—together with the smell, the insects and the clammy sogginess. ▪ In early spring, these blackbirds can be seen curiously probing into the heads of last year's cattails in search of larvae. ▪ *Xanthocephalus* is Greek for 'yellow-headed.'

Nesting: loosely colonial in cattail marshes and shoreline shrubs; bulky, deep basket nest is usually woven into emergent vegetation over water and is made with wet vegetation, which tightens when dry; female incubates 3–5 eggs for 11–13 days.

Feeding: gleans the ground for seeds, beetles, snails, waterbugs and dragonflies; also probes into cattail heads for larval invertebrates.

Voice: strained, metallic grating that seems prolonged by the bird's unmusical efforts.

Similar Species: male is distinctive. *Rusty Blackbird* (p. 292) and *Brewer's Blackbird* (p. 293): females lack the yellow throat and face.

I.D.: *Male:* yellow head and breast; black back; wings, tail and underparts; white wing patches; black lore; long tail; black bill. *Female:* dusky brown overall; yellow breast, throat and eyebrow; hints of yellow in the face.

Size: L 8–11 in. (20–28 cm).

Range: common summer breeder in the southern and central U.S. Rockies; rare migrant in the Canadian Rockies; rare winter resident in the southern U.S. Rockies.

Habitat: cattail marshes, croplands, shoreline vegetation and ranchlands up to the subalpine.

RUSTY BLACKBIRD
Euphagus carolinus

The Rusty Blackbird owes its name to the color of its fall plumage, but its name could just as well reflect this bird's pathetic, grating, squeaky song, which sounds very much a rusty hinge. ▪ When Rusty Blackbirds are migrating and during winter, they use a wide variety of habitats, but they typically roost in marshy or swampy areas. ▪ Unlike other blackbirds, the Rusty Blackbird is not a significant 'nuisance' bird, because it tends to avoid human-altered environments. ▪ *Euphagus* is Greek for 'good eater,' which is a rather puzzling name.

breeding

I.D.: *General:* yellow eyes; dark legs and bill. *Breeding:* dark plumage; male is darker and has a subtle green gloss. *Fall:* rusty wings, back and crown; male is darker; female has buffy underparts.
Size: *L* 9 in. (23 cm).
Range: rare migrant and summer visitor and very rare winter visitor to the Canadian Rockies; rare elsewhere in the Rockies.
Habitat: beaver ponds, roadsides, landfills, wet meadows and shoreline shrubs up to the lower subalpine.

Nesting: typically in the northern boreal forest; in a shrub or small tree, often near water; bulky nest is woven with twigs and lichens, with an inner cup of mud and grass; female incubates 4–5 eggs for 14 days.
Feeding: walks along shorelines gleaning waterbugs, beetles, dragonflies, snails, grasshoppers and small fish; also eats waste grain and seeds.
Voice: call is like a rusty door hinge.
Similar Species: *Brewer's Blackbird* (p. 293): male has 'whiter' eyes and glossier plumage; female has dark eyes. *Common Grackle* (p. 294): keeled tail; larger body and bill size.

BREWER'S BLACKBIRD

Euphagus cyanocephalus

These small, bold blackbirds have a two-note song that is very similar to the Brown-headed Cowbird's. They commonly squabble with pigeons and starlings for leftover scraps of food, and, along roadways, they can be seen strutting confidently in defiance of nearby, rapidly moving vehicles. ▪ The Brewer's Blackbird allows us to easily and intimately observe it. By studying the behavior of several birds in a flock, you can determine the hierarchy of the flock as it is perceived by the birds themselves. ▪ Brewer's Blackbird feathers, which superficially appear black, actually show an iridescent quality as reflected rainbows of sunlight move along the feather shafts.

I.D.: *Male:* glossy black plumage; dark blue on the head; green body iridescence; yellow eyes. *Female:* flat brown plumage; black eyes.
Size: *L* 8–10 in. (20–25 cm).
Range: common migrant and summer resident throughout the Rockies; uncommon winter visitor in the southern U.S. Rockies; rare winter visitor in the northern U.S. Rockies.
Habitat: wet meadows, grasslands, roadsides, landfills, stockyards and shrublands up to the lower subalpine.
Nesting: loosely colonial; on the ground or in a shrub or tree; well-built cup nest is woven with twigs, grass, mud, roots and fur; female incubates 4–6 eggs for 12–14 days.
Feeding: walks along shorelines and open areas, gleaning invertebrates and seeds.
Voice: song is a creaking, 2-noted *k-shee*.
Similar Species: *Rusty Blackbird* (p. 292): longer, more slender bill; lacks the blue and green gloss in the plumage; female has yellow eyes. *Brown-headed Cowbird* (p. 295): shorter tail; male has black eyes and a brown head. *Common Grackle* (p. 294): much longer, keeled tail; heavier bill.

COMMON GRACKLE
Quiscalus quiscula

The Common Grackle is a noisy, cocky bird that prefers to feed on the ground in open areas. Birdfeeders in rural areas can attract large numbers of these blackish birds, whose cranky disposition drives away most other birds (even the quarrelsome jays and House Sparrows). ▪ The Common Grackle is a poor, but spirited, singer. Usually while perched in a shrub, a male grackle will slowly take a deep breath that inflates his breast and causes his feathers to rise; then he closes his eyes and gives out a loud, surprising *swaaaack*. Despite our perception of the Common Grackle's musical weakness, after his 'song' the male proudly poses with his bill held high. ▪ The population of Common Grackles in the Rockies is increasing because of expansion from the east. ▪ *Quiscalus* is New Latin for 'quail,' which a grackle really does not resemble.

I.D.: *Sexes similar:* glossy black plumage; overall purple iridescence; long, keeled tail; yellow eyes; heavy bill; female is smaller and duller than the male. *In flight:* tail resembles a flattened, vertical rudder.
Size: *L* 11–13½ in. (28–34 cm).
Range: uncommon migrant and summer breeder in western Colorado valleys and in Utah; rare elsewhere in the Rockies.
Habitat: fields, wet meadows, urban areas, shorelines and willow shrublands up to the lower subalpine.
Nesting: semi-colonial; in a tree, often near water; bulky cup nest is made of twigs, grass,

mud, feathers and occasionally trash; female incubates 3–6 eggs for 12–14 days.
Feeding: slowly struts along the ground, gleaning, snatching and probing for beetles, earthworms, grasshoppers, larval invertebrates, seeds, grain and fruit; also catches insects in flight and eats small vertebrates, including bird eggs.
Voice: call is a quick, loud *swaaaack*.
Similar Species: *Rusty Blackbird* (p. 292) and *Brewer's Blackbird* (p. 293): smaller; lack the heavy bill and the keeled tail. *European Starling* (p. 232): very short tail; long, thin bill. *Red-winged Blackbird* (p. 289): male has a red shoulder patch and a shorter tail.

BROWN-HEADED COWBIRD
Molothrus ater

The cowbird is quickly becoming one of the most hated native birds in North America for its nest parasitism. Historically, Brown-headed Cowbirds followed bison herds—they now follow ranch mammals—and their nomadic lifestyle makes it impossible to tend a nest; instead, cowbirds lay their eggs in the nests of other songbirds. Many of the parasitized songbirds do not recognize the cowbird eggs and incubate them and raise the young cowbirds as their own. As the rapidly growing cowbird develops, it often outsizes its foster parent, whose own offspring often get squeezed out of the nest or die from lack of food. ▪ Cowbirds now parasitize more than 140 bird species in North America; the expansion of ranching and the fragmentation of forests has significantly increased the cowbird's range. Despite individual tragedies, however, many songbird's have adapted to the cowbird's parasitism.

I.D.: *Male:* glossy green-black plumage; soft brown head; short, squared tail; dark eyes; conical bill. *Female:* gray-brown plumage overall; slight streaking on underparts; dark eyes.

Size: L 6–8 in. (15–20 cm).

Range: common migrant and summer breeder throughout the Rockies.

Habitat: fields, shrublands, forest edges, roadsides, mountain meadows, landfills, campgrounds, day-use areas and around large mammals up to the subalpine.

Nesting: no nest is built; female lays up to 40 eggs a year in the nests of other birds, usually 1 egg per nest, but exceptionally up to 8 (probably from several different cowbirds); eggs hatch after 10–13 days.

Feeding: gleans the ground for seeds, waste grain and invertebrates, especially grasshoppers, beetles and true bugs.

Voice: call is a squeaky, high-pitched *wee-tse-tse;* song is a high, gurgling *bubble-bubble-zeee.*

Similar Species: *Rusty Blackbird* (p. 292) and *Brewer's Blackbird* (p. 293): lack the contrasting brown head and darker body; slimmer bills; longer tails. *Common Grackle* (p. 294): much longer tail; larger.

BALTIMORE ORIOLE
Icterus galbula

Every spring and summer day somewhere across North America, someone does a double-take at a Baltimore Oriole. Owing its familiarity to Major League Baseball, this bird is suprisingly easily identified: the male's vivid colors strike a distinctive pattern. ▪ Both the city and the bird bear the title of Irishman George Calvert, the Baron of Baltimore, who established a colony in Maryland. Mark Catesby, one of America's first naturalists, chose to grant this bird its name because the male's plumage mirrored the colors of the Baron's Coat of Arms. ▪ 'Oriole' is derived from the Latin for 'golden bird.'

I.D.: *Male:* black head, throat, back, wings, rump and central tail feathers; brilliant orange underparts, wing patches and outer tail feathers; small, white wing patches. *Female:* olive-brown upperparts, darkest on the head; dull orange underparts.

Size: *L* 7–8 in. (18–20 cm).

Range: rare migrant and summer visitor to the Canadian Rockies.

Habitat: deciduous, riparian and mixed forests up to the montane.

Nesting: typically east of the Rockies; high in a deciduous tree, suspended from a branch; hanging pouch nest is woven with fine plant fibers, hair, string and fishing line and lined with fine grass and fur; female incubates 4–6 eggs for 12–14 days.

Feeding: gleans canopy vegetation and shrubs for caterpillars, beetles, wasps and other invertebrates; also eats fruit and nectar; visits feeding stations that offer hummingbird feeders and orange halves.

Voice: song consists of slow, clear, purposeful whistles: *peter peter here here peter.*

Similar Species: *Bullock's Oriole* (p. 297): orange cheek; large, white wing patch. *Black-headed Grosbeak* (p. 285): heavy, conical bill; darker orange plumage; broad, white wing patches. *Western Tanager* (p. 260): yellow body plumage; lacks the black head.

BULLOCK'S ORIOLE

Icterus bullockii

The male Bullock's Oriole has a striking, Halloween-like, black-and-orange plumage that flashes like embers amidst the treetops, while its sibilant whistles drip to the ground. ■ This is the common oriole of the West. Once thought to interbreed freely with the Baltimore Oriole, the birds were lumped together as one species: the Northern Oriole. Just as the birding community adjusted to the changes, new work has shown that the birds interbreed rarely enough that they can be considered two distinct species. ■ In naming this bird, William Swainson honored a father-son team of hobby naturalists in Mexico (both of whom were named William Bullock).

I.D.: *Male:* bright orange eyebrow, cheek, underparts, rump and outer tail feathers; black throat, eye line, cap, back and central tail feathers; large, white wing patch. *Female:* dusky yellow face, throat and upper breast; gray underparts; olive-gray upperparts and tail; small, white wing patches.

Size: *L* 7–8¹/₂ in. (18–22 cm).

Range: uncommon to locally common migrant and summer visitor throughout the U.S. Rockies.

Habitat: riparian forests, willow shrublands, urban areas and deciduous river valleys up to the montane.

Nesting: typically west of the Rockies and locally on the Great Plains; high in a deciduous tree, suspended from a branch; hanging pouch nest is woven with fine plant fibers, hair, string and fishing line and lined with horsehair, plant down, fur and moss; female incubates 4–5 eggs for 12–14 days.

Feeding: gleans canopy vegetation and shrubs for caterpillars, beetles, wasps and other invertebrates; also eats fruit and nectar; occasionally visits feeding stations that offer hummingbird feeders and orange halves.

Voice: accented series of 6–8 whistled, rich and guttural notes.

Similar Species: *Baltimore Oriole* (p. 296): lacks the orange cheek and the large, white wing patch. *Black-headed Grosbeak* (p. 285): heavy, conical bill; black cheek; darker underparts. *Western Tanager* (p. 260): yellow body plumage; lacks the black cap and throat.

297

GRAY-CROWNED ROSY-FINCH

Leucosticte tephrocotis

During summer, Gray-crowned Rosy-Finches thrive on the alpine tundra, where the air is thin and the wind a frigid fixture. These 'ice-box' breeders nest on the isolated islands of tundra that are sprinkled along the spine of the northern Rockies. ▪ The Gray-crowned Rosy-Finch is the most widely distributed of the three similar rosy-finches. Until recently, these birds were classified as one species, but geographic breeding isolation is thought to contribute to the unique features of the three species. ▪ During the winter, Gray-crowned Rosy-Finches spill out of the attics of the Rockies to flock together widely at lower elevations.

breeding

I.D.: *Sexes similar:* dark bill; black forehead; gray crown; rosy shoulder, rump and belly; brown cheek, back and breast; black legs; dark tail and flight feathers.

Size: L 5¹/₂–6¹/₂ in. (14–17 cm).

Range: common migrant and summer breeder in the Canadian and northern U.S. Rockies; uncommon winter resident in Wyoming, Colorado and Utah.

Habitat: mountain meadows, alpine tundra, avalanche slopes, roadsides and occasionally towns, most commonly in the upper subalpine and the alpine.

Nesting: on the ground, among rocks or in a crevice; bulky nest is made of moss, grass, fur and feathers; female incubates 4–5 eggs for 12–14 days.

Feeding: hops on the ground or snow, gleaning small seeds; occasionally visits feeding stations.

Voice: calls are high, chirping notes and constant chattering; song is a long, goldfinch-like warble.

Similar Species: *Black Rosy-Finch* (p. 299): black breast, back and cheek. *Brown-capped Rosy-Finch* (p. 300): lacks the gray crown.

BLACK ROSY-FINCH
Leucosticte atrata

On mountain peaks rising up from the Great Basin, the Black Rosy-Finch strikes beauty into the delicate system of the high country. Like the fragile alpine flower it nests beside, this bird flashes its beauty in quick yearly pulses, hoping to successfully breed in this area of limited opportunity. ▪ During summer, rosy-finches develop cheek pouches so they can carry larger amounts of insects to their rapidly developing young. ▪ The rosy-finch 'Grand-Slam' could be a goal of Rocky Mountain naturalists, perhaps not just for checklist gratification, but as an avenue to explore all reaches of our mountainous region. ▪ The scientific name *atrata* is Latin for 'clothed in black,' a obvious allusion to the male's handsome plumage.

♂

breeding

I.D.: Male: black forehead, cheek, breast and back; gray crown; rosy shoulder (hard to see), belly, flanks and rump; black bill and legs; dark tail and flight feathers. Female: similar but paler.
Size: L 5¹/₂–6¹/₂ in. (14–17 cm).
Range: uncommon year-round resident in the greater Yellowstone area and in northern Utah; rare winter visitor in the southern U.S. Rockies.
Habitat: *Summer:* typically in alpine tundra. *Winter:* open areas and mountain meadows down to the montane.

Nesting: among rocks or in a crevice; bulky nest is made of moss, grass, fur and feathers; female incubates 4–5 eggs for 12–14 days.
Feeding: hops on the ground or snow, gleaning small seeds; occasionally visits feeding stations.
Voice: calls are single notes or a tripled *pert-pert-chew*.
Similar Species: *Gray-crowned Rosy-Finch* (p. 298): brown breast, cheek and back. *Brown-capped Rosy-Finch* (p. 300): brownish crown; brown breast, cheek and back.

BROWN-CAPPED ROSY-FINCH
Leucosticte australis

Where only the most resilient mountaineers dare go in the peaks of Wyoming, Colorado and New Mexico, you will find the breeding grounds of the Brown-capped Rosy-Finch. Where ice and boulders are permanent landmarks, these small alpine denizens find sufficient food to raise a small brood. ▪ When the bite of fall weather becomes too much for even these finches, they retire down-slope to more hospitable areas—but still at higher elevations than almost all other birds! ▪ The scientific name *australis* is Latin for 'southern'; this is the most southern resident in our guild of rosy-finches.

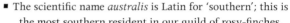

breeding

I.D.: *Male:* black forehead; brownish crown; brown breast, cheek and back; rosy shoulder, belly, flanks and rump; dark bill and legs; dark tail and flight feathers. *Female:* duller than the male; sometimes lacks the rosy plumage altogether.
Size: L 5¹/₂–6¹/₂ in. (14–17 cm).
Range: locally common summer breeder and irregular winter resident in the southern U.S. Rockies.
Habitat: *Summer:* around cliffs and rocky areas in the alpine. *Winter:* open areas, towns and roadsides up to the subalpine.

Nesting: on the ground, among rocks or in a crevice; bulky nest is made of moss, grass, fur and feathers; female incubates 4–5 eggs for 12–14 days.
Feeding: hops on the ground or snow, gleaning small seeds; occasionally visits feeding stations.
Voice: call is a harsh, 3-note *peyt-a-weet;* flight song is long and warbling.
Similar Species: *Black Rosy-Finch* (p. 299): gray crown; black breast and face. *Gray-crowned Rosy-Finch* (p. 298): gray crown.

PINE GROSBEAK

Pinicola enucleator

Perhaps one of the great moments in the long Rocky Mountain winter is when the Pine Grosbeaks emerge from the wilds to settle upon backyard feeders. There they might remain for the entire winter, or, like their erratic irruptive pattern, disappear for months. ▪ The prize when out 'pining' for grosbeaks is the sight of a mature male. Search the tops of spruce and pine trees; the spires are favorite perching sites for this grosbeak. The male's splendid red plumage strikes a vivid contrast against the snow and spruce bows. ▪ Cold human residents and winter visitors to the Rockies can be soothed somewhat by the soft warbles these snowbirds sing during the coldest days.
▪ *Pinicola* is Latin for 'pine dweller,' and *enucleator* is Latin for 'one who takes off shells.'

I.D.: *General:* stout, conical, dark bill; white wing bars; black wings and tail. *Male:* rosy red head, underparts and upperparts. *Female* and *Immature:* rusty crown, face and rump; ashy gray back and underparts.
Size: *L* 8–10 in. (20–25 cm).
Range: fairly common year-round resident in the Canadian Rockies; increasingly scarce year-round southward.
Habitat: *Summer:* subalpine fir and Engelmann spruce forests in the upper subalpine. *Fall to spring:* townsites, spruce-fir forests and pinyon-juniper woodlands in the foothills and the montane.

Nesting: in a conifer or tall shrub; bulky cup nest is loosely made of twigs, moss, grass, lichens and fur; female incubates 4 eggs for 13–15 days.
Feeding: gleans buds, berries and seeds from trees; also forages on the ground; visits feeding stations in winter.
Voice: song is a short, musical warble.
Similar Species: *White-winged Crossbill* (p. 306): much smaller; lacks the stubby bill. *Evening Grosbeak* (p. 312): female has a light-colored bill and broad, white wing patches.

PURPLE FINCH
Carpodacus purpureus

The courtship of Purple Finches is one of the most gentle and appealing mating rituals in the Rockies. The liquid warbling song of the male bubbles through conifer boughs, announcing his intentions to receptive mates. When a female approaches, the colorful male dances lightly around her, quickly beating his wings until he gently lifts off the ground. ▪ Their gentle nature and simple but stunning plumage endear Purple Finches to naturalists. They are a blessing, especially during winter, for their habit of offering a song to the crisp winter air.

▪ Purple (*purpureus*) is simply too harsh a description of this bird's delicate color. Roger Tory Peterson said it best when he described the the Purple Finch as a sparrow dipped in raspberry juice.

I.D.: *Male:* light bill; raspberry-red head, throat, breast and nape; brown- and reddish-streaked back and flanks; reddish-brown cheek; red rump; notched tail; light belly; brown wings and tail; unstreaked undertail coverts. *Female:* dark brown cheek and 'jaw' line; white eyebrow and 'drool'; heavily streaked underparts; unstreaked undertail coverts.

Size: L 5¹/₄–6 in. (13–15 cm).

Range: common spring migrant and uncommon summer resident in the Canadian Rockies.

Habitat: pine, spruce and mixed forests and townsites in the montane and the lower subalpine.

Nesting: typically across southern Canada and the northeastern U.S. and along the Pacific coast; in a conifer, far from the trunk; tight cup nest is woven with twigs, grass, moss, lichens and fur; female incubates 4–5 eggs for 13 days.

Feeding: gleans the ground and vegetation for seeds, buds, berries and insects; readily visits feeding stations.

Voice: song is a bubbly, continuous warble; call is a single *cheep* or *weet*.

Similar Species: *House Finch* (p. 304): squared tail; male lacks the reddish cap; female lacks the distinct cheek patch. *Cassin's Finch* (p. 303): male has a brown nape and lightly streaked, brown flanks; female lacks the distinct cheek patch and has streaked undertail coverts.

CASSIN'S FINCH
Carpodacus cassinii

In some parts of the Rockies, Cassin's Finches are the most common birds—but only for a few short days. These birds move to higher elevations during the breeding season, and their mass migration frequently finds them in townsites for a short time. During these days, it seems that scarcely a tree, not to mention a feeder, is free of these marauding migrants. Once the birds have moved off, they are more difficult to see, but their bubbling courtship song serves as a pleasant reminder of their time in towns. ■ John Cassin was one of the leading 19th-century bird taxonomists: his name graces four species of birds.

I.D.: *Male:* reddish crown, throat and rump; brown nape; white underparts; streaked undertail coverts and flanks; deeply notched tail; mottled brown upperparts. *Female:* indistinct facial patterning; streaked undertail coverts; finely streaked underparts.
Size: L 5³/₄–6¹/₄ in. (15–16 cm).
Range: common year-round resident in the southern U.S. Rockies; common migrant and summer breeder in the northern U.S. Rockies; irregular migrant in the southern Canadian Rockies.
Habitat: *Summer:* spruce-fir forests in the subalpine. *Migration and Winter:* pinyon-juniper, Douglas-fir and ponderosa pine forests up to the montane.

Nesting: on an outer limb in a conifer; cup nest is woven with grass, moss, bark shreds, fur and small roots; female incubates 4–5 eggs for 12–14 days.
Feeding: eats mostly seeds, but also eats insects and buds in spring and berries in winter; often visits birdfeeders.
Voice: call is a 2-syllable *kee-up;* song is a long, varied warble.
Similar Species: *Purple Finch* (p. 302): male has a reddish nape and flanks; female has a distinct cheek patch and unstreaked undertail coverts. *House Finch* (p. 304): squared tail; male has a brown cap; female has heavily streaked underparts.

HOUSE FINCH
Carpodacus mexicanus

Before cities began to dot America's soil, House Finches were restricted to the Southwest. During the 1920s and 1930s, however, they were popular cage birds, and they were sold across the continent as 'Hollywood Finches.' Illegal releases of the caged birds and expansion from their historic range into farmlands and cities have resulted in two separate distributions in North America that are converging like a zipper along the Rocky Mountains. ▪ The House Finch is becoming one of the most common birds in North America; its expansion symbolizes both the intentional and the indirect results of human influence on wildlife communities. If your backyard feeder is currently free of House Finches, be patient: they're on their way.

I.D.: *General:* streaked undertail coverts; square tail. *Male:* brown cap; red eyebrow, forecrown, throat and breast; heavily streaked flanks. *Female:* indistinct facial patterning; heavily streaked underparts.
Size: L 5–6 in. (13–15 cm).
Range: locally common year-round in the U.S. Rockies; increasingly scarce northward; currently absent from the Canadian Rockies, but its range is expanding.
Habitat: cities, towns and agricultural areas up to the montane.
Nesting: in a cavity, a building, dense foliage or an abandoned bird nest; cup nest is woven with grass, twigs, leaves, fur and string; female incubates 4–5 eggs for 12–14 days.

Feeding: gleans vegetation and the ground for seeds; visits feeding stations.
Voice: song is a warble lasting about 3 seconds, with the last note usually rising.
Similar Species: *Cassin's Finch* (p. 303): notched tail; male has a reddish cap and finely streaked flanks; female has finely streaked underparts. *Purple Finch* (p. 302): notched tail; male has a reddish upper back and flanks; female has a distinct cheek patch.

RED CROSSBILL
Loxia curvirostra

Red Crossbills are one of the great gypsies of the bird world, coming and going in response to food availability. These nomads scour Rocky Mountain forests for pine cones, and when an abundant supply is discovered, they might breed, regardless of the season. ■ By observing conifer cone crops, an attentive naturalist can predict with some accuracy whether crossbills will appear during the upcoming season. ■ There are few other birds in the Rockies as tied to a single food source as the crossbills. Apart from pine forests, try searching out Red Crossbills near sources of mineralized water, to which they will descend from the trees for a drink. ■ The scientific name *curvirostra* is Latin for 'curve-billed.'

♂

I.D.: *General:* crossed bill tips. *Male:* dull orange-red to brick red plumage; dark wings and tail; always has color on the throat. *Female:* olive-gray to dusky yellow plumage; plain, dark wings. *Immature:* streaked underparts; otherwise resembles female.
Size: L 5^1/$_2$–6^1/$_2$ in. (14–17 cm).
Range: fairly common, local year-round resident throughout the Rockies; populations fluctuate considerably from year to year.
Habitat: coniferous forests, especially ponderosa and lodgepole pine, but also spruce-fir, from the foothills to the subalpine.
Nesting: on an outer branch in a conifer;

cup nest is loosely woven with twigs, grass, moss, fur and bark strips; female incubates 3–4 eggs for 12–18 days; can breed any time of the year.
Feeding: prefers conifer seeds (especially pine); also eats buds, deciduous tree seeds and occasionally insects; often licks road salt or minerals in soil; occasionally visits feeders.
Voice: distinctive call note: *jip-jip*; song is a varied warble (similar to other finches).
Similar Species: *White-winged Crossbill* (p. 306): 2 broad, white wing bars. *Pine Siskin* (p. 309): similar to immature Red Crossbill, but lacks the crossed bill and is smaller.

WHITE-WINGED CROSSBILL
Loxia leucoptera

Novice birders frequently measure how exotic a bird is by its bill size and shape. The bills of tropical toucans, hornbills and cassowaries are elaborate, but the forests of Rockies also host a bird with a most particular bill. The tips of the crossbill's beak overlap, leaving the bird with a seemingly clumsy foraging instrument. Crossbills primarily eat spruce seeds, however, and their bills are perfectly designed to pry open the cones. When a crossbill closes its bill, the bill tips separate the overlapping scales, which allows the bird to seize the sought-after seed with its tongue. ■ Crossbills overwinter in flocks. The presence of a foraging group high in a spruce tree creates an unforgettable shower of spruce cone scales and crackling chatter. ■ When not foraging in spruce spires, White-winged Crossbills are frequently seen licking salt from winter roads. ■ The scientific name *leucoptera* means 'white wing.'

I.D.: *General:* crossed bill tips; 2 bold, white wing bars. *Male:* reddish-pink plumage overall; black wings and tail. *Female:* dusky yellow plumage overall; slightly streaked underparts; dark wings and tail. *Immature:* like the female, but more heavily streaked.

Size: L 6–6³/₄ in. (15–17 cm).

Range: fairly common year-round resident in the Canadian Rockies; populations fluctuate considerably from year to year.

Habitat: coniferous forests, primarily spruce-fir, and occasionally townsite and deciduous forests in the montane and the lower subalpine.

Nesting: on an outer branch in a conifer; cup nest is loosely woven with twigs, grass, moss, fur, cocoons and bark strips; female incubates 4 eggs for 12–14 days.

Feeding: prefers conifer seeds (mostly spruce and fir); also eats deciduous tree seeds and occasionally insects; occasionally licks salt and minerals from roads.

Voice: call is composed of harsh *chet* notes; song is a high-pitched series of trills.

Similar Species: *Red Crossbill* (p. 305): lacks the white wing bars; male is paler. *Pine Grosbeak* (p. 301): much larger; lacks the crossed bill tips.

COMMON REDPOLL

Carduelis flammea

Predictably unpredictable winter visitors to the Rockies, Common Redpolls are often seen snowplowing through soft powder. Wintering redpolls can forage atop the snow, picking fallen seeds from its surface or plucking at emergent grass heads. The redpoll does not sink deep into the snow, because its light, fluffy body allows it to float on the softest snow without sinking beyond its belly. ▪ Wintering redpolls are remarkably fearless of humans, and as long as you aren't too aggressive, most birdwatchers can have a prolonged, intimate look at these small wintering finches. ▪ The scientific name *flammea*, Latin for 'flame,' refers to the red cap.

non-breeding

I.D.: *Sexes similar:* red fore crown (cap); black chin; pale bill; streaked rump; lightly streaked flanks. *Male:* breast often pinkish. *Female:* light gray breast.

Size: L 5–5½ in. (13–14 cm).

Range: common migrant and winter visitor in the Canadian and northern U.S. Rockies; increasingly scarce southward; populations fluctuate from year to year.

Habitat: open fields, meadows, roadsides, townsites, railways and forest edges in the montane and the subalpine.

Nesting: on the taiga; in a shrub or among rocks, on a platform of twigs; cup nest is woven with small roots, grass, lichens and moss and thickly lined with ptarmigan feathers; female incubates 4–5 eggs for 10–11 days.

Feeding: gleans the ground, snow and vegetation in large flocks for seeds, especially birch; visits feeding stations.

Voice: song is a twittering series of trills; calls are a soft *chit-chit-chit-chit* and a faint *swe-eet*; indistinguishable from the Hoary Redpoll.

Similar Species: *Hoary Redpoll* (p. 308): unstreaked rump; very faintly streaked flanks; generally paler. *Pine Siskin* (p. 309): heavily streaked overall; yellow flashes in the wings and tail.

HOARY REDPOLL
Carduelis hornemanni

During winter, great flocks of redpolls descend into birch trees or to feeders along forest edges in the Rockies, and mixed in with the large flocks of Common Redpolls, there is often a lightly colored redpoll with an unstreaked rump. The Hoary Redpoll debate predictably arises and birdwatchers square off over the ambiguous field marks. ▪ Although the confirmation of a Hoary Redpoll is hard to come by, simply appreciate the bird's cold tolerance and its amazing migratory feats, rather than wasting the moment in second guesses and debate. ▪ The Hoary Redpoll is one of the most northerly wintering songbirds. ▪ Jens Wilken Hornemann was one of Denmark's leading botanists, and he helped organize an expedition to Greenland where this bird was first discovered.

non-breeding

I.D.: *Sexes similar:* red forecrown (cap); black chin; yellow bill; pale plumage overall; unstreaked rump; lightly streaked flanks. *Male:* pinkish-tinged breast. *Female:* light gray breast.
Size: L 5–5¹/₂ in. (13–14 cm).
Range: common migrant and winter resident in the Canadian Rockies; populations fluctuate from year to year.
Habitat: open fields, meadows, roadsides, townsites, railways and forest edges in the montane and the subalpine.

Nesting: on the taiga and arctic tundra; in a shrub or among rocks, often near water; cup nest is woven with twigs, grass and small roots and lined with fur and ptarmigan feathers; female incubates 4–5 eggs for 11 days.
Feeding: gleans the ground, snow and vegetation in flocks for seeds and buds; occasionally visits feeding stations.
Voice: song is a twittering series of trills; calls are a soft *chit-chit-chit-chit* and a faint *swe-eet;* indistinguishable from the Common Redpoll.
Similar Species: *Common Redpoll* (p. 307): streaked rump; more heavily streaked flanks; red cap is often less defined. *Pine Siskin* (p. 309): very heavily streaked; yellow flashes in the wings and tail.

PINE SISKIN
Carduelis pinus

Do not be confused by the dull, streaked plumage of the Pine Siskin; as its behavior truly shows, this is a goldfinch masquerading as a sparrow. ▪ Tight flocks of these gregarious birds are frequently heard before they are seen. Their characteristic call, *zzweeeet*, starts off slowly and then climbs to a high-pitched climax. Once you recognize this distinctive call, if you spot a flurry of activity in the treetops, showing occasional flashes of yellow, you can confirm the presence of these finches. ▪ After the first hard-won identification, Pine Siskins will be encountered frequently in coniferous woodlands, deciduous areas and even at backyard feeders.

I.D.: *Sexes similar:* heavily streaked underparts; yellow at the base of the tail feathers and in the wings (easily seen in flight); dull wing bars; darker, heavily streaked upperparts; slightly forked tail; indistinct facial pattern.
Size: L 4¹/₂–5¹/₄ in. (11–13 cm).
Range: common to abundant migrant and summer breeder throughout the Rockies; common winter visitor in the southern U.S. Rockies; increasingly scarce winter visitor northward.
Habitat: coniferous and aspen forests, forest edges, meadows, townsites, roadsides, agricultural areas and grasslands up to the subalpine.
Nesting: occasionally loosely communal;

often on an outer branch in a conifer; flat nest is woven with grass and small roots and lined with fur and feathers; female incubates 3–4 eggs for 13 days.
Feeding: gleans the ground and vegetation for seeds, buds, thistle seeds and some insects; attracted to road salts, mineral licks and ashes; regularly visits feeding stations.
Voice: song is a coarse but bubbling expression; call is a prolonged, accelerating, rising *zzweeeet*.
Similar Species: *Common Redpoll* (p. 307) and *Hoary Redpoll* (p. 308): red cap; no yellow in the wings. *Purple* (p. 302), *Cassin's* (p. 303) and *House* (p. 304) finches: females have a thicker bill and no yellow in the wings or tail.

LESSER GOLDFINCH
Carduelis psaltria

Searching through flocks of finches in the southern Rockies often rewards the viewer with the sight of the day-night plumage of the male Lesser Goldfinch. These birds frequently associate with Pine Siskins and American Goldfinches in small to large foraging flocks. ▪ First-year males, still without the contrasting plumage of the mature males, are often just as successful as their older peers in finding mates. It is thought that female Lesser Goldfinches are attracted by song rather than sight. ▪ Lesser Goldfinches will copy the songs of neighboring species, which is unusual for a finch. ▪ The scientific name *psaltria* means 'one who plays the lute'—an allusion to the bird's voice.

black-backed form

I.D.: *General:* yellow underparts and undertail coverts; black wings and tail; white wing patches; small, stubby, black bill; black legs. *Green-backed male:* black cap; green back. *Black-backed male:* black head, back and rump. *Female:* green upperparts.
Size: L 4–4¹/₂ in. (10–11 cm).
Range: uncommon migrant and summer resident in the southern U.S. Rockies; black-backed form is increasingly common southward.

Habitat: riparian and ponderosa pine forests, agricultural areas, townsites and grasslands up to the montane.
Nesting: saddled on a limb in a small tree or shrub; cup nest is woven with grass, plant fibers, bark strips, moss and a few feathers; female incubates 4–5 eggs for 12 days.
Feeding: gleans vegetation for thistle and other 'weed' seeds; attracted to salt-rich soils; visits bird baths and garden hoses for water.
Voice: song is similar to the American Goldfinch's; call is a mewing *tee-yee*.
Similar Species: *American Goldfinch* (p. 311): white undertail coverts; pale legs.

AMERICAN GOLDFINCH
Carduelis tristis

The American Goldfinch is a bright, cheery songbird that is commonly seen during summer in weedy fields, roadsides and backyards, where it often feeds on thistle seeds. It swings over fields in its distinctive undulating flight, filling the air with its jubilant *po-ta-to-chip* call. ■ The male's black cap and wings separate it from the other yellow birds that are also mistakenly called 'wild canaries.' ■ The American Goldfinch, the state bird of Washington, delays nesting until June to ensure a dependable source of thistles and dandelion seeds to feed its young. ■ The scientific name *tristis*, Latin for 'sad,' refers to the goldfinch's voice. It is an awful tribute to this pleasing and playful bird.

♂

breeding

I.D.: *Breeding male:* black forehead, wings and tail; bright yellow body; white wing bars, undertail coverts and tail base; orange bill and legs. *Non-breeding male:* olive-brown back; yellow-tinged head; gray underparts. *Female:* yellow-green upperparts; yellow throat and breast; yellow-green belly.
Size: *L* 4 1/2 – 5 1/2 in. (11–14 cm).
Range: uncommon to common migrant and summer resident in Glacier and Waterton Lakes NPs; uncommon migrant and summer resident elsewhere in the Rockies.
Habitat: open forests, fields, meadows, roadsides, townsites and agricultural areas up to the montane.
Nesting: in a fork in a shrub or dense bush; cup nest is tightly woven with plant fibers, grass and spider silk and lined with fur; female incubates 4–6 eggs for 10–12 days.

Feeding: gleans vegetation for thistle, birch and alder seeds, as well as for insects, berries and the seeds of many other plants; commonly visits feeding stations outside the Rockies.
Voice: calls are *po-ta-to-chip* (often delivered in flight) and *dear-me, see-me*; song is varied and long, with trills, twitters and sibilant notes.
Similar Species: *Evening Grosbeak* (p. 312): much larger; massive bill. *Wilson's Warbler* (p. 258): greenish wings without wing bars; thin bill. *Lesser Goldfinch* (p. 310): yellow undertail coverts; dark legs and bill.

EVENING GROSBEAK
Coccothraustes vespertinus

Unannounced, a flock of Evening Grosbeaks descends one chilly December day upon a feeder. For the proprietor of the feeder, the gold and black grosbeaks are both an aesthetic blessing and a financial curse. Although Evening Grosbeaks benefit from the sunflower seed bounty offered to them, they disappear suddenly in late winter in an expression of their wild and independent spirit, not to be seen again until they are driven out of their summer homes by the following December's snow and wind. ■ The force per unit area that this grosbeak can exert with its bill might make it the most powerful of any North American bird. ■ Large irruptions of Evening Grosbeaks occur every two to three years, with some birds ranging as far south as the Gulf states. ■ It was once thought that this bird sang only in the evening, a fact that is reflected in both its common and scientific names: *vespertinus* is Latin for 'of the evening.'

I.D.: *General:* massive, light-colored, conical bill; black wings and tail; broad, white wing patches. *Male:* black crown; yellow eyebrow; dark brown head gradually fading into golden yellow on the belly and lower back. *Female:* gray head and upper back; yellow-tinged underparts; white undertail coverts.
Size: L 7–8½ in. (18–22 cm).
Range: locally uncommon year-round resident throughout the Rockies.
Habitat: *Summer:* open coniferous forests. *Winter:* townsites and deciduous forests up to the subalpine.

Nesting: on an outer limb in a conifer; flimsy cup nest is loosely woven with twigs, small roots, plant fibers and grass; female incubates 3–4 eggs for 11–14 days.
Feeding: gleans the ground and vegetation for tree and shrub seeds, buds and berries; also eats insects and licks mineral-rich soil; visits feeding stations for sunflower seeds.
Voice: song is a wandering warble; call is a loud, sharp *clee-ip.*
Similar Species: *American Goldfinch* (p. 311): much smaller; small bill; smaller wing bars. *Pine Grosbeak* (p. 301): female has a black bill and smaller wing bars.

HOUSE SPARROW
Passer domesticus

Since its introduction to North America in the 1850s, the House Sparrow has managed to colonize most human-altered environments on the continent. The Rocky Mountains, for the most part, remain free from this aggressive and adaptable songbird. It is only in towns, ranchlands and agricultural areas that the House Sparrow has penetrated into the Rockies. ■ The House Sparrow is well known to most North Americans, because it lives in abundance in all North American cities and towns. It was introduced around Brooklyn, New York, as part of a plan to control the numbers of insects that were damaging grain and cereal crops. Contrary to popular opinion at the time, the diet of these Eurasian sparrows is largely vegetarian, and their impact on crop pests has been minimal. ■ House Sparrows are not closely related to the other North American sparrows; they belong to the family of Old World sparrows (Passeridae).

I.D.: *Breeding male:* gray crown; black bib and bill; chestnut nape; light gray cheek; white wing bar; dark, mottled upperparts; gray underparts. *Winter male:* smaller black bib; light-colored bill. *Female:* plain gray-brown overall; buffy eyebrow; streaked upperparts; indistinct facial patterns; grayish, unstreaked underparts.
Size: L 5¹/₂–6¹/₂ in. (14–17 cm).
Range: locally abundant year-round resident at middle to low elevations throughout the Rockies.
Habitat: townsites, agricultural areas, railyards and developed areas up to the montane; absent from undeveloped areas.

Nesting: often communal; in a nest box, natural cavity or building; when not in a cavity, a large, dome-shaped nest is woven with grass and other plant fibers; female incubates 4–6 eggs for 10–13 days.
Feeding: gleans the ground and vegetation for seeds, insects and fruit; frequently visits feeding stations.
Voice: familiar, plain *cheep-cheep-cheep-cheep.*
Similar Species: male is distinctive; female is distinctively drab.

CLARK'S GREBE

Aechmophorus clarkii

I.D.: *Sexes similar:* black upperparts; white underparts; face is mostly white (to above the eyes); long, slim, yellow-orange bill; short tail; long neck.
Size: L 21–23 in. (53–58 cm).
Range: uncommon in the central and southern U.S. Rockies; rare in the Rockies north of Yellowstone NP.
Habitat: large lakes and reservoirs with vegetated shallows in the foothills and the montane.

LEAST BITTERN

Ixobrychus exilis

I.D.: *General:* buffy yellow inner wing patches, sides and flanks; light-colored bill; yellow legs; lightly streaked throat and breast; short tail; dark outer wings. *Male:* black crown and back. *Female* and *Immature:* chestnut-brown head and back.
Size: L 11–14 in. (28–36 cm); W 17 in. (43 cm).
Range: rare migrant in the southern U.S. Rockies.
Habitat: among tall, dense grasses, willows, bulrushes and cattails in wetlands, lake edges and backwaters in the montane.

GREAT EGRET

Ardea alba

I.D.: *Sexes similar:* tall, white bird; long, black legs; straight, yellow bill; long, curving neck; short tail. *Breeding:* elegant, white plumes trailing from the throat and rump; green patch develops between the base of the bill and the eye. *In flight:* head is folded back over the shoulders; legs are extended back.
Size: L 37–41 in. (94–104 cm); W 51 in. (130 cm).
Range: rare local breeder in Idaho and Colorado; vagrant in the Canadian and northern U.S. Rockies.
Habitat: open riverbanks, lakeshores and marshes in the montane.

breeding

CATTLE EGRET

Bubulcus ibis

I.D.: *Sexes similar:* snow-white plumage; yellow-orange bill; all-yellow legs and feet. *Breeding:* elegant plumes on the throat and rump; buffy-orange throat, rump and erect crown; orange-red legs and bill; lore can become purple. *Immature:* similar to an adult, but with black feet. *In flight:* head folds back over shoulders; legs extend beyond tail.
Size: L 19–21 in. (48–53 cm); W 36 in. (91 cm).
Range: continually expanding; rare in Colorado and Idaho; vagrant in the Canadian and northern U.S. Rockies.
Habitat: agricultural fields, especially those with livestock; also in wetlands and along river edges and lakeshores.

non-breeding

GREEN HERON

Butorides virescens

I.D.: *Sexes similar:* small, stocky heron; green-black crown; chestnut face and neck; white streaks down the throat and underparts; blue-gray back and wings mixed with iridescent green; relatively short legs; dark bill; short tail. *Breeding male:* bright orange legs. *Immature:* heavy streaks on front and underparts; dull brown upperparts.
Size: *L* 15–22 in. (38–56 cm); *W* 26 in. (66 cm).
Range: rare migrant in the southern Rockies; rare vagrant in the northern Rockies.
Habitat: tree-lined or shrub-lined marshes and rivers and shallow wetlands with emergent vegetation.

GREATER WHITE-FRONTED GOOSE

Anser albifrons

I.D.: *Sexes similar. Adult:* dark brown overall; dark speckling on the belly; orange-pink bill and feet; white around the bill and on the forehead; white hindquarters; black band on the tail. *Immature:* pale belly without speckles; no white on the face.
Size: *L* 27–33 in. (69–84 cm).
Range: rare to very rare spring and fall migrant throughout the Rockies.
Habitat: *In migration:* croplands, fields, open areas and shallow marshes.

ROSS'S GOOSE

Chen rossii

I.D.: *Sexes similar:* white overall; black wing tips (primaries); dark pink feet and bill; plumage is occasionally stained rusty by iron in the water. *Blue phase:* white head; blue-gray body plumage. *Immature:* gray plumage; dark bill and feet.
Size: *L* 21–26 in. (53–66 cm); *W* 51 in. (130 cm).
Range: locally uncommon to rare migrant in most of the Rockies.
Habitat: shallow wetlands, lakes and fields.

EURASIAN WIGEON

Anas penelope

I.D.: *Male:* rufous head; cream forehead; rosy breast; gray sides; black hind end; dark feet; black-tipped, gray bill. *Female:* predominantly brown head and breast with rufous hints; black-tipped, blue bill. *In flight:* large, white wing patch.
Size: *L* 16¹/₂–20 in. (42–51 cm).
Range: rare to uncommon migrant throughout the Rockies.
Habitat: shallow wetlands, lake edges and ponds in the montane and the lower subalpine; usually mixed in flocks of American Wigeons.

GREATER SCAUP

Aythya marila

I.D.: *Male:* dark green, rounded head; dark breast; white belly and flanks; light gray back; dark hindquarters; blue, black-tipped bill; golden eyes. *Female:* brown overall; well-defined white patch at the base of the bill; rounded or flat-topped head. *In flight:* long white wing stripe.

Size: *L* 16–19 in. (41–48 cm).

Range: very rare spring and fall migrant throughout the Rockies.

Habitat: lakes, large marshes and reservoirs, usually far from the shore.

OLDSQUAW

Clangula hyemalis

I.D.: *Breeding male:* dark head with a white eye patch; dark neck and upperparts; white belly; pink bill with a dark base; long, dark central tail feathers. *Non-breeding male:* white head with a dark eye patch; white neck and belly; dark breast; white patches on the back; pink bill with a dark base; long, dark central tail feathers. *Breeding female:* short tail feathers; gray bill; dark head, throat, wings and back; white ear patch; white underparts. *Non-breeding female:* similar, but generally lighter, especially on the head.

non-breeding

Size: *L* 17–20 in. (43–51 cm).

Range: rare spring and fall migrant throughout the Rockies; very rare winter visitor to the southern U.S. Rockies.

Habitat: deep lakes, reservoirs, large rivers and large marshes in the montane.

WHOOPING CRANE

Grus americana

I.D.: *Sexes similar. Adult:* very tall, large bird; black wing primaries; all-white plumage; bare red skin on the forehead and the chin; long, pointed bill; black legs. *Immature:* orange-red head and upper neck. *In flight:* neck and legs are extended.

Size: *L* 50–60 in. (127–152 cm); *W* 78–90 in. (198–229 cm).

Range: accidental throughout the Rockies; historically rare (19th century); uncommon in Grays Lake NWR in Idaho.

Habitat: *In migration:* wetlands, croplands and fen areas.

BLACK-BELLIED PLOVER

Pluvialis squatarola

I.D.: *Sexes similar:* short, black bill; long, black legs. *Breeding:* black face, breast and belly; light gray crown; white shoulders; black back spotted with white; white undertail coverts. *Non-breeding:* gray-brown upperparts; light underparts. *In flight:* black 'wing pits'; white tail.

breeding

Size: *L* 10¹/₂–13 in. (27–33 cm).

Range: rare spring and fall migrant in low-elevation passes throughout the Rockies.

Habitat: edges of lakes and reservoirs; occasionally on plowed fields, short meadows or pasturelands.

AMERICAN GOLDEN-PLOVER

Pluvialis dominica

I.D.: *Sexes similar:* dark back speckled with gold; black mask, throat, belly and undertail coverts; straight, black bill; long legs; white stripe across the forehead and down through the shoulders.
Size: L 10–11 in. (25–28 cm).
Range: rare spring migrant throughout the Rockies.
Habitat: lake edges, shorelines, mudflats, agricultural fields, pastures, golf courses, airports and backwaters in the foothills and the montane.

breeding

MOUNTAIN PLOVER

Charadrius montanus

I.D.: *Sexes similar:* thin, dark bill; clean, light underparts; sandy upperparts; white forehead; black forecrown; thin, black eye line; light legs.
In flight: white wing stripe; dark tail band.
Size: L 8–9¹/₂ in. (20–24 cm).
Range: rare spring and fall migrant in the central and southern U.S. Rockies; breeds in small numbers on the high plains in Montana, within sight of the Rockies.
Habitat: short-grass prairie, heavily grazed pastures, mudflats and shorelines.

breeding

HUDSONIAN GODWIT

Limosa haemastica

I.D.: *Sexes similar:* long, slightly upturned bill; white rump; long, black legs; black tail. *Breeding:* heavily barred, chestnut underparts; dark-brown upperparts. *Non-breeding:* sandy brown body. *In flight:* black 'wing pits' and wing linings; light flight feathers.
Size: L 14–16 in. (36–41 cm).
Range: rare spring migrant along the eastern slopes of the Rockies and in the Canadian Rockies; very rare fall migrant throughout the Rockies.
Habitat: shorelines of prairie marshes.

breeding

SANDERLING

Calidris alba

I.D.: *Sexes similar:* straight, black bill; black legs. *Non-breeding:* white underparts; sandy upperparts; black line down the white rump and tail. *Breeding:* rufous-mottled head, neck and upperparts; white belly.
Size: L 7–8¹/₂ in. (18–22 cm).
Range: rare spring and fall migrant in the Rockies.
Habitat: shores of lakes, reservoirs and marshes.

breeding

DUNLIN

Calidris alpina

breeding

I.D.: *Sexes similar:* downcurved, black bill; black legs.
Breeding: jet black belly; rusty wings and crown; lightly
streaked, white breast. *Non-breeding:* gray-brown upperparts;
light underparts; light brown streaking on the breast and nape.
In flight: white wing stripe; white rump is split by a black line.
Size: L 7¹/₂–9 in. (19–23 cm).
Range: very rare migrant throughout the Rockies.
Habitat: mudflats and shorelines of ponds and lakes up to the montane.

STILT SANDPIPER

Calidris himantopus

breeding

I.D.: *Sexes similar:* long neck; long, yellow-green
legs; medium-sized bill. *Breeding:* red 'ear' patch;
vertically streaked head and neck; horizontally
streaked breast and belly. *Non-breeding:* gray overall; dark
upperparts; light underparts.
Size: L 7¹/₂–9 in. (19–23 cm).
Range: rare and accidental spring migrant throughout the Rockies;
uncommon to common fall migrant in the northern Rockies.
Habitat: lakeshores, ponds, sewage lagoons, wet meadows and mudflats.

SHORT-BILLED DOWITCHER

Limnodromus griseus

non-breeding

I.D.: *Sexes similar:* straight, long, dark bill; chunky
body; white rump. *Breeding:* cinnamon overall; dark
upperparts; light barring on the flanks; broad white
bands on the tail feathers; occasionally has a white belly.
Non-breeding: gray upperparts; dirty white underparts; white
eyebrow.
Size: L 11–12 in. (28–30 cm).
Range: locally uncommon to rare migrant in low-elevation passes
throughout the Rockies.
Habitat: along lakeshores, shallow marshes and mudflats in the montane and the subalpine;
usually in flocks with Long-billed Dowitchers.

PARASITIC JAEGER

Stercorarius parasiticus

light phase

I.D.: *Sexes similar:* long, pointed, dark wings; slightly
longer, pointed central tail feathers; brown upperparts;
dark cap; light underwing tips. *Light phase:* white
underparts; white to cream-colored collar; light brown neck
band. *Dark phase:* all brown underparts and collar. *Juvenile:* barred underparts; central tail
feather extends just past the tail.
Size: L 18 in. (46 cm).
Range: rare spring migrant and very rare fall migrant throughout the Rockies.
Habitat: migrant through open habitats.

MEW GULL

Larus canus

I.D.: *Sexes similar:* small bill; dark eyes; small body size. *Breeding:* light gray upperparts; white head and underparts; all-yellow bill; black wing tips with large white spots; yellow legs. *Non-breeding:* black-tipped bill; black, terminal tail band and wing tips; brown mottling on the head and underparts.
Size: *L* 15–16 in. (38–41 cm).
Range: accidental migrant in the southern U.S. Rockies; rare to uncommon migrant in the Canadian Rockies; winters in small numbers in western Montana.
Habitat: migrant through open habitats.

breeding

BARN OWL

Tyto alba

I.D.: *Sexes similar:* heart-shaped, white facial disk; brown eyes; golden brown upperparts spotted with black and gray; creamy white, black-spotted upperparts; long legs; white undertail and under wings; pale bill.
Size: *L* 12¹/₂–18 in. (32–46 cm); *W* 45 in. (112 cm).
Range: uncommon to rare migrant in the southern and central U.S. Rockies.
Habitat: cliffs, hollow trees, barns and banks in agricultural and riparian regions.

EASTERN SCREECH-OWL

Otus asio

I.D.: *Sexes similar:* small owl; yellow eyes: light-colored bill; ear tufts; vertically streaked underparts; dark upperparts; gray-brown phase is most likely in the Rockies.
Size: *L* 8–10 in. (20–25 cm); female is slightly larger.
Range: rare resident along the front ranges of the southern U.S. Rockies.
Habitat: open deciduous woodlands and riparian forests with a dense understorey, mostly in the foothills.

RED-HEADED WOODPECKER

Melanerpes erythrocephalus

I.D.: *Sexes similar. Adult:* flaming red head and throat; black back, wings and tail; white belly, rump and inner wing patches. *Immature:* brown head, back, wings and tail; slight brown streaking on the breast.
Size: *L* 7¹/₂–8¹/₂ in. (19–22 cm).
Range: rare migrant and summer resident in Colorado (east of the Continental Divide); very rare westward and elsewhere in the Rockies.
Habitat: lowlands; favors riparian deciduous forests.

ALDER FLYCATCHER

Empidonax alnorum

I.D.: *Sexes similar:* green upperparts; slight eye ring; 2 white wing bars; orange lower mandible; long tail; yellow-green underparts.
Size: L 5³/₄–6¹/₂ in. (15–17 cm).
Range: uncommon migrant and locally rare resident in the Canadian Rockies and northern Montana.
Habitat: edges of wet areas in willows and birch thickets, muskeg edges and streamside vegetation in the montane.

GRAY FLYCATCHER

Empidonax wrightii

breeding

I.D.: *Sexes similar:* gray upperparts; white belly and undertail coverts; faint eye ring; 2 faint wing bars; light lower mandible; long tail with thin, white border. *Fall birds:* olive-tinged.
Size: L 5¹/₄–6 in. (13–15 cm).
Range: uncommon migrant and summer resident in the southern U.S. Rockies.
Habitat: pinyon-juniper woodlands; also in sagebrush and juniper woodlands.

EASTERN PHOEBE

Sayornis phoebe

I.D.: *Sexes similar:* gray-brown upperparts; light underparts; no eye ring; no obvious wing bars; all-black bill; faint yellow-green belly; dark legs; frequently flicks its tail.
Size: L 6¹/₂–7 in. (17–18 cm).
Range: rare to very rare migrant and summer visitor throughout the Rockies.
Habitat: forest edges and clearings, usually near lakes or rivers.

ASH-THROATED FLYCATCHER

Myiarchus cinerascens

I.D.: *Sexes similar:* gray-brown upperparts; gray throat and breast; yellow belly and undertail coverts; dark bill; dense crest; 2 white wing bars; no eye ring; tail shows some rufous in the webbing.
Size: L 7–8 in. (18–20 cm)
Range: uncommon to common migrant and breeder in western Colorado and Utah; accidental elsewhere in the Rockies.
Habitat: semi-open areas with pinyon-juniper woodlands.

CASSIN'S KINGBIRD

Tyrannus vociferans

I.D.: *Sexes similar:* dark gray upperparts; whitish chin; yellow belly and undertail coverts; dark wings; brown tail; no white outer tail feathers; no wing bars; black bill.
Size: *L* 8–9 in. (20–23 cm).
Range: uncommon migrant and resident in the foothills and mesas of the southern U.S. Rockies; accidental elsewhere in the Rockies.
Habitat: open woodlands, agricultural areas, cholla grasslands and pinyon-juniper woodlands.

GRAY-CHEEKED THRUSH

Catharus minimus

I.D.: *Sexes similar:* gray-brown upperparts; gray cheek; bold spots on the throat and breast; light belly and undertail coverts; thin, gray eye ring.
Size: L 7 in. (18 cm).
Range: rare spring migrant in the eastern Rockies.
Habitat: migrates through woodlands up to the upper subalpine.

BLACK-THROATED GREEN WARBLER

Dendroica virens

I.D.: *Male:* yellow face; black throat; white belly; black flanks; olive-green cap, back and rump; 2 white wing bars. *Female:* paler overall.
Size: L 5 in. (13 cm).
Range: rare migrant in the Canadian Rockies; vagrant in the U.S. Rockies.
Habitat: mature coniferous and mixed woods in the montane.

♂

breeding

CANADA WARBLER

Wilsonia canadensis

I.D.: *General:* pale yellow 'spectacles'; yellow underparts; dark upperparts; orange legs; white undertail coverts. *Breeding male:* blue-black back; dark 'necklace.' *Female:* blue-green back; faint 'necklace.'
Size: *L* 5–5$^{1}/_{2}$ in. (13–14 cm).
Range: vagrant along the eastern slopes of the Rockies.
Habitat: willow and alder thickets, riparian shrublands and dense understoreys in the foothills and the montane.

♀

♂

BLACK-THROATED SPARROW

Amphispiza bilineata

I.D.: *Sexes similar:* black chin and throat; white 'jaw'
line and eyebrow; gray cheek and cap; unstreaked,
light underparts; gray upperparts; dark bill; black tail
with white outer tail feathers; dark legs.
Size: *L* 4¹/₂–5¹/₂ in. (11–14 cm).
Range: rare migrant and summer resident in the
southwestern Rockies.
Habitat: semi-desert shrublands, mesquite and
pinyon-juniper woodlands and agricultural areas in the
lowlands and the foothills.

BAIRD'S SPARROW

Ammodramus bairdii

I.D.: *Sexes similar:* finely streaked 'necklace';
2 black stripes bordering a white chin; buffy head
and nape; pale legs and bill; faint chestnut on the
wing covers.
Size: *L* 5–5¹/₂ in. (13–14 cm).
Range: very rare local breeder along the eastern
slopes of the Rockies.
Habitat: native grasslands and lightly grazed pastures up to the montane.

SWAMP SPARROW

Melospiza georgiana

breeding

I.D.: *Sexes similar:* chestnut crown; gray eyebrow and face
with a white 'jaw' line and throat; reddish-brown–streaked
upperparts; lightly streaked, gray breast; buffy sides.
Size: *L* 5³/₄ in. (15 cm).
Range: very rare migrant or vagrant throughout the
Rockies.
Habitat: wet shrublands, often near lakes or streams, and cattail
or bulrushes marshes in the foothills and the lower montane.

HARRIS'S SPARROW

Zonotrichia querula

non-breeding

I.D.: *Sexes similar. Breeding:* black crown, throat and
bib; gray face; white underparts; pink-orange bill;
black streaks on the flanks; mottled upperparts.
Non-breeding: brown face; buffy flanks.
Size: *L* 7¹/₂ in. (19 cm).
Range: very rare migrant along the eastern slopes of the
Rockies.
Habitat: roadsides, shrubby vegetation, forest edges and
thickets in the foothills and the montane.

McCOWN'S LONGSPUR

Calcarius mccownii

I.D.: *Breeding male*: black cap and bib; rufous shoulder; black whisker; light gray face and underparts; black bill; white outer tail feathers; black on the central and terminal area of the tail (like an inverted T). *Breeding female*: similar patterning, but not as bold; gray plumage.
Size: L 6 in. (15 cm).
Range: rare migrant in the Yellowstone area; local breeder on the eastern slopes of the southern Canadian and U.S. Rockies.
Habitat: shortgrass prairies, native grasslands, pastures and agricultural areas.

breeding

CHESTNUT-COLLARED LONGSPUR

Calcarius ornatus

I.D.: *Breeding male:* chestnut nape; black underparts; yellow throat; black cap; white eyebrow; mottled brown upperparts; white outer tail feathers; black central and terminal tail feathers; white undertail coverts. *Breeding female:* might show a chestnut nape; mottled brown overall; light breast streaks.
Size: L 5 1/2 in. (14 cm).
Range: rare migrant and local breeder along the eastern slopes of the Rockies.
Habitat: *In migration:* grasslands, prairies and meadows from the lowlands to the subalpine.

breeding

ROSE-BREASTED GROSBEAK

Pheucticus ludovicianus

I.D.: *General:* large, light-colored, conical bill. *Male:* black hood, back, tail and wings; red breast and inner underwings; white underparts, rump and wing patches. *Female:* brown upperparts; light underparts; streaked breast; light eyebrow and crown stripe; white wing bars.
Size: L 7–8 1/2 in. (18–22 cm).
Range: very rare migrant and summer visitor on the eastern slopes of the Rockies.
Habitat: pure deciduous and mixedwood forests, riparian woodlands and wooded urban areas in the foothills.

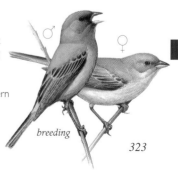

INDIGO BUNTING

Passerina cyanea

I.D.: *General:* dark, stout, conical bill; beady, black eyes; black legs; no wing bars. *Breeding male:* royal blue overall. *Breeding female:* soft brown overall; faintly streaked flanks.
Size: L 5 1/2 in. (14 cm).
Range: very rare migrant and summer visitor in the southern U.S. Rockies.
Habitat: forest edges, shrubby fields, orchards, overgrown pastures and hedgerows in the eastern lowlands.

breeding

323

GLOSSARY

accipiter: a forest hawk (genus *Accipiter*); characterized by a long tail and short, rounded wings; feeds mostly on birds.

brood: *n.* a family of young from one hatching; *v.* to sit on eggs so as to hatch them.

coniferous: cone-producing trees, usually softwood evergreens (e.g., spruce, pine, fir).

corvid: a member of the crow family (Corvidae); includes crows, jays, magpies and ravens.

covey: a brood or flock of partridges, quails or grouse.

crop: an enlargement of the esophagus, serving as a storage structure and (in pigeons) has glands which produce secretions.

dabbling: foraging technique used by ducks, where the head and neck are submerged but the body and tail remain on the water's surface.

dabbling duck: a duck that forages by dabbling; it can usually walk easily on land, it can take off without running, and it has a brightly colored speculum; includes Mallards, Gadwalls, teals and others.

deciduous: a tree that loses its leaves annually (e.g., oak, maple, aspen, birch).

dimorphism: the existence of two distinct forms of a species, such as between the sexes.

eclipse: the dull, female-like plumage that male ducks briefly acquire after molting from their breeding plumage.

elbow patches: dark spots at the bend of the outstretched wing, seen from below.

flycatching: feeding behavior where a bird leaves a perch, snatches an insect in mid-air, and returns to their previous perch; also known as 'hawking.'

fledgling: a young chick that has just acquired its permanent flight feathers, but is still dependent on its parents.

flushing: a behavior where frightened birds explode into flight in response to a disturbance.

gape: the size of the mouth opening.

irruption: a sporadic mass migration of birds into a non-breeding area.

larva: a development stage of an animal (usually an invertebrate) that has a different body form from the adult (e.g., caterpillar, maggot).

leading edge: the front edge of the wing as viewed from below.

litter: fallen plant material, such as twigs, leaves and needles, that forms a distinct layer above the soil, especially in forests.

lore: the small patch between the eye and the bill.

molting: the periodic replacement of worn out feathers (often twice a year).

morphology: the science of form and shape.

nape: the back of the neck.

neotropical migrant: a bird that nest in North America, but overwinters in the New World tropics.

niche: an ecological role filled by a species.

open country: a landscape that is primarily not forested.

parasitism: a relationship between two species where one benefits at the expense of the other.

phylogenetics: a method of classifying animals that puts the oldest ancestral groups before those that have arisen more recently.

pishing: making a sound to attract birds by saying *pishhh* as loudly and as wetly as comfortably possible.

polygynous: having a mating strategy where one male breeds with several females.

polyandrous: having a mating strategy where one female breeds with several males.

plucking post: a perch habitually used by an accipiter for plucking feathers from its prey.

raptor: a carnivorous (meat-eating) bird; includes eagles, hawks, falcons and owls.

rufous: rusty red in color.

speculum: a brightly colored patch in the wings of many dabbling ducks.

squeaking: making a sound to attract birds by loudly kissing the back of the hand, or by using a specially design squeaky bird call.

talons: the claws of birds of prey.

understorey: the shrub or thicket layer beneath a canopy of trees.

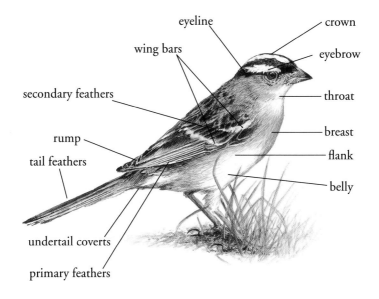

BIBLIOGRAPHY

American Ornithologists' Union. 1983. *Check-list of North American Birds.* 6th ed. (and its supplements). American Ornithologists' Union, Washington, D.C.

Andrews, R., and R. Righter. 1992. *Colorado Birds.* Denver Museum of Natural History, Denver.

Bent, A.C. 1921–68. Life histories of North American birds series. *U.S. National Museum Bulletin.* Washington, D.C.

Butler, J. 1989. *Alberta Wildlife Viewing Guide.* Lone Pine Publishing, Edmonton, Alberta.

Campbell, R.W., N.K. Dawe, I. McTaggart-Cowan, J.M. Cooper, G.W. Kaiser and M.C.E. McNall. 1990. *The Birds of British Columbia: Volumes 1 & 2: Nonpasserines.* Royal British Coumbia Museum, Victoria.

Chapman, F.M. 1968. *The Warblers of North America.* Dover Publishing, New York.

Dunne, P., D. Sibley and C. Sutton. 1988. *Hawks in Flight.* Houghton Mifflin Co., Boston.

Ehrlich, R.R., D.S. Dobkin and D. Wheye. 1988. *The Birder's Handbook.* Fireside, New York.

Evans, H.E. 1993. *Pioneering Naturalists: The Discovery and Naming of North American Plants and Animals.* Henry Holt and Co., New York.

Farrand, J., ed. 1983. *The Audubon Society Master Guide to Birding.* Vols. 1–3. Alfred A. Knopf, New York.

Folzenlogen, R. 1995. *Birding the Front Range: A Guide to Seasonal Highlights.* Willow Press, Littleton, Colorado.

Gaines, D. 1988. *Birds of Yosemite and the East Slope.* Artemisia Press, Lee Vining, California.

Godfry, W.E. 1986. *The Birds of Canada.* 2nd ed. National Museum of Natural Sciences, Ottawa.

Gotch, A.F. 1981. *Birds: Their Latin Names Explained.* Blandford Press, Dorset, England.

Gray, M.T. 1992a. *Watchable Birds of the Rocky Mountains.* Mountain Press Publishing Co., Missoula, Montana.

———. 1992b. *Colorado Wildlife Viewing Guide.* Falcon Press, Helena, Montana.

Gruson, E.S. 1972. *Words for Birds.* Quadrangle Books, New York.

Griscom, L., and A. Sprunt, Jr., eds. 1957. *The Warblers of America.* Doubleday and Co., Garden City, New York.

Holroyd, G.L., and H. Coneybeare. 1990. *The Compact Guide to Birds of the Rockies.* Lone Pine Publishing, Edmonton, Alberta.

Holroyd, G.L., and K.J. Van Tighem. 1983. *The Ecological (Biophysical) Land Classification of Banff and Jasper National Parks: Volume 3—The Wildlife Inventory.* Canadian Wildlife Service, Edmonton, Alberta.

Johnsgard, P.A. 1986. *Birds of the Rocky Mountains.* University of Nebraska Press, Lincoln.

Kaufman, K. 1996. *Lives of North American Birds.* Houghton Mifflin Co., Boston.

Leahy, C. 1982. *The Birdwatcher's Companion.* Hill and Wand, New York.

McEneaney, T. 1988. *Birds of Yellowstone.* Roberts Rinehart Publishers, Boulder Colorado.

———. 1993. *The Birder's Guide to Montana.* Falcon Press, Helena, Montana.

Mearns, B., and R. Mearns. 1992. *Audubon to Xantus: The lives of those Commemorated in North American Bird Names.* Academic Press, San Diego.

Peterson, R.T. 1990. *A Field Guide to the Western Birds.* 3rd ed. Houghton Mifflin Co., Boston.

Raynes, B., and D. Wile. 1994. *Finding the Birds of Jackson Hole.* Darwin Wile, Jackson, Wyoming.

Reader's Digest Association. 1990. *Book of North American Birds.* The Reader's Digest Association, Pleasantville, New York.

Richards, A. 1988. *Shorebirds of the Northern Hemisphere.* Dragon's World, Surrey, England.

Semenchuck, G.P., ed. 1992. *The Atlas of Breeding Birds of Alberta.* Federation of Alberta Naturalists, Edmonton, Alberta.

Scott, O.K. 1993. *A Birder's Guide to Wyoming.* American Birding Association, Colorado Springs.

Scott, S.S. 1987. *Field Guide to the Birds of North America.* National Geographic Society, Washington, D.C.

Slinger, J. 1996. *Down and Dirty Birding.* Fireside, New York.

Stokes, D., and L. Stokes. 1996. *Stokes Field Guide to Birds: Western Region.* Little, Brown and Co., Boston.

Terres, J.K. 1995. *The Audubon Society Encyclopedia of North American Birds.* Wings Books, New York.

Wareham, B. 1991. *British Columbia Wildlife Viewing Guide.* Lone Pine Publishing, Edmonton, Alberta.

Wauer, R.H. 1993. *The Visitor's Guide to the Birds of the Rocky Mountain National Parks: United States and Canada.* John Muir Publications, Santa Fe.

INDEX OF SCIENTIFIC NAMES

This index references only the primary, illustrated species descriptions.

INDEX OF COMMON NAMES

Boldface page numbers refer to the primary, illustrated species descriptions.

More Rocky Mountain fun and adventure from Lone Pine

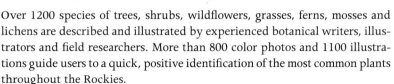

Plants of the Rocky Mountains
by Linda Kershaw, with contributions
  from Andy MacKinnon and Jim Pojar

Over 1200 species of trees, shrubs, wildflowers, grasses, ferns, mosses and lichens are described and illustrated by experienced botanical writers, illustrators and field researchers. More than 800 color photos and 1100 illustrations guide users to a quick, positive identification of the most common plants throughout the Rockies.
1-55105-088-9 • 5.5" x 8.5" • 352 pgs. • softcover • $24.95CDN/$19.95US

Compact Guide to Birds of the Rockies
by Geoffrey Holroyd and Howard Coneybeare

A habitat-based guide that includes unusual and useful notes for more than 100 birds. Its convenient size and full-page color illustrations make this guide a most useful part of your field kit. Slip it into your daypack or windbreaker pocket before every hike!
0-919433-52-9 • 4.25" x 5.75" • 144 pgs. • softcover • $9.95CDN/$7.95US

CANADIAN ORDERS
1-800-661-9017 PHONE
1-800-424-7173 FAX

U.S. ORDERS
1-800-518-3541 PHONE
1-800-548-1169 FAX